D0079021

Information Visualization

Information Visualization

Design for Interaction

Second edition

Robert Spence
Imperial College, London

PEARSON
Prentice Hall

Harlow, England • London • New York • Boston • San Francisco • Toronto
Sydney • Tokyo • Singapore • Hong Kong • Seoul • Taipei • New Delhi
Cape Town • Madrid • Mexico City • Amsterdam • Munich • Paris • Milan

Pearson Education Limited
Edinburgh Gate
Harlow
Essex CM20 2JE
England

and Associated Companies throughout the world

Visit us on the World Wide Web at:
www.pearsoned.co.uk

First published 2001
Second edition published 2007

© by the ACM Press, A Division of the Association for Computing Machinery, Inc. (ACM), 2001
© Pearson Education Limited 2007

The right of Robert Spence to be identified as author of this work has
been asserted by him in accordance with the Copyright, Designs and Patents Act 1988.

ISBN-13: 978-0-132-0655-04
ISBN-10: 0-132-0655-09

British Library Cataloguing-in-Publication Data
A catalogue record for this book can be obtained from the British Library

Library of Congress Cataloging-in-Publication Data
A catalog record for this book is available from the Library of Congress

10 9 8 7 6 5 4 3 2 1
10 09 08 07

Typeset in 10/12pt Caslon 224 by 30
Printed and bound by Mateu Cremo, Artes Graficas, Spain

The publisher's policy is to use paper manufactured from sustainable forests.

To the memory of Kathy

Contents

Chapter 6   Case Studies   185

Supporting resources
Visit **www.pearsoned.co.uk/spence** to find valuable online resources

Companion Website for students
- Links to sources of information on the web

For instructors
- PowerPoint slides including all key illustrations from the book
- An Instructor's Guide with teaching hints for each chapter
- Outline answers to design exercises

For more information please contact your local Pearson Education sales representative or visit **www.pearsoned.co.uk/spence**

About the Author

 Someone once remarked about Bob Spence that in the context of research he has led a double life. Experts in human–computer interaction (HCI) are unaware of his extensive and pioneering work on the theory and design of electronic circuits, and *vice versa*. Novel research in these two apparently disparate fields has won him not only a PhD but a couple of higher doctorates. The separation of the two fields is only apparent, however, because Bob's original research in HCI was specifically driven by the need for an effective tool for the electronic circuit designer. It resulted in the first interactive graphic facility for circuit design, called MINNIE; and MINNIE went on to be a commercial reality, developed and marketed by a company of which Bob was chairman. This early work in the late 1960s and early 1970s resulted in many original information visualization techniques, though that term had not then been invented. It has also been argued that Bob's team proposed and implemented the first on-screen calculator. His group's more recent work during the decade which saw an explosive expansion of information visualization tools (the 1990s) was also stimulated to a great degree by the needs of engineering designers.

The contribution to HCI for which Bob is perhaps best known is the invention, jointly with Mark Apperley (now of Waikato University, New Zealand), of the first focus+context display called the Bifocal Display. Since its invention in 1980 it has spawned a significant amount of research into information visualization and the underlying technique has reached commercial reality.

Currently Bob is Emeritus Professor of Information Engineering at Imperial College London, still teaching courses in both electrical engineering and human–computer interaction. His research is now focused on the relatively new topic of rapid serial visual presentation. Otherwise, much of his time is occupied by teaching courses in information visualization around the world: 'have courses, will travel' is his motto.

In 1990, Bob's achievements led to his election to Fellowship of the Royal Academy of Engineering, a professional body of a stature comparable to that of the US National Academy of Engineering.

Other books written by the author include:

Linear Active Networks (1970, Wiley)

Tellegen's Theorem and Electrical Networks (1970, MIT Press) with Penfield and Duinker. Translated into Russian and Chinese.

Resistive Circuit Theory (1974, McGraw-Hill)

Modern Network Theory – An Introduction (1978, Georgi) with Brayton, Chua and Rhodes

Sensitivity and Optimisation (1980, Elsevier) with Brayton

Computer-aided Circuit Design (1980, Prentice-Hall) with Burgess

Tolerance Design of Electrical Circuits (1988, Addison-Wesley) with Soin. Translated into Japanese

Information Visualization (2001, Addison-Wesley)

Foreword

We are awash in data. Whether it is corporate executives analysing profits in different markets in order to determine next year's sales strategy, parents examining the latest automobile specifications to select a new car to buy for their family, or students browsing facts and figures about universities as they plan upcoming applications, people use data in all aspects of their lives. Unfortunately, the data is too often an unorganised sea of numbers and text that is difficult to understand and to gain insight from.

How do we help people to make sense of all the data? By better organising it, giving it a structure, and providing it with a meaningful representation, we are able to transform the data into a format that people can more easily and quickly explore. That process is what information visualization is all about. Effective visual representations present data in a form that allows people to browse the display and understand the inherent information resident in the data. As Don Norman and Stuart Card have noted, visualizations serve as external cognition aids that assist people's memory and thinking. Information visualization systems such as those presented in this book combine illustrative representations of data with interactive user interfaces that allow people to examine data from many different perspectives.

The field of information visualization has two important components. First, the supporting technical foundations for creating representations of data are necessary. Underlying mathematics, computer graphics, and user interface techniques allow developers to create visualizations that are responsive, illuminating, and in some cases even beautiful. The second important component of information visualization is the human aspect. Without a deep understanding of the information-seeking tasks and goals of the consumer of the information visualizations, it is significantly more challenging to develop systems that are truly useful and informative. A careful understanding of the perceptual and cognitive capabilities of people is necessary to develop effective information visualizations.

In the first edition of this book, Bob Spence created an accessible introduction to information visualization, one ripe with examples that helped illustrate the concepts and theories developed by researchers. His long and noted history in the field with research ranging from the initial notions of focus+context displays to highly interactive, general information display systems such as the Influence and Attribute Explorer, as well as to dynamic animated RSVP displays, provided him with an ideal background to author an initial textbook for the field.

This book is the second edition of that text, but calling it a second edition is both limiting and misleading. Spence has completely reorganized the material, creating a significant revision that hinges on the three main concepts of representation, presentation and interaction. Much as information visualization developers do when designing a system for a new application area, Spence has created a structure and a form that allow his users (the book readers) to better understand the key concepts of information visualization. He writes with clarity and insight, carefully explaining the important ideas of the field as well as their significance.

This new edition of the book, much like the first, includes numerous examples and case studies of information visualizations and systems. These examples range from classic imagery such as Florence Nightingale's depiction of Crimean hospitals and Harry Beck's initial London subway maps to the most recent highly interactive computer graphics interfaces that are marvels of technical sophistication. The best way to understand visualizations is to see them, and Spence provides the reader with an extensive set of illustrated examples that inform and also inspire future developments. His inclusion of sample exercises and accompanying online resources such as lecture slides and videos makes this book an excellent teaching resource as well.

John Stasko
Georgia Institute of Technology

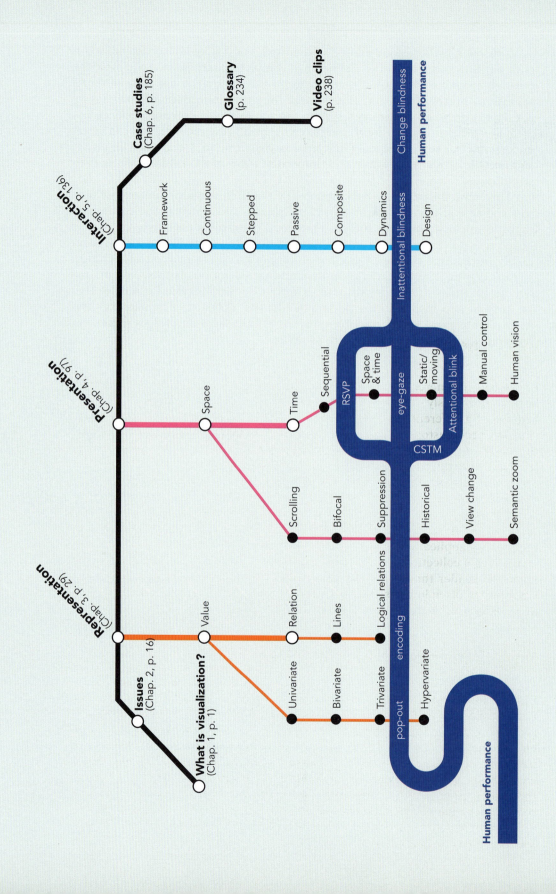

Preface

A second edition of *Information Visualization* (2001)? Well, yes and no. Yes in the sense that this revision is again intended to be at an introductory level and aimed principally at undergraduates and masters students in a wide range of courses. But no in the sense that its *structure* and other aspects are radically different from the earlier book. Let me explain.

The structure

I have become increasingly aware that the material in my original book would benefit enormously – by which I mean that the student reader and others would benefit – if a different structure were to be employed. Thus (see the map opposite) after the customary and essential introductory chapter (Chapter 1) I use the whole of Chapter 2 to identify, by means of a 'walk-through' of a visualization tool, the three principal issues underlying information visualization (IV). These are *representation* (the visual or aural encoding of data), *presentation* (the selection and layout of encoded data) and *interaction* (undertaken to acquire different 'views' of data). Also, because I feel that it is essential to see information visualization in context – acknowledging the many constraints imposed by application requirements – I have added a concluding chapter (6) comprising a collection of individual case studies. Hopefully its content will convince the reader that the application of information visualization, like many other design disciplines, is to a considerable extent a *craft*, calling upon the creative abilities of the interaction designer.

Definitions and references

Unlike most advocates of information visualization I stress that its definition refers to the development of a mental model of data. A related point is that it is grossly misleading to separate 'visual' from 'visualization': the potential to encode data in sound, though not extensively employed, should nevertheless not be ignored. A glossary of terms that I have provided also reflects my permanent concern that many of the terms employed in information visualization – 'browsing', 'navigation' and 'search' are some examples – lack precise definition, requests for their clarification often being met with more than the usual amount of arm waving. Students deserve better. If readers disagree with any definition at least we have a point of departure.

With regard to references I have tried, where possible, to acknowledge the originator of a concept or technique by giving the primary reference: many advances in information visualization first made in the 1960s, 1970s and 1980s either fail to be referenced or have been forgotten. Thus, while this book is not intended to be a research monograph, references to primary and significant sources should enable the interested student to 'dig deeper'. In this connection they should also be aware of the well-respected compilation of seminal papers contained in *Information Visualization: Using Vision to Think* by Card, Shneiderman and Mackinlay.

Human performance

Another departure from the first edition concerns human cognitive behaviour. Users look at presented data, often in a series of rapid eye movements, interpret what they see, call upon relevant experience and make decisions about how next to view the data, all the time creating and modifying a mental model of that data in human memory and even modifying the problem they are solving. The design of a visualization tool carried out without even a passing understanding of such human behaviour is likely not to be making full use of either human ability or the potential of information visualization. However, bearing in mind that this book is about information visualization rather than human perception and cognition, I have decided to introduce aspects of human performance at the point where they are particularly relevant rather than in a separate chapter, but briefly so as not to disturb the flow: blue text is used to help identification. Readers can always dig deeper in Colin Ware's excellent *Information Visualization: Perception for Design* (2004).

Readership

Let me return to the intended readership. Not surprisingly the first edition has primarily been adopted for university courses falling within the general area of computer science, though it is slowly being recognized that information visualization is relevant to an extremely wide range of fields. I hope, therefore, that in addition to student use, this book will be of interest not only to software engineers whose implementations can benefit from awareness of the potential of information visualization but also to the huge population of professionals – police officers, bankers, managers, online vendors and many others – whose activity can potentially be immensely enhanced through the application of information visualization: they will not expect to become IV experts but should expect, in view of their valuable domain expertise, to play a useful part in the commissioning and evaluation of visualization tools.

Visual analytics

I recently encountered a new term, 'visual analytics', and wondered what it was, only to discover that I had been actively associated with it for the past 30 years. The definition of this 'new' discipline – 'the science of analytical reasoning facilitated by interactive visual interfaces' – suggests that this book is extremely relevant to the discipline. Additional relevance is present in that the 'new' field emphasizes the importance of cognitive science which, as pointed out earlier, is introduced as and when relevant in the book.

Teaching resources

For the more than 50 adopters of the first edition who are known to me I have freely supplied my PowerPoint files, mindful of the enormous effort needed to assemble all the many images and diagrams from scratch when first teaching the subject of information visualization. These are now available, again freely, from the publisher's website. Similarly available on the accompanying DVD is a collection of video clips which, in my opinion, can be immensely helpful in illustrating various concepts and techniques. They are sufficiently brief (as short as four seconds) so as not to detract from the flow of a lecture. Each clip is fully described in the Appendix.

Pedagogy

I believe that the best way to learn about information visualization is to do it. Thus, rather than require my students to sit an exam paper, I ask them to undertake design exercises ranging from the simple (but challenging) to the substantial. I also require them to justify their designs, typically pasted to the wall of the classroom, so that discussion by both teacher and other students can enhance the learning process. It is worth pointing out that the student can benefit from many of the design exercises provided in the book by making sketches using coloured pencils and paper.

I would particularly draw the teacher's attention to the exercises associated with Chapter 6 (case studies). I have used these myself as the final activity of a two-week module within the masters course at the Technical University of Eindhoven and elsewhere. The students organize themselves into groups of four and spend approximately four days full-time on the project; some groups put forward their own projects for approval. These design exercises do not demand programming expertise beyond what is needed to provide an illustration of the design: we are, after all, testing creativity and critical ability within the context of information visualization, not programming skill. After about two days of work each group makes an interim 20-minute presentation describing their progress so far and responds to questions from the class and teacher. The final submission is restricted to four pages in ACM conference format – with no extra appendices or figures! – to provide a realistic reporting medium.

Bob Spence
London
June 2006

Acknowledgements

The writing of this book has been made possible only through the many interactions I have had – some brief, some intense – with many people. Where do I start?

I'll begin with the students undertaking the User System Interaction Masters course at the Technical University of Eindhoven in The Netherlands. For two weeks each year I teach a module on information visualization, and the need to rethink that course every year, combined with the lively discourse that takes place, has helped immensely to shape the structure of the book and its contents. Thank you – you know who you are! The constant rethink required for other courses given around the world – London, Konstanz, Kuala Lumpur, Singapore and elsewhere – has helped in the same way.

I have also been privileged to learn from those who have collaborated with me in my research. Ongoing interaction with Mark Apperley dates back to 1971, with Lisa Tweedie to the early 1990s and with Oscar de Bruijn to the late 1990s. More recently the help I have received from Mark Witkowski, Catherine Fawcett and Katy Cooper has been crucial to my research and hence this book.

There are many others who have contributed by sharing their thoughts with me on a variety of occasions: at conferences, on a Thames sightseeing boat, at regular meals at an excellent Greek restaurant and elsewhere. They include the interaction designer Ron Bird, Kent Wittenburg of Mitsubishi Research Labs, Brock Craft of University College London, the pilots Paul Hough, Herr Rudensteimer and Varnavas Serghides, Par-Anders Albinsson of the Swedish Defence Research Agency and Bill Buxton. Many people have been generous with their time in providing me with advice, information and often figures. They include Dr Mary Potter of MIT (human visual processing), Barbara Tversky of Stanford (memory), Tom Oldfield (bioinformatics), George Furnas (history of fisheye lenses), Andy Cockburn (zoom and pan), Carl Gutwin (distortion evaluation), Harri Siirtola (parallel coordinate plots), Pourang Irani (mobile cells), Ed Chi and Peter Pirolli of Xerox PARC (scent), the interaction designer Alison Black, Chris Ahlberg (CEO of Spotfire Inc.), Gerard Conway (pharmaceuticals), Soon Tee Teoh (coherence and correlation), Lin Freeman (social networks), Christiaan Fluit of Adena (cluster maps), Ben Bederson (PDA calendars), Wendy Hodges and Timothy Rowe (horned lizards), Keith Andrews (InfoSky), Chia Shen (interactive tables) and Marcus Watson (audio encoding). I'm most grateful to all of you.

Especially valuable were the critiques provided by referees of various drafts of the book, some resulting in significant changes in the content and structure. I'm therefore most appreciative of the advice received from John Stasko, Lisa Tweedie, Catherine Plaisant, Par-Anders Albinsson, Harri Siirtola and Pourang Irani.

Colin Grimshaw, Martin Sayers and Neville Miles of the Imperial College Media Centre are to be thanked for the many occasions on which they have very patiently, professionally and often innovatively provided me with the static and dynamic images that are essential to the teaching of information visualization. Also at Imperial College, Ellen and Don have often found the unfindable in my search for references.

At Pearson Education Simon Plumtree, Elizabeth Rix and Vivienne Church have been enormously supportive in minimising the pain suffered by this author in the tasks needed to get the book into production. Their friendliness and patience has been both impressive and welcome, and it has been a pleasure interacting with them.

Finally, there is a group of people who would lay no claim to expertise in information visualization, but who nevertheless valuably supported my activities in a variety of ways: Annie, Bill, Wendy and Wiesia deserve my warm appreciation.

The author and publishers are grateful to the following for permission to reproduce copyright material:

Fig. 1.5, photograph of Harry Beck, reprinted courtesy of Ken Garland. Fig. 3.19 courtesy of David Mintz from the Air Quality Analysis Group at the Office of Air Quality Planning and Standards U.S. Environmental Agency; Figure 3.25 Reprinted with permission from *The State of the World Atlas* (6th edition) by Dan Smith copyright © Myriad Editions/www.MyriadEditions.com; Figure 3.78 from London Underground Map designed by H.F. Stingmore (1927) and Figure 3.79, London Underground Map designed by Harry Beck (1933), London's Transport Museum © Transport for London; Fig. 4.29 from www.streetmap.co.uk reprinted with permission from Collins Maps and Atlases.

In some instances we have been unable to trace the owners of copyright material, and we would appreciate any information that would enable us to do so.

The cover design by Andrea Bannuscher of Pearson Education is based on a mosaic created by the author and photographed by Neville Miles, formerly of Imperial College. The mosaic, composed of smalti, was inspired by the visualization technique called prosections. It is illustrated in Figure 5.50.

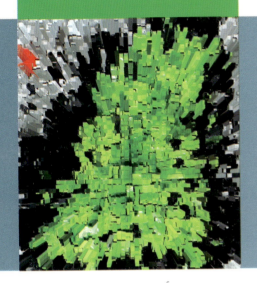

CHAPTER 1

What is Visualization?

Application of the potential offered by information visualization has seen a meteoric rise during the last 15–20 years. However, although this development has been triggered by the availability of computers and related technologies, the very essence of information visualization can be appreciated by looking at four examples produced long before the invention of computers and all now regarded as classics.

The first is the map (Figure 1.1) drawn by Monsieur Minard, Napoleon's mapmaker, to represent the easterly advance of Napoleon's army from the Polish–Russian border towards Moscow and its subsequent retreat. Most viewers of this map do not need to ask whether the thickness of the lines depicts the number of soldiers in the army or whether brown indicates advance and black

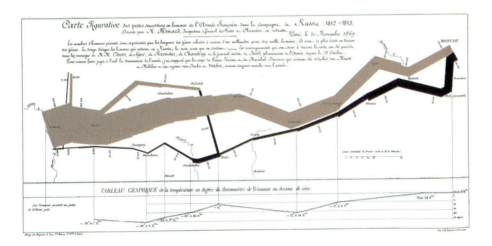

FIGURE 1.1
Minard's map of Napoleon's march to, and retreat from, Moscow
Source: *Tufte (1983)*

retreat. We see that of 440,000 soldiers who set out with Napoleon, only 10,000 returned. At the lower part of the map the temperatures endured (and frequently not endured) by the army during the retreat are recorded. The sudden and very noticeable fall in the number of soldiers as they crossed the Berezina river during retreat was in fact due to the ice not being quite thick enough. Overall, we gain considerable understanding from Minard's map without the need to read about the expedition, and the map's essential features remain in our memory long after we have ceased looking at it. In passing we may note that the map might not be entirely suitable as a recruitment poster.

The second example is taken from a report written by Florence Nightingale (1858) to the British government in which she records the improvements she made to the ghastly hospitals in Scutari during the Crimean war of 1858. She devised the diagram shown in Figure 1.2 in which radial segments have an area proportional to the number of deaths in the hospital in a particular month and subtend an angle proportional to the number of days in that month. It is immediately apparent that hospital conditions improved from month to month after she introduced her reforms. Moreover, the inner circle provides, for comparison, the same information for a military hospital situated in England. Thus, in one elegant but simple diagram, Florence Nightingale was able to impress upon the British government the magnitude of her achievement. Again, without even looking back at the diagram, we carry away in our mind an appreciation of her achievement and a visual memory of her 'rose-petal' diagram.[1]

FIGURE 1.2
Florence Nightingale's diagram showing the dramatic reduction in death rates in the hospitals of Scutari following the changes she introduced
Source: *Nightingale (1858)*

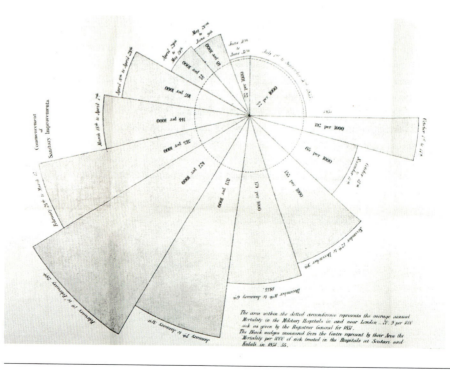

---

[1] Nightingale's report has a fascinating appendix containing recipes. It is strongly recommended that details of the Crimean hospitals are not perused before eating the results of Nightingale's – or anyone else's – recipes.

FIGURE 1.3
An 1845 map of London's Soho district, showing deaths from cholera (points) and the location of water pumps (crosses)
Source: *Tufte (1983)*

The third example is provided by a cholera epidemic that struck the Soho district of London in 1854. The medical officer for London at that time, a Dr John Snow, had the task of bringing the outbreak under control. He examined the map shown in Figure 1.3 in which, superimposed on a background of streets, dots denote deaths and crosses denote the pumps from which people obtained water. Snow observed that most of the deaths were concentrated around the Broad Street pump and drew the (now) obvious conclusion and put a lock on the pump. His disablement of the pump was followed by a decrease in the number of deaths from cholera (Tufte, 1997). Workers at the nearby brewery were noted to be relatively free of cholera, for reasons that can be left to the imagination. Snow's achievement is commemorated by a public house (Figure 1.4) situated close to the Broad Street pump in what has inexplicably been renamed Broad*wick* Street.

The last example is more recent. In 1931, Harry Beck (Figure 1.5) was an unemployed draughtsman. However, in the words of Bill Bryson (1998), Harry Beck 'realized that when you are underground it doesn't matter where you are. Beck saw – and what an intuitive stroke this was – that as long as the stations were presented in their correct sequence with their interchanges clearly delin-eated, he could freely distort the scale and, indeed, abandon it altogether! He gave his map the orderly precision of an electrical wiring system, and in so doing created an entirely new, imaginary London that has little to do with the disorderly geography of the city above'. The small payment he received from

FIGURE 1.4
The John Snow pub in Broadwick Street, London

FIGURE 1.5
Harry Beck, creator of the famous London Underground map
Source: *Ken Garland*

London Underground – which at first was not sure whether the new map was a good idea – contrasts sharply with Beck's influence on the maps of most transport systems in the world (Ovenden, 2003). The story of Harry Beck is a fascinating one (Garland, 1994). As with the other three examples, the viewer departs with an image in their mind. Indeed, for people living and working in London, the image of the 'Tube' map is certainly well remembered (albeit not in full detail) and usefully so when planning many journeys.

Visualization

The common aspect of these four examples is the nature of the *result* of looking at the diagrams. Nothing was written down or sketched, and nothing appeared in the memory of any computer. The result was created entirely in the mind of the viewer; we might say that **insight** or understanding was acquired. This is in fact consistent with the dictionary definition of visualization:

> **visualize**: to form a mental model or mental image of something.

Thus, visualization is solely a human cognitive activity *and has nothing to do with computers*. It should also be said at this point that the activity need not involve a visual experience, as might be suggested by the term 'visual' in visualization, because sound and other sensory modalities – not only graphics – can be employed to represent data.

From what we have seen, the activity of information visualization can be summarized in the simple diagram of Figure 1.6. Data – in whatever form – is transformed into pictures, and the pictures are interpreted by a human being. The diagram emphasizes the fact that, quite often, the sight of a graphical encoding of data causes an 'Ah Ha!' reaction in the viewer in the sense that a useful discovery has been made. In illustrating the process by which a user can be informed about data the figure makes the point that data and information are very different things. The principal task of information visualization is to allow information to be derived from data. We often hear mention of information overload whereas, in fact, the problem is one of data overload: information overload is perhaps a luxury we can only contemplate!

The data in Figure 1.6 can be of many different types. The temperatures depicted in Minard's map, for example, constitute numerical or *quantitative* data, while the colours brown (originally red) and black depict *ordinal* data (advance followed by retreat). *Categorical* data is exemplified by the deaths and

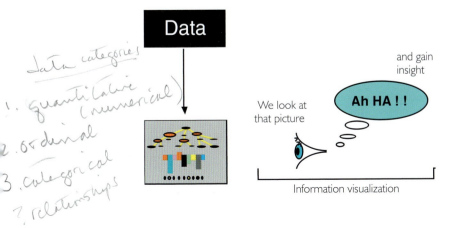

FIGURE 1.6
The process of information visualization. Graphically encoded data is viewed in order to form a mental model of that data

pumps seen in the map of Soho. Data concerned with *relationships* is well illustrated by Beck's Tube map. Text, of rapidly increasing importance as a source of data, is categorical data, containing no inherent ordering or numerical value. Whatever the nature of the data, the underlying philosophy of information visualization was concisely encapsulated by Simon (1996) who remarked that:

> *. . . solving a problem simply means representing it so as to make the solution transparent*

The term 'simple' refers, of course, to the concept. Choosing an effective way to encode data to make the solution transparent is far from simple and continues to challenge and fascinate practitioners and researchers.

Before even attempting to see how and why computers can assist the activity of visualization it is important to stress how valuable a *paper-based* display of data can be. Just as an elegant diagram helped Florence Nightingale to impress and persuade the British government, a similarly simple diagram might impress and persuade a venture capitalist from whom you wish to obtain investment, a professor who must assess your research or a jury sitting in a fraud trial. In these and many other situations much might depend upon the creation of an effective representation of relevant data. For a reader, the memory of a diagram may well be more durable and easily recalled than a description put forward in words, a description which has somehow to be succinctly modelled and remembered. For example, without turning back the page the reader can probably remember the essence of the diagrams created by Minard, Nightingale, Snow and Beck.[2]

1.2 Computational support

In the last 15–20 years especially computers have been responsible for massive advances in the field of information visualization.

There are three principal reasons. First, increasingly inexpensive and rapid access *memory* makes possible the storage of the truly vast amounts of data owned by business and government; insurance houses and pharmaceutical companies readily come to mind. Second, increasingly powerful and fast *computation* allows the rapid interactive selection of subsets of that data for flexible exploration.[3] Third, the availability of *high-resolution graphic displays* ensures

---

[2] Many other memorable encodings of information can be found in the book by Tufte (1983) and the fascinating 'gallery' of Michael Friendly (http://www.math.yorku.ca/SCS/Gallery).

[3] A contrast arises in the case where data *cannot* be selected according to need prior to its display. The design of printed posters to enable anyone at any railway station in The Netherlands to discover how to get from their current location to their desired destination is an exceedingly challenging one: here, there is no facility for selection except the direction of eye gaze. The alternative, which often comes quickly and uncritically to mind, in which an individual traveller can select personalized data, is fraught with difficulties of many kinds, as should become apparent in the course of this book. Advances in interactive information visualization have not diminished the challenge or value of static representations of data. Indeed, later in the book we shall encounter situations in which a suitably designed *static* representation demands much less cognitive effort for its interpretation than does an interactive dynamic display of the same information.

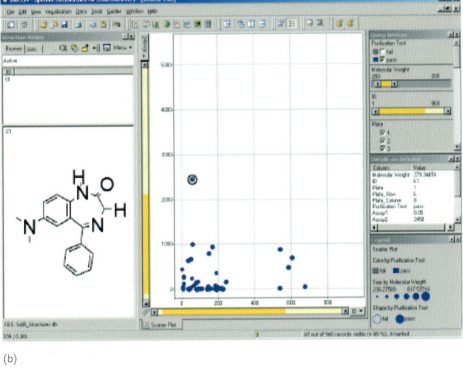

(a)

(b)

FIGURE 1.7(a)
A table
associated with
the exploration
of potentially
useful drugs
may involve
many rows
corresponding
to compounds
and 14 columns
associated with
specific
properties.
Gaining insight
into such a table
is difficult

FIGURE 1.7(b)
The visual
encoding of the
table data can
enhance
understanding.
In this example
a property 'ID'
is plotted against
'Assay1'. Colour
and shape both
encode the
passing or
failure of a
purification test
and size
encodes
molecular
weight.
Identification of
one compound
reveals its
molecular
structure.
*(Courtesy of
Spotfire Inc.)*

that the presentation of data matches the power of the human visual and cognitive systems. Two examples will briefly illustrate the consequences of these
three technological advances.

The powerful Spotfire™ **visualization tool** supports the development of new drugs by the pharmaceutical industry.[4] In the very early stages of drug development thousands or even hundreds of thousands of substances characterized by many properties must be examined. Presentation of the vast amount of data in a conventional table (Figure 1.7(a)) does not lead to ease of understanding. Spotfire™ allows the trained user to select a subset of that data, to have it presented in one or more easily assimilated visual forms and to interact with it, for example to investigate molecular structure (Figure 1.7(b)). Many such visual representations of data are examined in the course of drug development.

A second and very simple example illustrates the potential benefit of rearrangement of the visual representation of data. Figure 1.8(a) shows the result of an experiment in which ten crops all received seven different treatments (e.g. sprays, fertilizers). A black square indicates that the treatment was successful, a white one that it was not. Simply by appropriately reordering rows and columns of the matrix, Figure 1.8(b) is obtained, from which it is immediately noted that certain groups of treatments seem to be effective for particular groups of crops. That discovery, of course, will in its turn lead to many questions in the mind of the agricultural expert who begins to examine other data to explain what has been discovered, emphasizing the fact that visualization typically requires the iterative examination of different visual representations of data. This second example is also a reminder that advances in the representation of data and its interactive exploration have often been enhanced by the development of appropriate algorithms, of which the one involved in Figure 1.8 is one of the simplest.

FIGURE 1.8
An example of a simple rearrangement of the representation of data that can lead to insight
Source: *Courtesy of Bob Waddington*

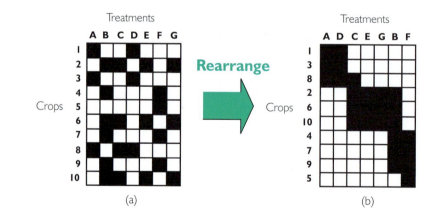

To the two examples provided above the reader will be able to add, from their own experience, many examples in which flexible movement from one view of a subset of data to another is required. One is the familiar task of arranging a flight to a holiday destination. If that task is carried out via the Web it will

---

[4] Compatible with our definition of visualization we shall refer to a visualization tool as a computer-based system designed to display (normally) visually encoded data with a view to supporting the process of visualization. We shall not – as is unfortunately common – use the term 'visualization' to refer to what is seen on a display.

normally be the case that a variety of pages (i.e. views) of available data will be examined to create a mental model, including available flight times ('Can Granny be ready in time for such an early flight?'), possible routes ('Be nice to stop over in Pisa to see the Tower'), total costs, special deals, different airlines and so on. Industry and commerce provide many other examples: decisions regarding the development of a drug (Spotfire), the control of a silicon chip production line (Inselberg, 1997) and the investigation of criminal activity (Davidson, 1993; Westphal and Blaxton, 1998). In all these examples modern computers beneficially facilitate the display of many different views of data. All also benefit from the availability of high-resolution graphical displays: in some cases (Keim *et al.*, 1993) every available pixel is harnessed to provide a display that can lead to understanding.

To place the above examples in perspective we should note that the potential for information visualization offered by rapid computation and high-quality displays was recognized more than 30 years ago. Figure 1.9 shows, for example, the representation, by circle size, of the effect of changes in every component in an electronic circuit on some property of that circuit (Spence and Drew, 1971). Again in the context of electronic circuit design, Figure 1.10 shows an interface whose responsive interaction allowed a designer to manually vary the value of a component (the slider on the right) and immediately (e.g. within 0.2 seconds) see the effect on a plot describing some circuit property (Spence and Apperley, 1974): an early example of 'dynamic querying'.

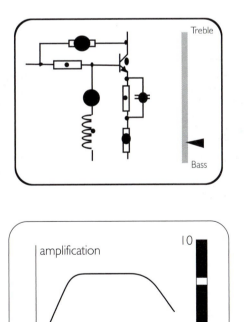

FIGURE 1.9
Circle size encodes the influence of components on the performance of a circuit

FIGURE 1.10
An interface permitting dynamic exploration of the effect of a component value on a circuit property

1.3 The human user

Having acknowledged the immense contribution that computers and associated artifacts have made to information visualization, especially in the last decade or two, we shall in this book almost take them for granted: it is how *human beings* interact with data, and therefore how best to encode and present data graphically, that is of crucial concern to the interaction designer – the person who has to be aware of the needs of a user as well as the characteristics of human behaviour. To emphasize the importance of such awareness we mention just three experimentally observed aspects of behaviour directly relevant to information visualization and which are remarkable in the sense that people find them difficult to believe.

In one experiment people were asked to view a video showing a group of six people running in a small area and passing a ball to each other, and to count the number of times that one particular girl touched the ball, a task lasting one minute. Most of those people were completely unaware of an additional person, dressed as a gorilla, walking into the midst of the young people, pausing to beat its chest and then walking off scene. Even though this intrusion – not only bizarre but unexpected – occurred *within the scene being attended to*, it was not noticed! On seeing a replay of the video some people even questioned whether they were seeing the same video. This phenomenon is called *inattentional blindness* (Simons and Chabris, 1999). Since visualization involves a user's attention to what is being displayed, the relevance of inattentional blindness is clear. One wonders how many accident reports ('the information was staring the operator in the face and he didn't see it') might be revised in the light of our knowledge of this phenomenon.

In the second experiment people were shown two pictures in a repeated sequence and told that they differed. Even though the difference was gross it often took people 15 or more seconds to detect it. This phenomenon is called *change blindness* (Rensink, 2002). Since most uses of visualization tools involve the observation of a change of view of some data, the relevance of change blindness is clear.

The third example emphasizes the fact that visualization relies on the formation of a mental model of some data, often called an *internal model* or a *cognitive map*. Tversky (1993) usefully pointed out, however, the danger of regarding what is remembered as a single entity and pointed out the existence of what she called a *cognitive collage*. This is illustrated by asking a person, 'Which is further west, Reno or Los Angeles?' A common but incorrect answer (Figure 1.11) is 'Los Angeles' because that city is associated with the state of California and Reno is associated with the state of Nevada, which is generally east of California. Association of Reno with Nevada and Los Angeles with California can be thought of as items in memory and the relative locations of Nevada and California as another – the danger lies in a simple but inappropriate combination of these models.

These three examples – and there are many more in the literature – make the point very strongly that, if an interaction designer is to exploit the undoubted potential of information visualization, they must be aware of the characteristics of the human user. It is for this reason that aspects of human cognitive and perceptual processing are introduced *as and when appropriate* and printed in blue

FIGURE 1.11
A map showing the states of California and Nevada and the cities of Los Angeles and Reno, to illustrate the concept of 'cognitive collage'

text. The reader wishing to dig deeper into these matters is referred to the excellent text by Ware (2004).

1.4 The value of information visualization

Though the topic of information visualization is undoubtedly fascinating, questions quite rightly arise concerning its value. The most effective way of answering those questions is to provide concrete examples, three of which now follow.

1.4.1 Fraud

The Serious Fraud Office of the United Kingdom spent eight person years examining 48 file drawers of paper-based data to identify the perpetrator of a suspected building society fraud (Davidson, 1993). An alleged perpetrator was identified, sent for trial and judged guilty. The same task was then set to a single investigator who was provided with a visualization tool which had access to the same data. The same alleged perpetrator was identified within four weeks, a time improvement of about 100 times. But that was not all – the visualization tool made it possible, within the same time frame, to additionally identify the master criminal behind the perpetrator. The fascinating aspect of this story is the fact that the manner in which the data was displayed was extremely simple and based on straight lines (see Chapter 3).

1.4.2 Silicon chips

For the major industry involved in the manufacture of silicon chips, an article in *Fortune* magazine illustrated the benefits of information visualization:

> *Texas Instruments manufactures microprocessors on silicon wafers that are routed through 400 steps in many weeks. This process is monitored, gathering 140,000 pieces of information about each wafer. Somewhere in that heap of data can be warnings about things going wrong. Detect a bug early before bad chips are made.*

1.4.3 Pharmaceutical industry

A similar message comes from people who, among other things, develop drugs. In the words of Sheldon Ort, speaking to *Fortune* magazine:

> *Eli Lilly has 1,500 scientists using an advanced information visualization tool (Spotfire) for decision making. With its ability to represent multiple sources of information and interactively change your view, it's helpful for homing in on specific molecules and deciding whether we should be doing further testing on them.*

The fact that the revenue announced by Spotfire Inc. for the year 2005 was US$ 35 million speaks volumes for the value that its users attach to the benefits of information visualization.

1.5 Questions of taxonomy

There are related, and somewhat overlapping, fields called *scientific visualization,* and *geovisualization,* both sharing, with information visualization, the general aim of helping a user to be informed about data of some kind. With scientific visualization it is generally agreed that what is seen by a user primarily relates to a physical 'thing' such as a horned lizard for which the distance between outer skin and interior bone is colour coded (Figure 1.12) or a mountain range over which the formation of clouds is of concern. By contrast, *information visualization* is more concerned with 'abstract' concepts such as price, baseball scores, currency fluctuations and family relations which, while undoubtedly associated with physical things such as pound coins, baseball bats, dollar bills and human beings, do not often require those physical things to be portrayed: the currency trader presumably knows (though he need not) what a $10 bill looks like and doesn't require an image of one to assist in his trading.

FIGURE 1.12
Reconstruction from X-ray CT showing distance to bone (colour map on skin surface) of the Texas horned lizard and the Mexican horned lizard
(Courtesy of Dr Wendy Hodges and Dr Timothy Rowe, and Digimorph.org)

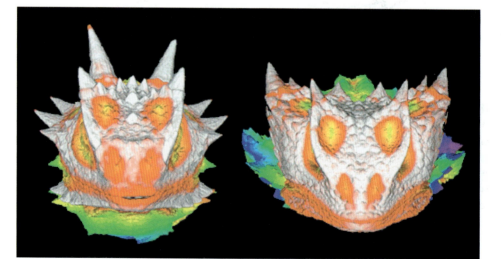

Geovisualization is similar to scientific visualization in that a map of some sort is usually at the heart of any display of data. Figure 1.13, for example, shows the concentration of people having the surname Spence in the United Kingdom in 1881 and 1998, and can validly be said to employ encoding techniques that will be discussed in this book. So do the maps of Minard, Snow and Beck. Scientific and geovisualization tend to embody a spatial content, whereas information visualization typically involves abstract and non-spatial data such as engineering data and financial transactions. However, as we have seen, there can be a substantial degree of overlap.[5]

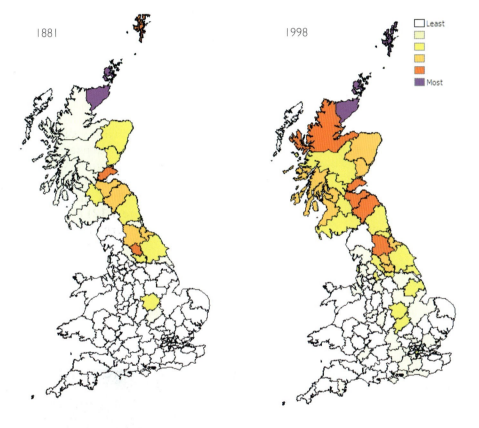

FIGURE 1.13
Incidence of the surname Spence by region of England, Scotland and Wales, in 1881 and 1998

The reader would be correct in observing that the distinction between the three types of visualization, as described above, lacks precision, reflecting the need for a better taxonomy. Tory and Moller (2004) have in fact challenged the traditional taxonomy by proposing one that is based on the user's mental model of the information that is to be gleaned from available data, a basis compatible with the cognitive focus of our definition of visualization. It will be interesting to see how their proposed taxonomy is adopted and the benefits that will accrue to interaction design.

---

[5] The reader interested in geovisualization is referred to the book by MacEachren (2004).

1.6 Issues

This introductory discussion of information visualization – what it is, how it is achieved, how useful it is and how human processes are crucial to its success – does not explicitly identify the principal issues that must be understood to achieve its effective application. We have in fact encountered many of those issues in the course of this chapter, albeit informally. They are *representation* (the manner in which data is encoded, usually in visual form), *presentation* (the way in which suitably encoded data is laid out within available display area and time) and *interaction* (the actions undertaken by a user to move from one view of data to another). In the following chapter we employ a specific task – the selection of a car to buy – to gradually design a visualization tool that illustrates these three issues prior to their detailed consideration in later chapters.

Exercises

The value of many of these exercises can be enhanced by discussing the results in open class.

Exercise 1.1 (Review)

What is the meaning of 'visualization'? Is it carried out by a human being or a computer?

Exercise 1.2 (Review)

In what essential ways have improvements in technology enhanced the potential of information visualization?

Exercise 1.3

Without consulting the chapter you have just read, sketch the essential details of what you remember of the representations created by Minard, Nightingale, Snow and Beck. In other words, externalize your mental models of those representations.

Exercise 1.4

In the course of a normal day, make notes of examples in which data is represented visually, aurally or by tactile means. Afterwards identify whether, for each case, the data has value (numeric, ordinal, categorical) or is a relation.

Exercise 1.5

Preferably by means of sketches rather than computer-drawn diagrams, explore alternative ways of representing the data encoded in the representations of Minard, Nightingale, Snow and Beck.

Exercise 1.6

Select a physical object (e.g. a car, yourself, a house) and identify some of its attributes that can usefully be represented visually. Sketch a possible visual representation of that selected object.

CHAPTER 2

The Issues

What are the basic issues that need to be addressed by a book about information visualization? To answer this question we examine how and why an information visualization tool is typically used. To this end we select one representative task and study it in some detail. At this stage there is little danger in selecting just one task for study because we shall find that the issues identified are relevant to most applications of information visualization. During the discussion certain concepts that will later be seen to be important are presented in **boldface**.[1]

2.1 The task

The **task** we address is that of selecting a car to buy, a specific but representative example of the generic and widespread task of selecting one object from among many on the basis of its attributes. A variant would be the 'whittling down' of a large number of objects to identify a few worthy of further consideration. An associated – and crucial – subtask, that of **gaining insight** into a collection of data, is equally widespread and an essential component of data mining and decision support. Although we shall address the task of selecting a car using a *digital* information space, there are useful parallels from the physical world of car showrooms.

---

[1] In this chapter only. In subsequent chapters boldface is used to denote the first occasion on which a term is defined additionally in the Glossary.

2.2 Nature of the problem

To be realistic it must be accepted that the sort of problem we are addressing in order to complete the task is frequently characterized by a lack of precision. Requirements such as 'nice looking', 'sporty' and 'affordable' may be articulated in the context of car purchase. Others of which the buyer is aware but which may not be articulated could include fashion and colour. There may, in fact, be other criteria of which the prospective buyer is unaware but which will unconsciously influence choice. Not surprisingly, therefore, it is frequently the case that *a problem is formulated as it is being solved* (Schon, 1983). We often do not know what we do not know.

2.3 The data

Data describing a collection of cars can usually be recorded in tabular form and is often **presented** to the user in this way (Figure 2.1). Each row corresponds to a car (in general, an **object**), while each column refers to a different **attribute** of that car. Not all attributes are of the same type: some are numerical (e.g. *Price*), some are categorical (e.g. *Make*) while others are ordinal (e.g. *Rating*); some might involve text, as in a recommendation.

Make	Price (£)	MPG	Rating	Age (yrs)
Ford	15,450	31	*****	3
Chevy	12,450	27	***	4

FIGURE 2.1
A table recording the attribute values (columns) of a collection of objects (rows)

2.4 Table presentation

Notwithstanding the public's widespread familiarity with tables, such a presentation is often of limited help, especially if there are many rows and ten or more columns. In the unusual situation where a precise requirement exists, the table can certainly be searched, by eye or by some automatic search mechanism, until a car satisfying those requirements is found (or not). Nevertheless, even if a precise match is found, the purchaser may still wonder what else may have been acceptable and, on further reflection, perhaps more desirable. Even if a precise match fails to be found, it is unlikely that a line-by-line search of the table will have contributed much to the user's mental model of the data. It is true, as we shall see later when discussing the Table Lens, that an interactive facility to rearrange table rows according to some criterion (e.g. *Price*) can be immensely helpful, emphasizing the power of **interactive rearrangement**.

2.5 Bargrams

When the problem is first addressed a feature of the data that may well be of interest is the approximate range of prices. Unless the cars are arranged in the table in ascending or descending order of price – and there is no reason why *Price*, among many attributes, should be the basis of such preordained ordering – the range of prices will not be easy to ascertain from the table. An alternative **representation** of price data takes the form of a bargram as shown in Figure 2.2.[2] This **semi-qualitative** representation assumes that price *ranges* – rather than specific values – are sufficiently informative, at least initially. Moreover, the length of each bar can **represent** – indeed, can be made directly proportional to – the number of cars in that price range, thereby providing additional information regarding populations within each range. A quick glance at the bargram assists the formation of a useful **mental model** of the range of prices and the distribution of cars within the price ranges. We might say that the bargram is providing an **overview** of prices and population.

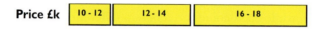

Price £k   10 - 12   12 - 14   16 - 18

FIGURE 2.2 A bargram representation of the price ranges associated with a collection of cars for sale, with the width of each bargram proportional to the number of corresponding cars

2.6 Interactive object selection

Rather than begin by acquiring an overview of prices, the user may instead happen to notice, among a collection of car images, one that seems particularly attractive (Figure 2.3). It would then be natural to wonder how much that car would cost and begin to seek some **detail**. The price could, of course, be placed in a label just below the image, but again there is no reason why *Price* should be chosen, out of ten or more attributes, for that label. Alternatively, the position of that car on the *Price* bargram can be indicated by an icon. Indeed, to allow the price of any car to be so indicated, an 'object vector' containing car icons can usefully be positioned above the bargram, as shown in Figure 2.4; the object vector also provides a useful immediate indication of the population of cars. Normally, the icons would be ordered in the object vector according to price, to

FIGURE 2.3 One (unquantifiable) attribute of a car – its appearance – may well attract the buyer's attention

---

[2] Many of the illustrations which follow have been inspired by concepts embodied in a visualization tool called the EZChooser (Wittenburg *et al.*, 2001), whose design is considered in Section 6.2.

allow comparison.[3] The **relation** between a car's image (Figure 2.3) and the corresponding price range (Figure 2.4) could be shown by a line connecting image to icon, but a more effective approach may be to use colour coding: place a coloured border around the image (Figure 2.5) and use the same colour for the icon. The relation between car image and price is reasonably clear and the user will probably then remember it for some time, thereby extending their mental model of the car collection.

Price £k | 10 - 12 | 12 - 14 | 16 - 18

FIGURE 2.4 Icons positioned above a bargram represent individual cars

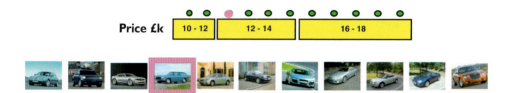

Price £k | 10 - 12 | 12 - 14 | 16 - 18

FIGURE 2.5 The price of a car selected via its image is indicated by colour coding both on the image and on the corresponding icon above the bargram

2.7 Overview

The term **overview**, just introduced, deserves further discussion. Although the term is not easy to define with precision, it can be argued that it implies a *qualitative awareness* of *one aspect* of some data, preferably acquired *rapidly* and, even better, pre-attentively: that is, without cognitive effort. An example drawn from this chapter would be an estimate of the number of cars available ('about 20' or 'worth looking into') and the price range ('about ten to twenty k'). There is no implication that the data overviewed is the entire data set, though the larger the data set that can be overviewed, the more useful the process may be. Advantages ensuing from an overview can include the shape of the data set ('most cars are far too expensive') and significant features ('cars are cheap or expensive – nothing in between') and may serve to suggest parts of the data set that could subsequently be filtered out to enable a task to be accomplished more effectively (Cairns and Craft, 2005).

---

[3] Equal spacing of object icons in the object vector precludes the precise representation of price.

2.8 Multiple attributes

Price is not usually the sole criterion for choosing a car. If the miles-per-gallon (MPG) performance is also of interest, another bargram can be shown (Figure 2.6) above the *Price* bargram. Again it is advantageous to position an object vector above the new bargram: clearly the same number of icons will be associated with it, though in general the cars they represent will not be in the same order. When a car image is identified by mouse click or mouse-over, the relevant icon above *both* bargrams can be appropriately colour coded, effectively **relating** the image to two attribute value ranges. Again, we see the user accumulating **detail** about cars.

FIGURE 2.6
The position of a selected car is indicated on all attribute bargrams by colour coding

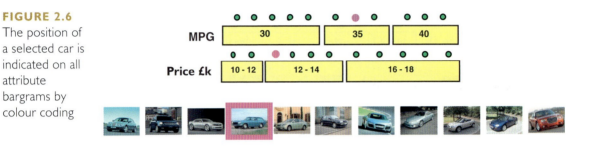

2.9 Detail

In contrast to overview, the term **detail** implies the aggregation of a *number of different features* of an object, awareness of which would usually involve *cognitive effort* and would not occur quickly unless the encoding of the data was extremely well designed to support rapid awareness. Thus, for a car, detail might be 'cost about £12k, low MPG, highly recommended, 1990 Buick, better deal than the Chevy'. Precision is *not* a requirement of detail.

Though it is often suggested otherwise (Shneiderman, 1996), it is not required that an overview should precede the awareness of detail, and the reason is to be found in the definition of information visualization – the acquisition of a mental model of some data. For example, the car buyer may select one car and discover detail – its price, MPG, year and HP – simply to discover the sort of car that is on offer. A different example is provided by a person who is house-hunting in an unfamiliar geographical region or country, who might arbitrarily select for view a card describing one house, simply to obtain some 'ball-park' feeling for what might be available. Such actions provide one 'point' on a 'surface' and act as a starting point for a mental model, to be followed either by more detail or an overview.

2.10 Significant objects

The display of another form of **relation** can be helpful. A buyer will often have in their mind the attributes of an ideal car. Although that car may not exist in the current collection, it may be useful, nevertheless, to *represent* the **ideal car** (Figure 2.7) in the same way as for a real car, but with a distinctive icon of its own to avoid confusion. Visually, the **relation** between an available car and the ideal is immediately obvious and the 'distance' between ideal and actual icons provides some idea of the extent to which an available car differs from the ideal. In the same way an existing car may be identified to indicate that it is a 'possible' in the buyer's mind and is usefully **tagged** by some means (Figure 2.8), thereby reducing the need to commit that information to memory.

FIGURE 2.7 An icon above a bargram can represent an 'ideal' (and possibly nonexistent) car to act as a point of reference

FIGURE 2.8 A car that is potentially of interest and worth remembering can be 'tagged' for later re-examination

2.11 Interactive attribute selection

Rather than acquiring detail regarding a car by identification of its image, the buyer may prefer to indicate an affordable price range by clicking on the relevant range in the bargram (Figure 2.9). In response, all icons above the *Price* bargram representing cars within that price range will be highlighted and a coloured frame will be assigned to the images of the corresponding cars. Additionally, and without the need for further interaction, the position of those icons on the *MPG* bargram will indicate the corresponding *MPG* attribute value

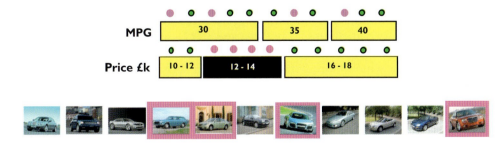

FIGURE 2.9
The interactive selection of a bargram range (here *price* £12–14k) identifies four cars whose price falls within that range

for each of those cars. In this activity a **focusing** operation is being carried out, the user effectively saying – even if only temporarily – 'Let's concentrate on cars within this affordable price range'.

Because it is now impossible to know which purple icon above a bargram corresponds to a given purple-framed car image, we can usefully introduce an immensely powerful – but simple – technique called 'brushing'. Mouse-over of a car image will cause the icon associated with that car to be highlighted in some way (in both *Price* and *MPG* object vectors) and *vice versa*. Subsequent **interactive selection** of an *MPG* range (Figure 2.10) will introduce additional focusing to identify cars that satisfy requirements on *both* attributes, *Price* and *MPG*. Further selections (and deselections) of attribute ranges may be made in the course of exploring the car data, in which case – as before – only those cars satisfying *all* selected ranges on *all* attribute scales will be identified. The interpretation of such selections and deselections as they take place will allow the user's internal model to be enhanced and, in all probability, cause the problem to be refined.

FIGURE 2.10
Subsequent interactive selection of an MPG range identifies only cars which satisfy both requirements

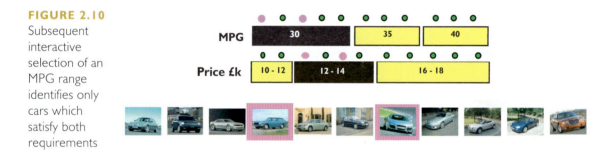

2.12 Space limitations

Typically, as many as ten attributes of a car may be examined before a decision to purchase is made. Unfortunately, there will be no room on a typical display for more than a few bargrams of the form and detail shown in earlier figures. A conventional scrolling function (Figure 2.11) may be thought appropriate, but carries with it the considerable disadvantage that the location of a given car on many attribute bargrams will be hidden. An alternative approach to the **presentation** of the many attribute scales is to reduce the vertical size of many of them by **suppressing** range values while keeping the icons, colour coded as before, superimposed on diminished bargrams (Figure 2.12). In this way, if the user is concentrating on two attributes – say *Price* and *MPG* – any significant change on another bargram is immediately apparent. For those attributes in the 'peripheral' area and for which more detail is required, a scrolling action brings them into full view so that range values can be discerned.

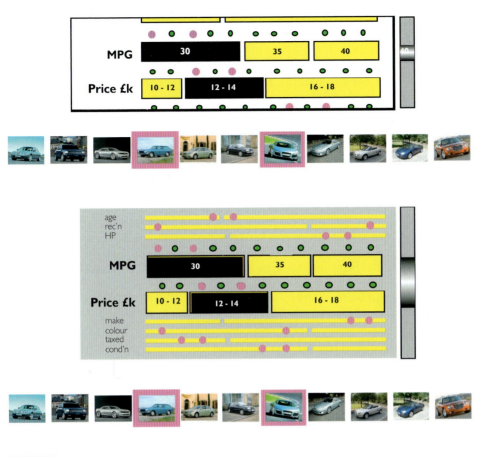

FIGURE 2.11
There may be insufficient room to display all attribute bargrams. One solution is to scroll bargrams through a window

FIGURE 2.11
There may be insufficient room to display all attribute bargrams. One solution is to scroll bargrams through a window

FIGURE 2.12
If space is too limited to accommodate all bargrams, many can be diminished so that some aspects of all bargrams are visible. A scrolling action determines which bargrams are fully displayed

2.13 Filtering

One option that could be made available to the car buyer is that of filtering. For example, if the price range from £16k to £18k was deemed to be the *only* one of interest, some interaction could ensure the **presentation** only of data associated with cars within that price range (Figure 2.13). A possible advantage of such **filtering**, involving the **suppression** of data, might be the reduction of cognitive effort required from the user arising from their ability now to concentrate on a subset of cars. A disadvantage might be the loss of valuable context information, as we shall see below.

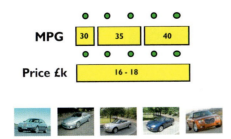

FIGURE 2.13
If a selected *Price* range is the only one of interest, other irrelevant detail can be suppressed

2.14 Taking stock

The reason we have been discussing a system which supports online car purchase is that we need to identify the principal issues that must be addressed if we are to understand and then exploit the phenomenon of information visualization. So far we have identified two issues: those of **representation** (the visual or aural encoding of data) and **presentation** (the selection and layout of encoded data in the available display area and available time). These issues receive separate treatment respectively in Chapters 3 and 4. But there is a third principal issue we must discuss, that of **interaction**. The importance of this issue arises from the fact that one of the major reasons why information visualization has increased in importance so rapidly over the last 15–20 years is that technology can now support *responsive* interaction: we can have an idea, or formulate a question, and get essentially immediate feedback to enhance our understanding. Interaction allows us, in fact, to select different *views* of our data, and because we typically move from one view to another quite briskly before reaching that 'Ah HA!' experience, we must decide how to 'navigate' between these different views (Woods and Watts, 1997).

2.15 Navigational guidance

It is quite common, when selecting an object to purchase and having specified limits to various attributes, to wonder what would happen 'if we had another £1,000 to spend'. An answer to this 'what if?' question could be obtained by selecting the next higher price range and observing any changes that occur. But such a step would have to be cancelled and repeated to answer a new question, for example, 'What if we kept the same price range as before but accepted a lower MPG?' A much more effective answer to many 'what if?' questions can be provided by a simple modification to the icon vector and can be *immensely* helpful. It is possible to indicate, with an 'outline' icon (Figure 2.14), those cars which do not satisfy all selected attribute ranges but which, if the attribute range immediately below the icon were to be selected, would *then* satisfy all requirements. In other words, the unselected range below the outline icon is the only one that the car does not satisfy. What this encoding is doing is providing **sensitivity information** which, because it can reveal latent possibilities not previously considered, can be extremely helpful in guiding the user's **exploration** of information space. An implementation of this sensitivity technique can be seen (Figure 2.15) in a visualization

FIGURE 2.14 An 'outline' icon above a bargram range indicates that the range is the only requirement not satisfied by the outlined car. Thus, if that range is interactively selected to indicate its acceptability, the icon will change to indicate that the car satisfies all requirements

tool called the EZChooser (Wittenburg *et al.*, 2001), which provided the original inspiration for most of the illustrations used in this chapter.

Vehicles matching your feature selections. (Color a vehicle in all rows by selecting a color over the picture.)

FIGURE 2.15
A view of the EZChooser, showing sensitivity information in the form of outline car icons
Source: *Courtesy of Kent Wittenburg*

Dodge/Plymouth Neon   Ford Escort/ZX2   Mazda Protege   Toyota Corolla

2.16 Movement in information space

The principal feature which separates modern information visualization tools from the works (albeit inspirational) of Minard, Snow and Nightingale is **interaction**: the facility we have to **change our view** of the available data. Our car purchaser, in taking the sequence of actions recorded in earlier figures, employed interaction to examine a sequence of different views of the car data. The progression was essentially incremental, appropriate to the gradual process of learning about (i.e. forming a mental model of) the collection of cars and gradually approaching a decision. In the course of this activity the user's mental model may well undergo considerable change: an early accumulation of insight followed by additions to and deletions from that model. The progression from one view of data to another can be viewed as **movement** within the **information space** which is the totality of the car data.

Superficially a quite different example of movement is provided (Figure 2.16) by a couple seeking an evening's entertainment. They search sequentially, using a simple menu system, through a pre-designed set of frames, a situation in distinct contrast to the purchaser of a car who has the freedom to view a multitude of different views and many different ways in which it is possible to interact with the system. In both cases, however, the fundamental activity, controlled by interaction, is the examination of many different views of available data by movement through **information space**.

Interactive movement in information space is referred to as **navigation**. While seeking entertainment may involve only a few movements in the relevant information space, the selection of a car to buy – as well as many other common tasks

FIGURE 2.16
The search through a menu system for an evening's entertainment constitutes movement through a discrete information space which is populated by frames such as these

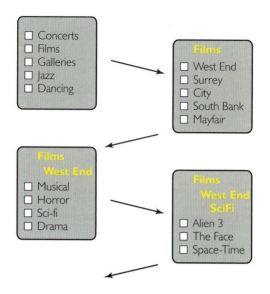

– may easily involve 100 or more such movements before the task is completed. Especially when many steps are involved, a particular concern of the interaction designer is the provision of **cues** to enhance navigation. We have seen one example in the outlined car icons in Figure 2.14 and 2.15: another example is seen at the top of each frame in Figure 2.16, showing the 'route' taken to the current frame, thereby providing an easy way of returning to a previous frame.

In view of its importance we now add **interaction**, discussed later in Chapter 5, to the issues of **representation** (Chapter 3) and **presentation** (Chapter 4) to form the core of this book: they can be viewed (Figure 2.17) as the essential link between available data and the human user seeking insight. However, before addressing these three issues separately and in some depth, we recall that information visualization is essentially the formation of a mental model of data: we must therefore identify those aspects of human performance that are directly relevant to information visualization.

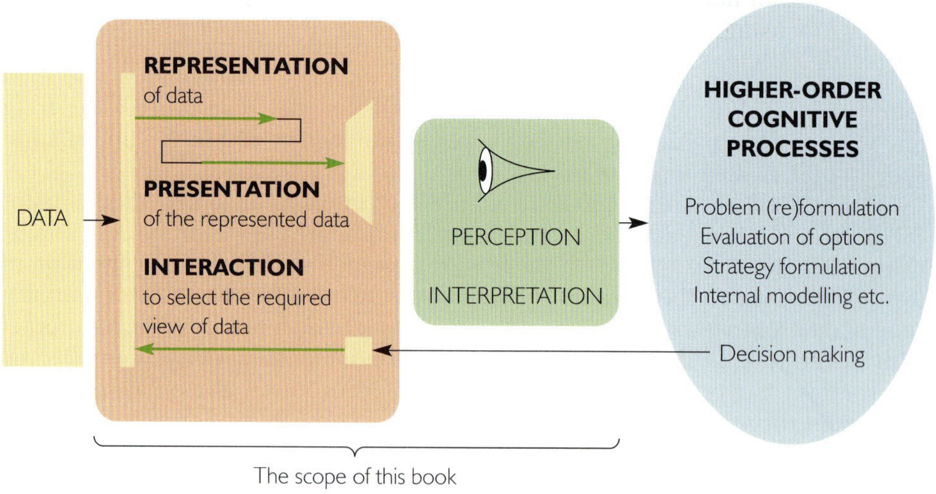

FIGURE 2.17
Identification of the interaction with data governed by high-order cognitive processes, highlighting the emphasis of the book

REPRESENTATION
of data

PRESENTATION
of the represented data

INTERACTION
to select the required view of data

DATA

PERCEPTION

INTERPRETATION

HIGHER-ORDER COGNITIVE PROCESSES

Problem (re)formulation
Evaluation of options
Strategy formulation
Internal modelling etc.

Decision making

The scope of this book

2.17 Perception and interpretation

In our discussion of car purchase we identified aspects of human performance that are involved in the activity of visualization. Two essential activities are those of **perception** and **interpretation** (Figure 2.17). Visual perception – simply *seeing* a representation of data – must precede an interpretation of the meaning of that representation, whether it be a purple circle above a bargram or the scroll bar beside those bargrams. Current understanding is such that it is both possible and useful in the context of information visualization to say something about these aspects of human behaviour. However, rather than devote a separate chapter to these topics they will be introduced as and when appropriate so that their relevance is directly evident: this material will be distinguished by blue text. To 'dig deeper' into these topics the reader is referred to Colin Ware's excellent book *Information Visualization: Perception for Design*.

Perception and interpretation are not the only aspects of human performance relevant to information visualization: there are many others that can be classified as '**higher-order cognitive processes**' (Figure 2.17), processes that are harnessed to support whatever task is being facilitated by information visualization. For example, choice of the next movement to make in information space is undoubtedly influenced by the state of the user's internal model, by their current expression of the problem being solved, by the strategy being adopted to enhance the model and by the criteria adopted to assess the relative benefits of available movements. And all these influences are undoubtedly affected by the user's previous experience, stored in long-term memory. However, understanding of these highly complex processes is not as advanced as for perception and cognition and, while they are sufficiently important to an interaction designer to receive mention in this book, their detailed discussion here is inappropriate.

2.18 Summary

By examining an illustrative application we have identified activities such as filtering and focusing, as well as the acquisition of both detail and overviews which support the activity of information visualization. We have seen how these activities depend for their effectiveness upon the way in which data – both values and relations – is represented and presented. We have also become aware of the benefits that can accrue from interaction. The three chapters which now follow discuss those principal issues of information visualization: representation (Chapter 3), presentation (Chapter 4) and interaction (Chapter 5).

Exercises

The value of many of these exercises can be enhanced by discussing the results in open class.

Exercise 2.1 (Review)

What are the drawbacks of the bargram representation of data? What are the advantages?

Exercise 2.2 (Review)

Explain the value of the outline cars which appear above the bargrams in the EZChooser.

Exercise 2.3 (Review)

What are the relative advantages and disadvantages of filtering and focusing?

Exercise 2.4 (Review)

A car is described by a number of attributes: price, appearance, make, recommendation, horse power, year of manufacture and age. Say which of these attributes are numerical, ordinal and categorical.

Exercise 2.5

Based on your experience of buying a mobile phone, washing machine, bicycle, car or other multi-attribute object, express your view as to the meaning of 'overview' and 'detail' and give some examples.

Exercise 2.6

For which of the attributes mentioned in Exercise 2.4 would it be possible to order the objects above a given bar of a bargram?

C H A P T E R   3

Representation

Our discussion of the previous chapter, together with examples introduced in Chapter 1, has shown that the power of information visualization stems to a considerable degree from our ability to take raw data, often in the form of numbers, and present it again – that is, *represent* it – in a different way, with the aim of informing a user. We repeat Simon's (1996) succinct remark that

> . . . *solving a problem simply means representing it so as to make the solution transparent.*

Our terminology is consistent with a dictionary definition of 'represent':

> **represent** (v): to depict, portray.

We have seen a number of ways in which values can be represented – or, as we often say, encoded – visually. Minard used colour and line thickness, John Snow used dots and crosses, Florence Nightingale used 'rose petals' and Harry Beck used colour to differentiate underground lines. There are, in fact, so many ways in which data can be represented visually or aurally that we cannot visit them all. What can be useful before we look at different techniques is to establish three important aspects of representation: the *type* of data we want to represent, the *complexity* of that data and the way in which a user *interprets* the encoded data.

Data types

One aspect of representation has to do with the *relation* between two or more items of data, also referred to as *structure*. The car purchase system used colour (Figure 3.1) to draw attention to the link between the price of a car and its appearance, and in Chapter 1 coloured lines were used to represent the connection between London Underground stations. The potential offered by interaction can additionally help to encode relationships if **brushing** is employed (Becker and Cleveland, 1987): a mouse-over of a list of doctors (Figure 3.2) can easily identify the hospital beds for which they have responsibility and, equally importantly, vice versa.

FIGURE 3.1
Part of the car purchase interface from Chapter 2: purple identifies a relation

FIGURE 3.2
Interaction to identify a doctor highlights the hospital beds under his or her care, and vice versa: an example of brushing

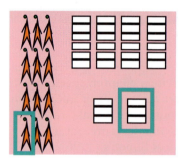

We also saw the need to represent *values*. Sometimes a user seeks precision and needs to know that the cost of a car is £16,995, but there are many situations where a **derived value** (Tweedie, 1997) such as an average or a range is primarily of interest. We must also be ready to facilitate answers not only to the precise question 'How much does it cost?' but also to the more qualitative enquiry as to how highly it is recommended.

These two classes of data – value and structure – will be examined separately later in this chapter.

Data complexity

Choosing a car on the basis of one or two attributes is reasonably straightforward. One could imagine the use of a scatterplot (Figure 3.3) to represent the position of each car in a space with two dimensions, *Price* and *Miles per gallon* . Realistically, of course, there may be ten or more car attributes of interest to a buyer, with the requirement that a visualization tool must somehow encode information about ten attributes for each of possibly 40 cars. It is not the

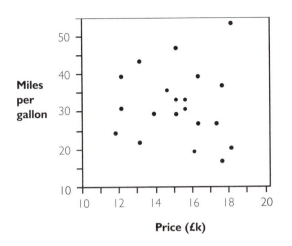

FIGURE 3.3
A point indicates, for each car, its Price and MPG attribute values

number of *cars* that presents the problem but the number of *dimensions* or *attributes*. Thus, in our discussion of techniques, we shall direct attention first to *univariate data* (where only one attribute is involved), then to *bivariate data* (two dimensions) and, after *trivariate data*, to the much more challenging task of representing multi-dimensional – often called *hypervariate – data*.[1]

Perception and cognition

We ignore, at our peril, the manner in which users behave when they view representations of data. As mentioned in Chapter 2, we shall introduce aspects of human behaviour as and when they are relevant to the techniques being discussed: the treatment will be brief (and in blue), but hopefully adequate to allow appreciation of its significance for interaction design. Also, rather than simply presenting a number of useful techniques without explaining *why* they should be of interest, we shall discuss measures by which the value of a particular technique may be judged.

3.1 The encoding of value

3.1.1 Univariate data

A single number
It may be difficult to believe that the task of making a person aware of just one number can be fraught with difficulty. Nevertheless, a striking example is provided by the old aircraft altimeter (Figure 3.4) whose purpose is to make an aircraft pilot aware of the height of an aircraft above sea level. As it happens, a number of fatal crashes can be linked to the manner of representation employed in that altimeter.

---

[1] This is, in fact, the taxonomy and pedagogical approach used by Cleveland (1993).

FIGURE 3.4
The original
aircraft
altimeter,
responsible for
many accidents

The smallest of the three hands of the altimeter indicates the number of tens of thousands of feet, the next largest the number of thousands of feet and the largest one of all shows hundreds of feet. Familiarity may enable the altimeter of Figure 3.4 to be interpreted quite rapidly as indicating a height of about 13,460 feet. The major problem arises when the pilot's gaze moves away from the altimeter, perhaps to interpret another indicator, perhaps to take in the view out of the window or to converse with a co-pilot. On returning visual attention to the altimeter it is possible that any change will not be noticed: for example, Figures 3.5 and 3.6 are representations of an altimeter and at first sight appear identical. But there is a difference of 10,000 feet between the heights they encode. The effect, already introduced in Chapter 1, is called *change blindness* (Rensink, 2002) and its relevance to information visualization is considerable. For example, if some interaction takes place and it is intended that the user be aware of a corresponding change in a visual display, it is essential that the change be noticed. Another example is shown in Figures 3.7 and 3.8. The two images differ, but it may not be immediately apparent to the reader that this is the case.

The modern aircraft altimeter, summarized diagrammatically in Figure 3.9, acknowledges the use to which an altimeter will be put and the characteristics of its human observer, the pilot. It reflects the need for a quick assessment of potential danger by separating the height scale into two sections, appropriately colouring them green and purple, and marking the position of the aircraft on that scale by a mainly black image. Thus, a quick glance (e.g. a maximum of 200 ms) will confirm that the aircraft is flying at a safe height. If more detail is

FIGURE 3.5 Representation of the view of an altimeter

FIGURE 3.6 An altimeter representation easily assumed to be the same as that in Figure 3.5

FIGURE 3.7 A picture which differs from that in Figure 3.8 *(Courtesy Ron Rensink)*

FIGURE 3.8 A picture which differs from that in Figure 3.7 *(Courtesy Ron Rensink)*

needed, the position of the black pointer may be noted as roughly between 1600 and 2000 feet. If even further detail is needed – for example when on a landing approach – numerical information is available within the black box. Additionally, the speed of rotation of the tens and units indicator (a single indicator, not two separate ones) can provide the pilot with a feeling for rate of descent or ascent. The need to understand the context of an application when applying visualization techniques is emphasized by the fact that, in the black box, the numerals representing thousands and hundreds are larger than those representing tens and units: this is because pilots 'think' in terms of hundreds of feet. The use of equal height numerals in the box would diminish the value of the altimeter and point to the fact that the interaction designer did not really understand the application context.

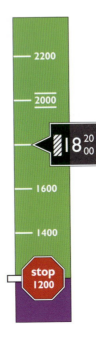

FIGURE 3.9
A modern aircraft altimeter

A second scenario in which the awareness of a single number is crucial is a surgical operation and particularly a major one lasting many hours. Any change in vital human signs such as blood pressure is a cause for concern, especially for the anaesthetist (as well as the patient), so it is essential that any change in such a vital sign be noticed immediately. The anaesthetist is, of course, presented with comprehensive visual information in the manner illustrated in Figure 3.10, but the effort of paying careful attention to such a presentation for many hours would be considerable. The simple solution is to encode vital signs in sound (Watson *et al.*, 1999; Watson and Sanderson, 2004): whatever the anaesthetist is attending to (perhaps on the telephone to respond to an urgent enquiry from a ward), he or she will immediately be aware of a change in the pitch or repetition rate of a constant sequence of 'beeps'. Another reason for introducing this example is that it emphasizes the fact that data can be encoded in ways other than visual and that the 'visual' in visualization should not be misinterpreted.

FIGURE 3.10
Representations of the vital signs of a patient during an operation. The difficulty of paying constant attention to such a display throughout a long operation has led to the encoding of vital signs in the pitch of a frequently repeated 'beep'. A change in pitch is immediately apparent wherever the gaze of the anaesthetist is directed
(Image by kind permission of Marcus Watson)

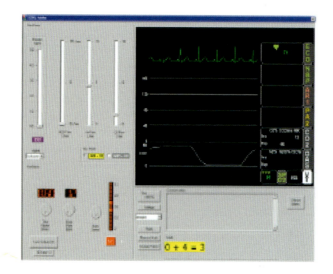

A collection of numbers

Notwithstanding the importance of representing a single number, as in an altimeter, a more common situation is one in which univariate data about a *number* of objects is of interest. Not surprisingly, well-established techniques are available (Cleveland, 1994; Tufte, 1983), though the field of information visualization is such that new ones continue to be invented.

Price data for a number of cars can, for example, be represented as dots on a linear scale (Figure 3.11). But how effective is this representation? A quick overview shows the general distribution of car prices; a more detailed examination will estimate the average price accurately enough to judge 'affordability'; further examination will disclose maximum and minimum prices. A valid question, therefore, for any representation is, 'How will the representation be used?' Many of the *initial* questions in the mind of a car buyer would be answered by a Tukey Box Plot of the same data (Figure 3.12). The box contains the *median* price (the middle line, which divides the number of data items into halves). The two ends of the box represent the 25 percentile (below which one quarter of the data items are to be found) and the 75 percentile. The 5 and 95 percentiles are indicated by the horizontal bars and the outliers are retained as points. Here, much of the data is being *aggregated*, to reflect the fact that precise detail is often not needed; we are now representing *derived values*.

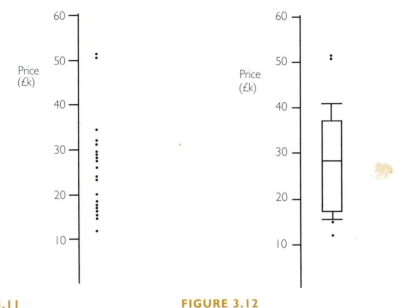

FIGURE 3.11

Each dot represents the price of a car

FIGURE 3.12

A Tukey Box Plot of the data represented in Figure 3.11

Another familiar representation of univariate data is the *histogram* (Figure 3.13). Much has been written about the need for appropriate choice of bin sizes and will not be repeated here. The essential point to note is that we are again representing *aggregate* properties – or derived values – of the data in a manner that can support both 'at a glance' awareness and the need for more precise understanding. The histogram is only one of many useful representations of numerical data that are more concerned with derived values. For example, if we 'push over' the columns of the histogram and join them together we obtain the *bargram* (Figure 3.14), already familiar from Chapter 2. While the relative count in a bin is now reflected in the bin's width, certain characteristics of the data are lost or not obvious at first sight – for example, the existence of outliers and the emptiness of a particular range. This omission may be immaterial in certain applications.

Values need not be numerical – they can be *categorical* or *ordinal*. The makes of cars can include Ford, Nissan, Toyota, Ferrari, etc., so that a bargram appearing in an online car sales display like the EZChooser (Wittenburg *et al.*, 2001) might contain this univariate categorical data as shown in Figure 3.15. Ordinal data can be found in the sales volume of a shop for the various ordered days of the week (Figure 3.16).

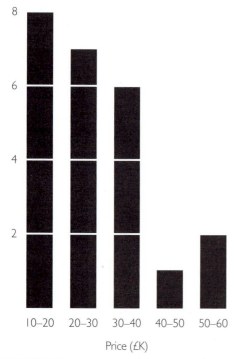

Price £k	10–12	12–14	16–18

FIGURE 3.14 A bargram representation of univariate data, obtained by 'tipping over' the columns (bars) of a histogram and joining them end to end, ignoring any null bins

FIGURE 3.13 A histogram of univariate data

FIGURE 3.15 A bargram representation of univariate categorical data

FIGURE 3.16 A histogram of univariate ordinal data.

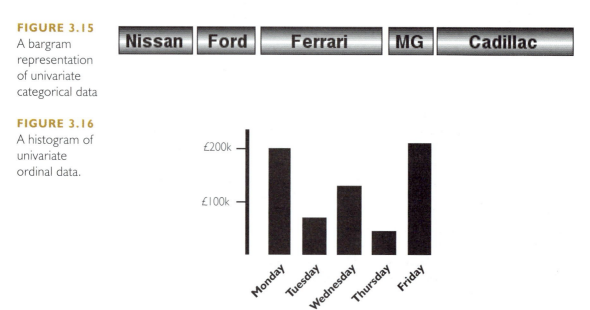

3.1.2 Bivariate data

A conventional approach to the representation of bivariate data is the *scatter-plot*. For a collection of houses, all characterized by a price and the number of bedrooms, each house is represented by a point in two-dimensional space with

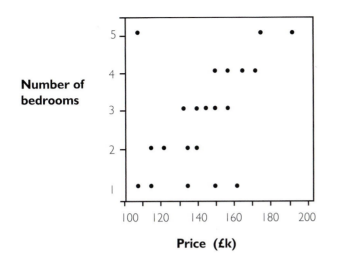

FIGURE 3.17
A scatterplot of bivariate data. Each point indicates the price and number of bedrooms associated with a house

axes associated with these two attributes (Figure 3.17). This representation affords an awareness of a general trend (more money, more bedrooms), of local trade-offs (less money, more bedrooms) and of outliers that may be interesting and might not have been anticipated (a five-bed house for £110,000). Any conventional query system requiring a precise formulation of housing needs would not encourage the specification of such an unanticipated result and is one of the many reasons why information visualization can be so valuable.

A special case of the scatterplot is a time series, in which one axis represents time and the other some function of time. The importance of time-varying data, for example in medical and climate studies, is such that many representation techniques as well as visualization tools have been developed to allow understanding to be derived from a time-series plot. The performance of one time-series query tool is illustrated in Figure 3.18 in the context of a data set containing 52 weekly stock prices for 1,430 stocks (Hochheiser and Shneiderman, 2004). The graph overview of Figure 3.18(a) shows the entire data set, providing some idea of density and distributions. In Figure 3.18(b) a single timebox limits the display to those items with prices between $70 and $250 during days 1 to 4. Subsequent queries add additional constraints, selecting items that have prices between $70 and $95 during days 7 to 12 (Figure 3.18(c)) and for prices between $90 and $115 for days 15 to 18 (Figure 3.18(d)).

An alternative representation of a time series (Figure 3.19), perhaps more suited for gaining an initial impression of data, is illustrated by the level of ozone concentration above Los Angeles, each square associated with one day and coloured to indicate the ozone level. The figure, which represents ten years of data, shows that ozone levels are higher in the summer months and that concentrations during those months have decreased with time.

Perhaps unexpectedly, insight into bivariate data can benefit from an apparent separation of the two attributes. For example, each of two attributes can be assigned to a separate histogram, as shown in Figure 3.20(a). A single house is represented once on each histogram, as illustrated by the highlighted house in Figure 3.20(b). If the histograms are static there is no opportunity to see the relation between the two attributes and there is little to commend the use of two

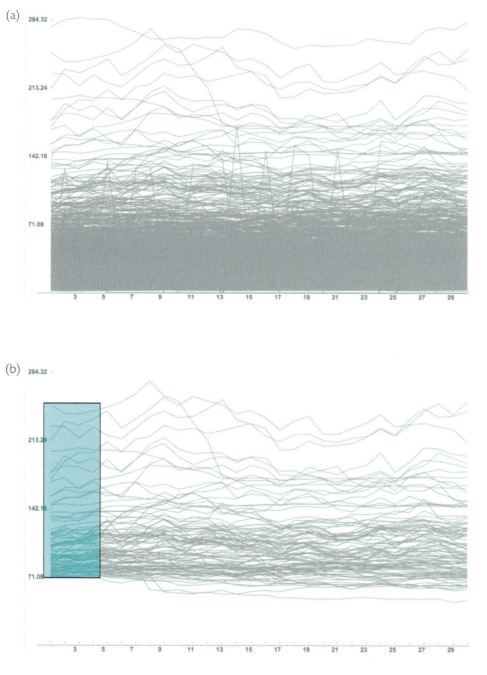

separate histograms. However, if interaction allows the placement of limits on one of the attribute scales (Figure 3.20(c)), then the houses thereby identified can usefully be encoded by colour not only on one attribute histogram but on the other as well (Figure 3.20(c)), thereby providing insight into the relation between the two attributes. This is another example of the powerful technique of brushing, whose value is difficult to overstate. Especially if the histogram display is modified to 'range down' selected objects, as in Figure 3.20(d), another

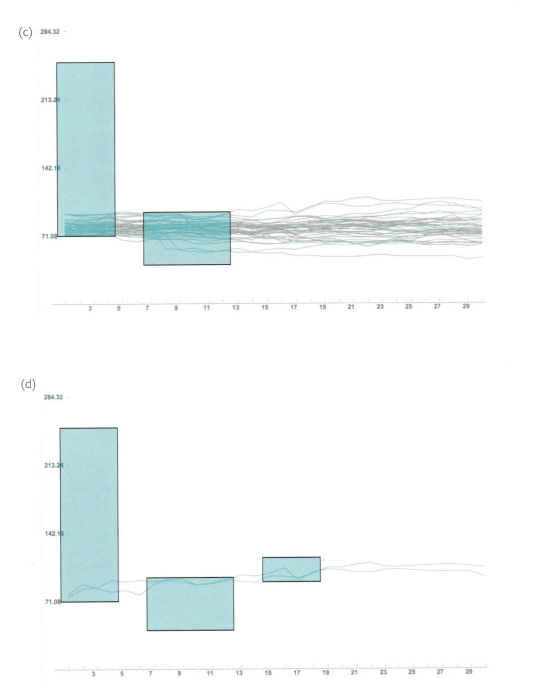

benefit accruing from brushing is illustrated if it is possible to move the entire selected *range* of one attribute from side to side and see how that affects the selected houses on the second attribute. If lower and upper limits on both attribute scales can be adjusted separately, a very flexible exploratory visualization tool results (Tweedie *et al.*, 1994; Spence and Tweedie, 1998; Albinsson *et al.*, 2003).

FIGURE 3.19

Representation of the level of ozone concentration above Los Angeles over a period of ten years

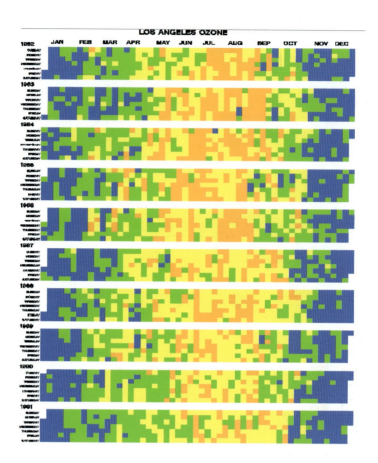

It may well be the case that, of two attributes, one is either far more important than the other or must be examined first. In this case it may be appropriate to employ 'logical' or *'semantic' zoom*. If the price of cars is of prime interest, a representation such as that shown in Figure 3.21(a) might be the first to be examined. It is then possible to arrange for a semantic zoom that will show, for a subset of the cars, the make of car in addition to the price (Figure 3.21(b)). This technique, which dates back to 1980 at least (Herot, 1980; Herot *et al.,* 1981), is quite general: it can encompass many attributes and many discrete levels of progressive zoom, as we shall see in the next chapter.

The frequent need for a *qualitative* understanding of data is illustrated in the representation of Figure 3.22. The domain is that of electronic circuit design and the situation is one in which the designer has proposed a design and needs a first appreciation of a particular property of that circuit, for example the magnitude of the voltage at each point in the circuit. These values are encoded by the size of a red square in Figure 3.22. Why? First because the designer will already have a mental model of the expected voltage magnitudes and the display will either confirm that model or, in the case of Figure 3.22, make it clear that a mistake has been made in choosing a value for a particular component (because the two squares at top right are not of equal area). In this example the designer has made a useful discovery, one that might not have been made if the voltage values had

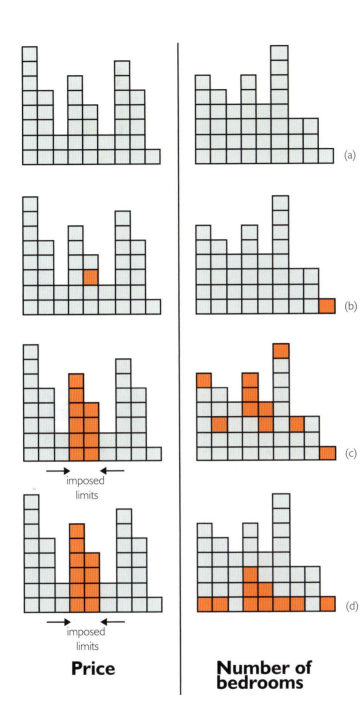

Price

Number of bedrooms

imposed limits

imposed limits

FIGURE 3.20
Linked histograms.
(a) The price and number of bedrooms associated with a collection of houses are represented by separate histograms;
(b) a single house is represented once on each histogram;
(c) upper and lower limits placed on price define a subset of houses which are coded red on *both* histograms;
(d) interpretation is enhanced by 'ranging down' the colour-coded houses, especially if exploration involves the dynamic alteration of limits

FIGURE 3.21
Semantic zoom reveals data about a second attribute

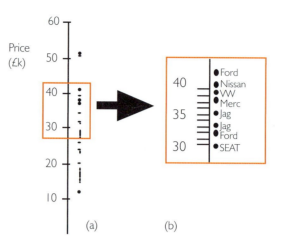

FIGURE 3.22
The area of each red square encodes the value of the voltage occurring at the point in the circuit at which the square is located

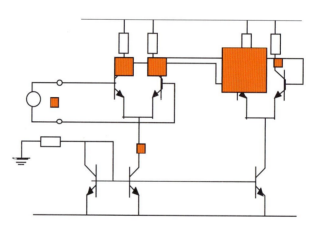

been displayed in numerical form. The difference between the two red squares 'pops out'. When numerical values are of interest, a simple mouse click or mouse-over can always replace the red squares with the corresponding numerical values.

A similar technique exists for representing value in such a way as to afford a qualitative understanding. Many people have a mental model of the representation of Australia and New Zealand on a map of the world (Figure 3.23), so that the fact that New Zealanders possess ten times as many bicycles as Australians (if that were true!) could be encoded by correspondingly magnifying the representation of New Zealand on a map, as shown in Figure 3.24. That such magnification encoding can lead to useful insight is demonstrated by *The State of the World Atlas* (Smith, 1999) of which one page, concerned with population density, is shown in Figure 3.25. The familiar large land mass normally located at top left is now replaced by a thin strip representing Canada's low population density, as is the case with Australia. Other pages in this atlas are equally illuminating.

3.1.3 Trivariate data

Since we live in a three-dimensional world there is a temptation to represent data about objects characterized by three attributes by points in three-

FIGURE 3.23
A representation of Australia and New Zealand on a conventional map

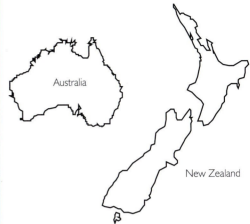

FIGURE 3.24
A representation of Australia and New Zealand indicating that some attribute of New Zealand is ten times its value for Australia

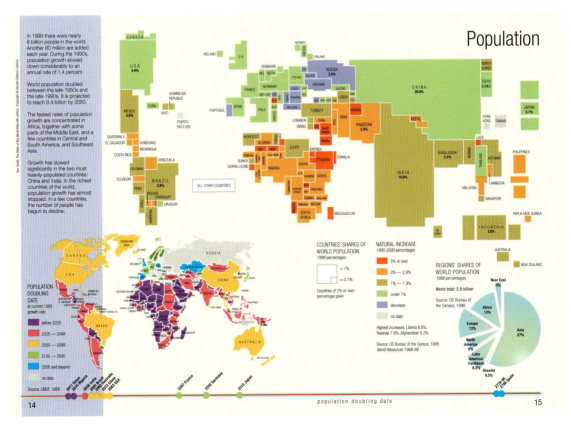

FIGURE 3.25 In *The State of the World Atlas*, magnification encoding is used to give a first impression of population densities. Note the reduced 'size' of Canada and Australia when compared with a conventional map
Source: *Smith (1999)*

dimensional space and to display a 2D view of that space (Figure 3.26). A problem is immediately apparent, however. It is impossible to know, for example, whether house A costs more than house C.

FIGURE 3.26
It is impossible, with a '3D' representation of data, to compare the attributes of Price, Number of bedrooms and Journey time to work values

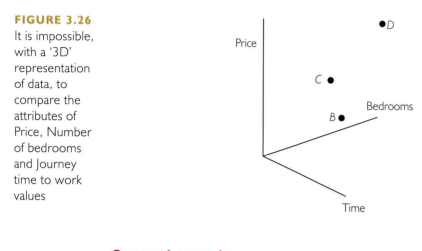

Scatterplot matrix

One solution is again to bring interaction to the problem and allow a user to reorient the 3D representation so that, for example, the view is the scatterplot shown in Figure 3.27 from which it is clear that house A costs less than house C.

FIGURE 3.27
A projection of the data shown in Figure 3.26, allowing comparison of *price* and *bedrooms* values

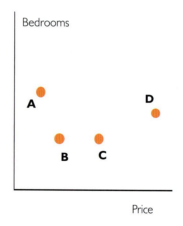

This was the origin of the comment that 'for 3D to be useful, you've got to be able to move it'.

For trivariate data – and, as we shall soon see, for hypervariate data – an alternative representation is a systematic structure formed from the three possible 2D views of the data, as shown in the scatterplot matrix in Figure 3.28: in essence, the user has reoriented the 3D plot in three different ways. Although two houses can now be compared easily with respect to three attributes, another problem is present. There are now three times as many points as houses, potentially increasing the cognitive load on the user, and often there will be no room for labels. Here again interaction can offer a solution by allowing the user to identify, for example, low-cost houses in the Price–Time plane, whereupon the same houses are highlighted in some way in the other two planes (Figure 3.29). Again, we are *brushing* houses from one plane to the other two. But, mindful of the phenomenon of change blindness, we must ensure that the user *notices* the highlighting. Thus, rather than simply changing the colour of a small dot from black to red in all three scatterplots, we might choose to highlight by magnification – even if only temporarily – as well as by colour, as shown in Figure 3.29.

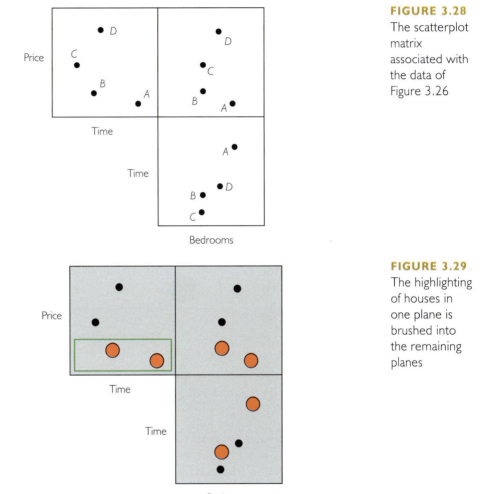

FIGURE 3.28
The scatterplot matrix associated with the data of Figure 3.26

FIGURE 3.29
The highlighting of houses in one plane is brushed into the remaining planes

The above example does not imply that three scatterplots comprising a scatterplot matrix are needed for trivariate data, a fact that can be illustrated by the representation of product fault data. Almost every mass-produced product designed for domestic use will encounter the problem of failure of some kind due to a variety of causes. The fact that a car radio, for example, has failed is easy to record but, and especially in the absence of the faulty product, it is a very expensive matter to find the cause of the fault. Information visualization can help, as shown in the representation of Figure 3.30. Two attributes represent independent variables: one is the month in which the product was manufactured and the other is the number of months it had been in service before the fault occurred. The radius of each circle indicates the number of products manufactured in a particular month and which had been in service for a specific number of months before failing. This representation alone is of considerable help in identifying the types of fault that may be occurring. For example, if many faults occur for one particular month of production irrespective of how long after production the fault occurs (as suggested by Figure 3.30), they are characterized as 'epidemical failure' and can guide the production manager in detecting the underlying cause. If, however, many faults are located on the rising diagonal (again as is the case in Figure 3.30) then a seasonal influence is indicated, since points along such a diagonal refer to products which all fail at roughly the same time.

FIGURE 3.30
A representation of reported product failure, based on month of production (MOP) of the failed product and total months in service (MIS) before the fault occurred. The radius of each circle indicates the number of faults reported for a given MOP and MIS

Another example of the representation of trivariate data, and which is similar to Figure 3.22, is concerned with a property of an electronic circuit. Figure 3.31 shows a diagram of an electronic circuit in which circles are superimposed on components to provide some idea as to their importance for – that is, their effect upon – a critical property of the circuit. But if the circuit is a hi-fi amplifier, the designer needs to know this information at a number of frequencies between the bass and treble extremes. It is a simple matter to animate the representation, with circle sizes changing accordingly as a pointer moves continuously up and down the frequency scale.

A special category of trivariate data is to be found in maps showing the location (latitude and longitude) and value of some object or attribute. Figure 3.32 shows the population of major cities in England, Wales and Scotland. By its use of circle size to encode each city's population, we can quickly gain an impression of how population is distributed. We might say that the information in this figure 'pops out'. We do not have to examine numbers to discover where the largest city is and what the relative sizes of the populations are. Thus, if we can arrange that information of interest to a user 'pops out' *without* the need for

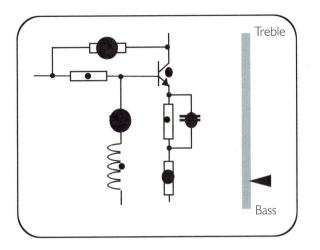

Treble

Bass

cognitive effort, then the user is at a huge advantage compared with a situation wherein careful attention has to be given to acquire that insight. How information can be encoded to result in essentially immediate comprehension is closely associated with the human visual system and is discussed immediately below.

Pre-attentive processing: 'things that pop out'

The desirability of information 'popping out', without the need for careful scrutiny, has been mentioned frequently. As Colin Ware (2004) remarks, 'We can do certain things to symbols to make it much more likely that they will be visually identified even after a very brief exposure. Certain shapes or colours "pop out" from their surroundings. The theoretical mechanism underlying pop-out is called **pre-attentive processing** because, logically, it must occur prior to conscious attention.' The 'very brief exposure' mentioned by Ware is typically in the region from 30 to 300 milliseconds. The importance of pre-attentive processing is reflected in Ware's comment (Ware, 2004, page 149) that:

> *An understanding of what is processed pre-attentively is probably the most important contribution that visual science can make to data visualization.*

In view of the immense advantage of deriving insight without the need for conscious attention, an obvious question for the interaction designer is, 'How do we *make* information pop out?' An in-depth discussion of pre-attentive processing in the context of the human visual system is available elsewhere (Ware, 2004): here we examine some examples which are sufficient to provide an initial understanding for an interaction designer.

A glance at Figure 3.32 immediately establishes where, in the United Kingdom, the greatest density of city population is to be found (and, for users familiar with a map of the UK, the fact that it *is* a map of the UK). Similarly, in Figure 3.33, the 'odd one out' can quickly be identified, as it can in Figures 3.34 and 3.35. Pre-attentive processing also allows us to quickly identify where, in Figure 3.36, the blue square is located. A cautionary example, however, is provided by the task of locating, in Figure 3.37, the red square in a collection of items which can be either red or blue *and* a square or a circle. Here, pre-attentive processing does not occur; careful scrutiny is required to locate the red square. This is because something which is both square (as opposed to circular) and red (as opposed to blue) is identified by 'conjunction encoding'.

FIGURE 3.33
The 'odd one out' can quickly be identified, by pre-attentive processing

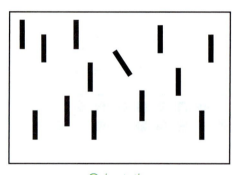

Orientation

FIGURE 3.34
Different shapes can often pop out

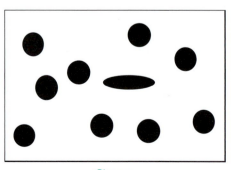

Shape

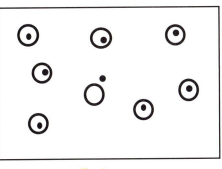

Enclosure

FIGURE 3.35
A single lack of enclosure can quickly be identified pre-attentively

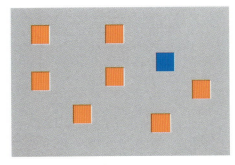

Colour

FIGURE 3.36
A different colour can be pre-attentively identified

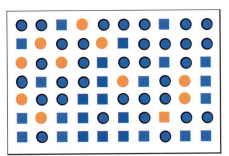

FIGURE 3.37
With conjunction encoding the red square is not pre-attentively identified

The last example does not imply that what might be called 'multiple pop-outs' are not possible. Evidence is provided by a novel representation (Irani and Eskicioglu, 2003) of mobile telephone network cell performance. Each cell is represented as shown in Figure 3.38, with colours and dimensions encoding critical performance measures. The outer boundary of a cell representation is chosen to allow their 'packing', as shown in Figure 3.39. As soon as a specialist user decides upon a specific interest – new call blockage rate, for example – the relevant information pops out without interference from other attribute encodings. An interesting and advantageous aspect of the chosen cell representation is that the potential for and general location of additional cells 'pop out' as a result of the arrows, as seen in the upper region of Figure 3.39.

FIGURE 3.38
Representation
of attributes
associated with
a mobile
telephone
network cell

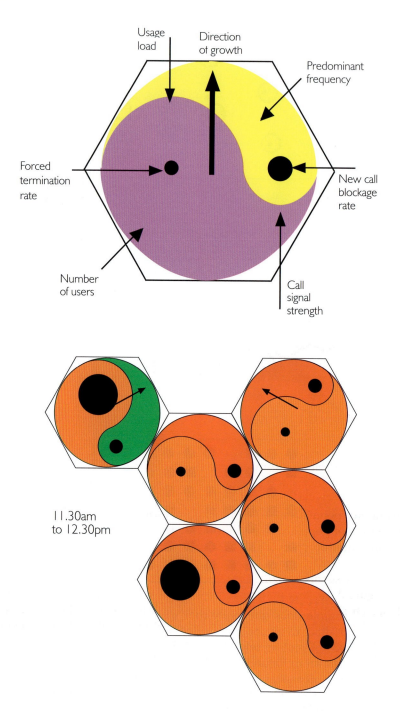

Usage
load

Direction
of growth

Predominant
frequency

Forced
termination
rate

New call
blockage
rate

Number
of users

Call
signal
strength

FIGURE 3.39
Representation
of attributes
associated with
a network of
mobile
telephone cells,
averaged over
one hour

11.30am
to 12.30pm

The examples provided above involve *static* representations of data. Fortunately, the advantages to be gained from pre-attentive processing can be extended through the use of animation, whether automatically or manually controlled. For example, Figure 3.40 shows the map display of Figure 3.32 but with

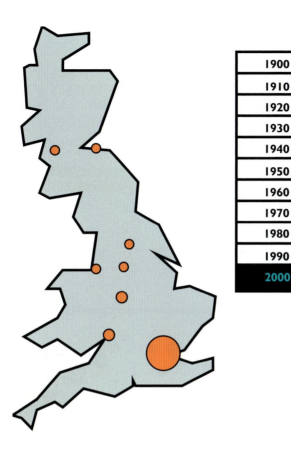

1900
1910
1920
1930
1940
1950
1960
1970
1980
1990
2000

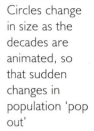

FIGURE 3.40
Circles change in size as the decades are animated, so that sudden changes in population 'pop out'

the addition of a scale calibrated in the decades since 1900 AD. If successive steps on the scale are now highlighted in sequence at a rate of about 5–10 per second, and circles are correspondingly sized, then a mental model of the changes in city populations could quickly be formed. Especially, the emergence of new centres of population would immediately be apparent and, just as with a static representation, 'pop out'. The idea that animation can facilitate 'pop-out' is examined further in Chapter 5.

Although it seems reasonable to employ circle size to encode city populations in Figure 3.40, it is natural to ask 'Why?' Why not use shading? Or bars? Or colour? Or shape? We have seen examples (e.g. Minard) where circle or line size or thickness are suited to the encoding of quantity, and where colour or shape would be inappropriate; colour and shape are perhaps more suited to situations where objects must be perceived as similar or different. Obviously guidance is needed as to the most appropriate encoding for a given task, though it must be realized that the most appropriate encoding depends upon many factors. We briefly discuss this matter below.

Choice of encoding

Although, as Mackinlay (1986) stated, 'there does not exist an empirically verified theory of human perceptual capabilities that can be used to prove theorems about the effectiveness of graphical languages', guidance regarding a choice of encoding is available from many sources, of which three are considered here. The first example is provided by Bertin (1967, 1983), a French pioneer of information visualization. The second comes from the statisticians Cleveland and McGill (1984) following an experiment in which they assessed the accuracy of judging variously encoded quantitative variables. The third is provided by Mackinlay (1986) who considered ordinal and categorical as well as quantitative data.

Bertin's guidance

Bertin identified four *tasks* common to information visualization and identified the encoding mechanisms he considered to be suited to those tasks. He presented his conclusions in a diagram similar to that shown in Figure 3.41, using

FIGURE 3.41

Interpretation of Bertin's guidance regarding the suitability of various encoding methods to support common tasks

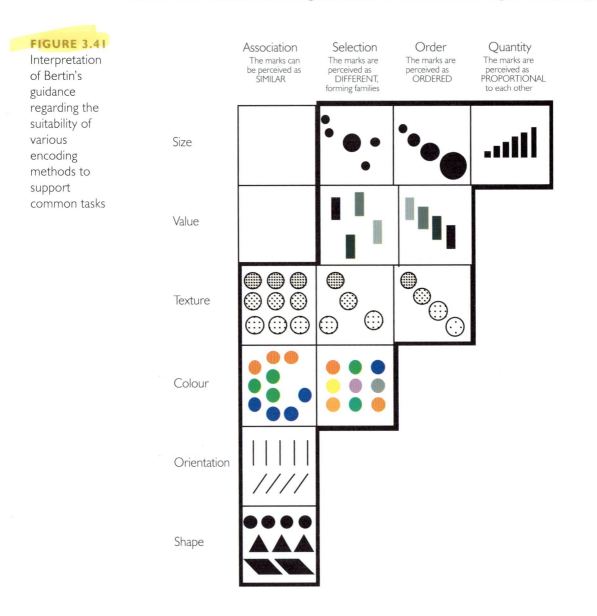

the term 'mark' to denote the result of encoding (e.g. a line or a coloured circle). There are four columns associated with some fundamental tasks. They are:

ASSOCIATION: the question here is how well the marks can be perceived as similar.

SELECTION: here Bertin was concerned with whether the marks can be perceived as different, 'forming families'.

ORDER: Can the marks be perceived as ordered?

QUANTITY: The question here is whether the marks can be perceived as proportional to each other.

The encoding mechanisms – *retinal variables* as they are often called – that he considered were size, value,[2] texture, colour, orientation and shape. As seen from Figure 3.41, Bertin ordered these roughly according to the number of tasks each encoding mechanism can usefully support. Detailed examination of Figure 3.41 shows the guidance to be intuitively reasonable. However, the most appropriate encoding mechanism is very dependent upon context and the guidance is certainly open to debate.

An example related to Bertin's diagram, and illustrating the influence of task, is provided by the TileBars interface (Hearst, 1995). The task supported by TileBars is that of identifying, among a collection of documents, a subset that may be relevant to a particular enquiry. TileBars accepts, from a user, a set of topics and a collection of documents that may or may not be relevant. For example, an investigator interested in research into the prevention of osteoporosis would make the entry shown in Figure 3.42. In response, the TileBars system would return, for each document, a representation of the form shown in the upper portion of Figure 3.43. On the left is a colour-coded reminder of the topics. The TileBar itself contains the same number of rows as there are topics and columns corresponding to segments of the document: these can be paragraphs, pages or chapters. By its density of shading, each rectangle shows, for the corresponding topic and segment, the relative frequency of occurrence of that topic word. Thus, the example shows that in the first segment of the document 'Recent advances in the world of drugs' there is mention of *prevention* but little of *research* or *osteoporosis*. The fifth segment of the document, however, contains substantial mention of all three topics, from which it may be judged

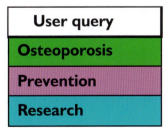

FIGURE 3.42
The specification of three topics of interest

---

2 As defined by Bertin (1967; 1983, page 73), 'value' is not restricted to a grey scale. As Bertin remarks, 'One can pass from black to white by grays, by blues or by reds . . .'

that the document may be worth examining, perhaps beginning with that fifth segment. Interaction with the fifth column then leads to the representation in the lower part of Figure 3.43 showing the relevant paragraph with the topic words highlighted. TileBars provides yet another example of the benefit to be obtained from derived values.

FIGURE 3.43
(top) The TileBar representation of the relevance of paragraphs to the topic words; (bottom) a selected paragraph with topic words highlighted

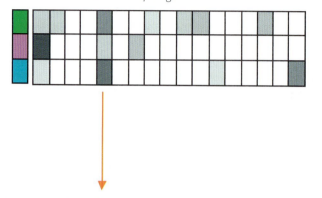

"Recent advances in the world of drugs"

Fortunately, scientific knowledge about this disease has grown, and there is reason for hope. Research is revealing that prevention may be achieved through estrogen replacement therapy for older women and through adequate calcium intake and regular weight-bearing exercise for people of all ages. New approaches to diagnosis and treatment are also under active investigation. For this work to continue and for use to take advantage of the knowledge we have already gained, public awareness of osteoporosis and of the importance of further scientific research is essential.

Accuracy of judgement of encoded quantitative data

The statisticians Cleveland and McGill (1984) addressed a different problem, concerned only with the accuracy with which subjects could assess *quantitative* data encoded in a variety of ways, some identical to the encoding mechanisms considered by Bertin. In one sense they investigated the last column of Bertin's matrix, concerned with quantity and which contained only one entry. Their result is shown in Figure 3.44, where the encoding mechanisms are ordered according to the accuracy with which they were found to support judgement of quantity.

Quantitative, ordinal and categorical data

Mackinlay (1986) addressed the encoding of non-quantitative as well as quantitative data and presented the rankings shown in Figure 3.45. The different positions of a given encoding mechanism on the three rankings are due, as Mackinlay points out, to 'the fact that additional perceptual tasks are involved'.

Representations we have already encountered have been located within Mackinlay's rankings in Figure 3.45, partly as illustrative examples but also because they do not appear at the top of the rankings; they illustrate the fact that many factors influence the choice of encoding. Minard, for example, might have had difficulty, in the context of other desirable features of his map, in encoding the population of the army by position as opposed to length (i.e. the width of a line) and Beck might have faced a similar problem in encoding differ-

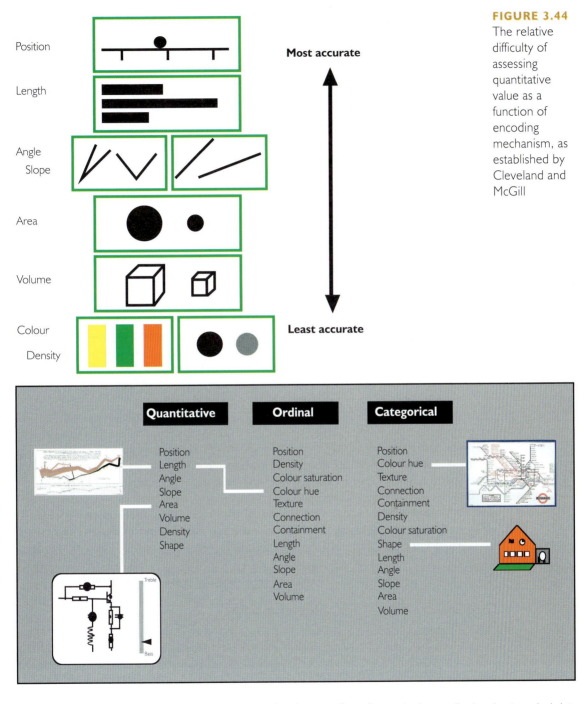

FIGURE 3.44 The relative difficulty of assessing quantitative value as a function of encoding mechanism, as established by Cleveland and McGill

FIGURE 3.45 Taken from Mackinlay's guidance for the encoding of quantitative, ordinal and categorical data

ent Tube lines in anything but colour. It is also difficult to see how Minard could have employed 'position' to indicate the ordering 'advance, retreat'. One must additionally bear in mind that the map was designed to ensure that information 'pops out', with an emphasis on qualitative understanding (e.g. 'Wow! Only a fraction of the soldiers who departed actually returned'), which, if interest persists, can be converted to quantitative understanding by close examination of numbers. Similarly, the 'circle size' representation (Figure 3.31) of the effect of components in an electronic circuit was chosen primarily because a designer is, at least in the initial stages, principally interested in whether some effect is large or small. A different consideration is associated with the multi-dimensional icon employed to represent the attributes of a house and which we discuss later in this chapter. Here we encounter *iconic encoding*, and this introduces yet another factor to be taken into consideration in the choice of encoding for a multi-attribute representation.

3.1.4 Hypervariate data

The challenge of representing hypervariate (also termed multivariate) data is substantial and continues to stimulate invention. It is an important challenge because so many real problems that are potentially amenable to at least partial solution via information visualization are of high dimensionality. The design of even the simplest silicon chip, for example, can involve over 100 components whose value has to be chosen by the designer in such a way that over 200 performance limits are satisfied. A decision regarding an investment portfolio is equally complex, as is the decision whether or not to continue with the development of a new drug. Even a basis for representing only eight scholastic achievements of a pupil can be challenging, as Exercise 3.3 will reveal.

It should first be mentioned that some of the representation techniques already discussed can be scaled, though sometimes to a limited extent, to handle hypervariate data. Thus, the TileBars scheme for the representation of text can handle more than three keywords, interactive histograms (as we shall see below) can be extended to many attributes and, as shown in Chapter 2, bargrams can be effective in the representation of many attributes of a collection of objects.

Coordinate plots

Parallel coordinate plots

One of the most popular and valued techniques for the representation of hypervariate data has a very simple basis and is called the method of parallel coordinate plots (Inselberg, 1985, 1997; Wegman, 1990). To explain the underlying principle we consider a simple case of bivariate data for which the details of two houses can be represented within a scatterplot (Figure 3.46), each house being represented by a single point. Imagine now the two axes to be detached and placed parallel to each other (Figure 3.47). Necessarily, each house will have to be represented by a point on both axes, thereby doubling the number of points required.

A further disadvantage would appear to be the need to show the relation between the two points characterizing a given house, here achieved (Figure 3.48) for each house by a straight line together with an identifying label. What is to be gained? For the case of two attributes, nothing. However, if we are dealing with objects characterized by more than two or three attributes the so-called parallel coordinate plot offers many advantages. Figure 3.49 shows the parallel

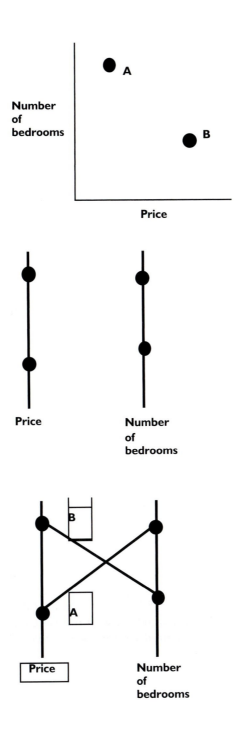

FIGURE 3.46
A simple scatterplot representing the price and number of bedrooms associated with two houses

FIGURE 3.47
An alternative representation to the scatterplot in which the two attribute scales are presented in parallel, thereby requiring two points to represent each house

FIGURE 3.48
To avoid ambiguity the pair of points representing a house are joined and labelled

coordinate plot for six objects, each characterized by seven attributes A to G. Each object is represented by a point on each axis and hence by the piecewise linear line ('polyline') joining them. It is immediately (i.e. pre-attentively) apparent that there is a 'trade-off' between attributes A and B, as well as a strong correlation between B and C. Nevertheless, even though a parallel coordinate plot facility is available in many commercial information visualization packages, limitations can be identified. For example, for the data shown in Figure 3.49, it is not apparent that there is also a 'trade-off' between B and E and a strong correlation between C and G; in other words, the ordering of the attributes can significantly affect the ease with which relationships can be identified.

FIGURE 3.49
A parallel coordinate plot for six objects, each characterized by seven attributes. The trade-off between A and B, and the correlation between B and C, are immediately apparent. The trade-off between B and E, and the correlation between C and G, are not.

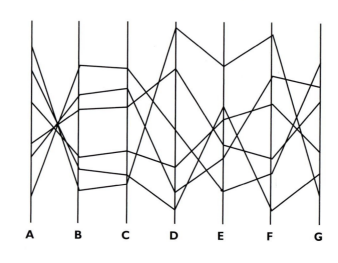

As with many other visualization tools, the potential offered by interaction is considerable (Siirtola, 2000). For example, a range of one attribute can be identified, thereby highlighting all the object lines which pass through that range (Figure 3.50); furthermore, that range can be dynamically explored manually, allowing a user to gain quick insight into relationships between different attributes. Other facilities are normally available, including averages, standard deviations and Tukey box plots. Selected ranges of two different attributes can, for example, be 'ANDed' or 'ORed' highlighting, respectively, only those object lines that pass through *both*

FIGURE 3.50
A parallel coordinate plot representation of a collection of cars, in which a range of the attribute *Year* has been selected to cause all those cars manufactured during that period to be highlighted.
Source: *Harri Siirtola*

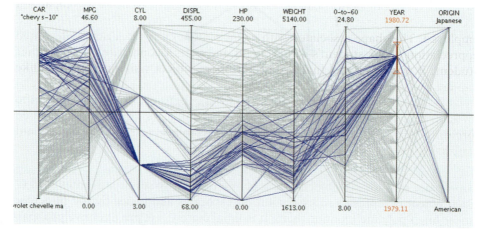

selected ranges and those which pass through either or both.[3] The parallel coordinate plot technique of representation has found a wide range of application. Inselberg (1997), for example, has shown how such plots can be used to enhance the manufacturing yield of a process of making silicon chips.

It is useful to be able to characterize the sort of insight that can readily be gleaned from a parallel coordinate plot. Whereas with the scatterplot each object was easily identified and discriminable in the company of other objects, that is not the case with parallel coordinate plots because each object is now represented by a polyline which usually intersects with many other such curves. What *is* particularly visible from a parallel coordinate plot are the characteristics of the separate attributes and, in some cases, the nature of the relation between them. Thus, remarks such as 'the majority of cars appear to have four cylinders' and 'it seems that low MPG inevitably means high price' can be based on rapidly acquired 'pop-out' insight. Thus, we may observe that the parallel coordinate plot technique can support **attribute visibility**. By visibility we mean the ability to gain insight pre-attentively or without involving a great detail of cognitive effort. We return later to the concept of visibility, and the associated concept of correlation, when more encoding examples have been accumulated.

A major attraction of parallel coordinate plots, which they share with some but not all other techniques, is that their complexity (here, the number of axes) is directly proportional to the number of attributes. They also have the advantage, which is sometimes not present with other techniques (Feiner and Beshers, 1990), that all attributes receive uniform treatment. The literature (e.g. Bendix *et al.*, 2005; Siirtola, 2006)) provides many examples of the continual development of the parallel coordinate technique.

Star plots

A star plot (Coekin, 1969) has many features in common with parallel coordinate plots in that an attribute value is represented by a point on a coordinate axis and, for a given object, those points are joined by straight lines. The difference is that attribute axes now radiate from a common origin. Thus, a star plot of my school report (Figure 3.51) shows, relative to a class average indicated by the extremities of the grey region, good performance in mathematics and chemistry but very poor performance in sport and literature. To make a comparison with the talents of my friend Tony, a separate star plot (Figure 3.52) can be employed. The shape associated with a star plot can provide a reasonably rapid appreciation of the student's achievement and permit comparison with another student. It can be argued that a star plot offers '**object visibility**'. Thus, unlike parallel coordinate plots which are especially suited to the identification of relations between attributes, star plots are perhaps better for comparing specific objects. Star plots have been used to compare objects as different as police forces and mortgage options. Other encoding techniques, such as colour and thickness, can provide additional flexibility.

---

[3] The observant reader may have noticed cars apparently characterized by zero HP or zero miles per gallon, neither constituting a very desirable attribute of a car. In fact, these are misleading representations associated with missing data and illustrate a challenge to the designer of a visualization technique.

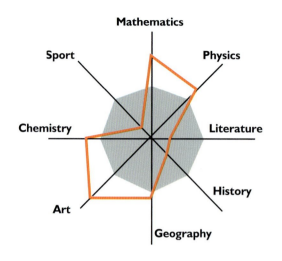

FIGURE 3.51 In a star plot attribute scales radiate from a common origin. Because shape can often effectively represent the combined attribute values of a single object, the points on each attribute scale can usefully be joined. Other useful information such as average values or thresholds can be encoded on the star plot

FIGURE 3.52
Star plots can be used to compare the attributes of two different objects, here the exam performance of two people in the subjects identified in Figure 3.51

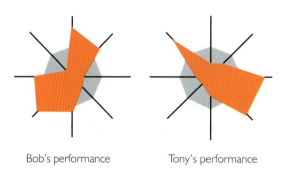

Bob's performance   Tony's performance

Scatterplot matrix

The scatterplot matrix discussed in the context of trivariate data is equally applicable to higher dimensions, but with one major disadvantage arising from the fact that, as the number of attributes increases, the number of different *pairs* of attributes increases rapidly. With two attributes we needed one scatterplot, with three we needed three and with four attributes there are six unique pairs. Thus, for 100 houses each associated with four attributes, the scatterplot matrix would contain 600 points. This is in contrast to the linear increase in complexity associated with parallel coordinate plots and, as we shall see, the Attribute Explorer to be discussed immediately below. While there is no theoretical limit to the number of attributes a scatterplot can handle, this unwelcome dependence of complexity on dimension is always present.

The use of a single scatterplot together with other encoding techniques to represent hypervariate data was demonstrated very effectively by Ahlberg (Ahlberg *et al.*, 1992; Ahlberg and Shneiderman, 1994) with an interactive representation designed to allow a user to select a film to watch on video (Figure 3.53). On the main (scatterplot) display each coloured square identifies a film. Colour encodes type (horror, musical, etc.), horizontal position indicates the year of production and vertical position indicates duration. On the right, sliders can be used to specify other attributes of a film such as director or actor. Scroll bars can be used to confine attention to a particular span of years and film length, whereupon more detail can be displayed (Figure 3.54). The Film Finder, as the interface was called, provides a good illustration of the potential of combining different representation techniques.

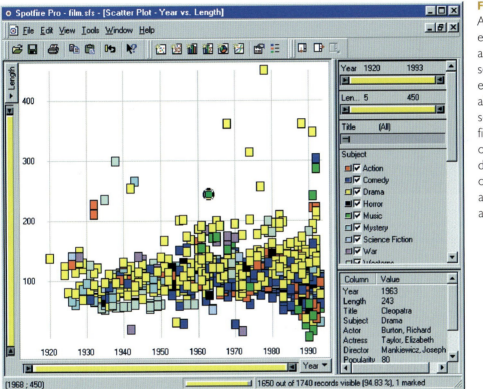

FIGURE 3.53

A scatterplot enhanced by additional and selective encoding, allowing the selection of a film on the basis of type, duration, year of production and other attributes

Linked histograms

The technique of linked histograms presented in the discussion of bivariate data (see Figure 3.20) can be extended to hypervariate data and, in the Attribute Explorer, can be considerably enhanced in value by additional encoding (Tweedie *et al.*, 1994; Spence and Tweedie, 1998). We shall first illustrate the technique in the context of buying a house, a task which, like that of buying a car, can usefully be generalized:

> *Given a collection of objects, each described by the values associated with a set of attributes, find the most acceptable such object or, perhaps, a small number of candidate objects worthy of more detailed consideration.*

FIGURE 3.54
The automatic
display of
additional detail
following the
selection of
narrower limits
on years of
production and
film length

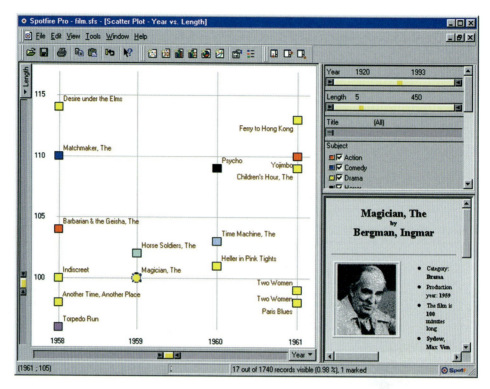

However, in the course of illustrating the use of the Attribute Explorer, we shall see that an equally important task for which it (and many other techniques) is suited is:

the acquisition of insight into multivariate data.

We begin by examining a histogram (Figure 3.55) of one attribute of a collection of houses, that of *Price*. Here, each house contributes one small rectangle to the histogram. Upper and lower limits to *Price* can easily be positioned (Figure 3.56) to identify a subset of houses that may initially and experimentally be regarded as affordable. The result is that the houses so identified are encoded green. For reasons soon to be apparent, houses outside the limits continue to be displayed. Many house attributes will normally be of interest and we shall consider just three to establish the concepts underlying the Attribute Explorer: *Price, Number of bedrooms* and *Garden Size*. Figure 3.57 shows the corresponding attribute histograms, but with the same limits on *Price* as in Figure 3.56. Those houses satisfying the limits on *Price* are now coded green not only on the *Price* histogram but also on the other two histograms, another example of brushing. Immediately, the consequences of the *Price* limits for the availability of houses with given garden sizes and numbers of bedrooms are apparent and can, in fact, be dynamically explored by moving the range bar between the *Price* limits to and fro: some idea of any correlation between *Price* and *Number of bedrooms* could easily be acquired. If limits are now additionally placed on the remaining attributes (Figure 3.58), green encoding applies only to those houses which sat-

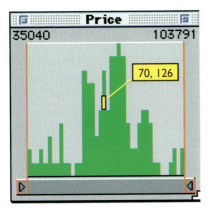

FIGURE 3.55 A histogram representing the prices of a collection of houses. The contribution of one house is shown in yellow

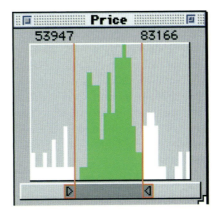

FIGURE 3.56 Limits on *Price* identify a subset of houses, coded green

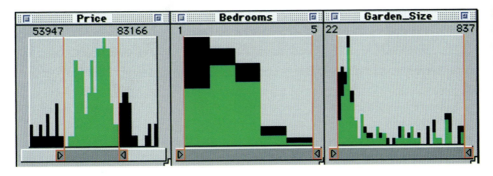

FIGURE 3.57 Houses defined by the limits on *Price* in Figure 3.56 are coded green in other attribute histograms

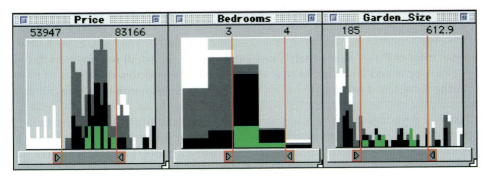

FIGURE 3.58 Green coding applies only to houses which satisfy all attribute limits. Houses which fail one limit are coded black, so if a black house is positioned outside a limit it will turn green if the limit is extended to include it

isfy *all* the attribute limits. Again, dynamic exploration achieved by adjusting either range positions or individual limits can help the user to gain insight into the house data and gradually come to a decision about which house or houses are worthy of more detailed consideration. It is because houses can be explored on the basis of their attributes that the technique described is called the Attribute Explorer.

Of major importance in the Attribute Explorer is the colour coding involved. Black houses are those which fail only one limit; therefore, if a black house is located outside a limit, that must be the limit it fails. This can be very useful

information. If a user has set an upper limit on the price they are prepared to pay, they would almost certainly wish to know about any house which failed only that limit and by a very small amount. Movement of a limit to enclose a black house will cause it to turn green, confirming that it now satisfies all limits.

The black encoding is extremely valuable in those circumstances wherein there are no houses that satisfy the stated limits, a situation depicted in Figure 3.59. In this example we see that by spending a little more, one house becomes available, whereas by accepting a house with three bedrooms a number of houses become available. Astonishingly, it is rare to find such guidance in online house sales.

FIGURE 3.59
Even if no houses satisfy all attribute limits, black houses, which fail only one limit, provide guidance as to the effect of relaxing limits

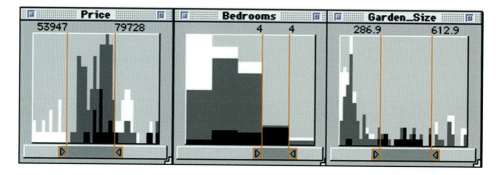

Potential applications of the Attribute Explorer technique will no doubt occur to the reader, especially after experiencing, for example, the frustration of trying to arrange flights on specific dates at convenient times or trying to decide which mobile telephone or washing machine to buy. Combination with other techniques could prove useful, such as providing an Attribute Explorer histogram along each axis of a parallel coordinate plot to enable better insight into the distribution of attribute values and, by brushing, the correlation between them. The Explorer is, of course, not restricted to numerical data: it can handle a combination of numerical, categorical and ordinal data. Concurrently with the invention of the Attribute Explorer, Eick (1994) proposed the technique of Data Visualization Sliders. He drew attention to the fact that, as well as providing a mechanism for the interactive specification of limits to an attribute, 'the effectiveness of sliders may be increased by using the space inside . . . as an interactive colour scale, a bar plot for discrete data, [or] a density plot for continuous data'. The effectiveness of the Attribute Explorer has been studied (Li and North, 2003) by comparing it with a Dynamic queries interface (see Chapter 5, Figure 5.23) in the context of a number of tasks. It was observed that the 'brushing histograms', as the Explorer was called, tended to offer advantages with the more complex tasks. It was commented that brushing histograms could be extended in various ways, for example to be zoomable and to possess granularity controls.

While originally invented to support the selection of one object from many on the basis of its attributes, the Attribute Explorer also offers considerable potential to support exploration with the goal of acquiring **insight** into data. An example is provided in its use as an investigative tool by the Swedish Defence Research Agency and illustrated briefly in Figure 3.60. (A more extensive

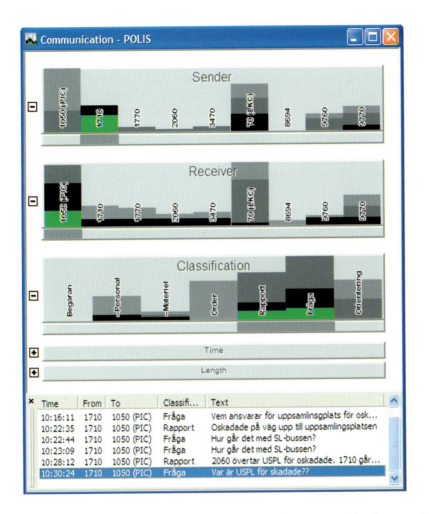

FIGURE 3.60
An Attribute
Explorer
representation
of three
dimensions of
communication
data captured
during an
emergency
services
exercise,
supporting
interactive
exploration by
an analyst

account is the subject of one of the case studies in Chapter 6.) The figure relates to communication data accumulated during a practice scenario of a train derailment on the Stockholm subway (Morin and Albinsson, 2005) involving three data dimensions. A single sender (1710) has been identified and a single receiver (1050), the on-site commander, as well as two categories of classification (reports and questions). The green 'hits' indicate that a large part of the total communication initiated by 1710 is indeed reports and questions directed to 1050. These 'hits' are also shown in the list below the Attribute Explorer.

Mosaic plots

The idea behind mosaic plots (Friendly, 1994) can be demonstrated by an example related to the Titanic disaster of April 1912, when 1,731 of the 2,201 passengers and crew were lost (Dawson, 1995). Table 3.1 shows the raw numerical data, involving four attributes: gender, survival, class and adult/child. Whereas it is difficult without careful examination to obtain much insight from the table, a so-called mosaic plot (Friendly, 1992, 1994, 2000) can profitably be generated as follows. We start with a rectangle whose area is proportional to the number of passengers and crew (Figure 3.61(a)). We then break down that area according to class of travel (Figure 3.61(b)), again representing number by area. Next we break down the resulting rectangles according to gender (Figure 3.61(c)), from which we can already begin to gain immediate insight into, for example, the male/female ratio in first-, second- and third-class accommodation. Finally, we break down the existing rectangles according to two attributes: survival (green) or otherwise (black), and adult/child (Figure 3.61(d)). The resulting mosaic plot is capable of providing rapid insight into the nature of the Titanic disaster and, of course, generating new questions – Who were the females travelling third class? Why did the vast majority of first-class females survive? Why, proportionately, did more female children survive than male children?

TABLE 3.1 Details of the Titanic disaster

Survived	Age	Gender	Class			
			1st	2nd	3rd	Crew
No	Adult	Male	118	154	387	670
Yes			57	14	75	192
No	Child		0	0	35	0
Yes			5	11	13	0
No	Adult	Female	4	13	89	3
Yes			140	80	76	20
No	Child		0	0	17	0
Yes			1	13	14	0

The order in which the original rectangle is broken down is, of course, open to choice, and the reader may wish to experiment with different orders to gain some feeling for the potential offered (see Exercises). Many other examples, and a fuller discussion, are provided by Friendly (2000) whose website is well worth visiting in this respect.

Icons

Object visibility is a property of representation techniques in which a single object is so portrayed that a number of its attributes can easily be assimilated, qualitatively if not quantitatively. Two examples are discussed here. One was originally invented to characterize the properties of geological samples, whereas the other was evaluated in the context of house selection.

Professor Chernoff, a statistician at Stanford University, observed that human beings are very sensitive to a wide range of human facial characteristics and suggested that facial features – such as eye size and the length of a nose – are not only numerous (he identified 18) but could, in a cartoon face, take on a sufficiently large number of 'values' to offer a useful encoding mechanism (Figure 3.62). He applied this idea (Chernoff, 1973) to the study of geological

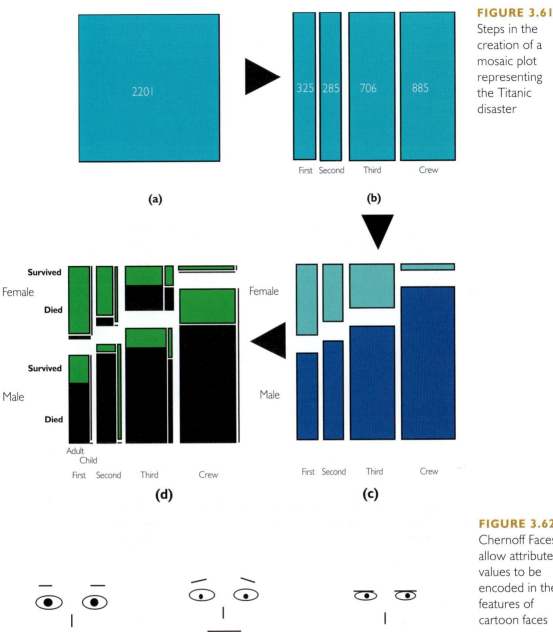

FIGURE 3.61
Steps in the creation of a mosaic plot representing the Titanic disaster

FIGURE 3.62
Chernoff Faces allow attribute values to be encoded in the features of cartoon faces

samples, each characterized by 18 attributes such as salt content and water content, and found that the display of so-called Chernoff Faces facilitated the identification of interesting groups of samples. If this use of computer-generated cartoon faces should appear frivolous it should be remarked that accountants, not usually associated with frivolity, have nevertheless explored the use of Chernoff Faces to display accountancy data (Stock and Watson, 1984). Since one would expect some facial features to be more informative than others (Morris *et al.*, 1999), it is useful to note that a study by De Soete (1986) established the relative value of various facial features. Ware (2004, page 253) comments that we may have special neural hardware to deal with faces.

In the context of house purchase the multidimensional icons shown in Figure 3.63 attempted to portray attributes more directly, for example representing a houseboat by a shape suggestive of a boat and a garage by a rectangular box containing a simple representation of a car. A total of eight house attributes were represented in this way. A question that immediately arises, of course, is whether such multidimensional icons offer any advantage over an equivalent textual description, shown in Figure 3.64. To investigate this issue, controlled experiments were undertaken (Spence and Parr, 1991). Subjects were given a number of tasks to complete, of which the following is representative:

You can spend up to £200,000 on accommodation. Locate the best you can with regard to the number of bedrooms and the size of garden, but it must have central heating.

FIGURE 3.63
Multidimensional icons representing eight attributes of a dwelling

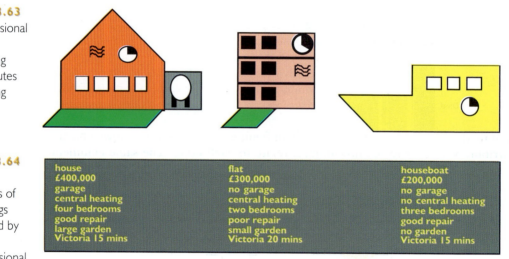

FIGURE 3.64
Textual descriptions of the dwellings represented by the multidimensional icons shown in Figure 3.63

house	flat	houseboat
£400,000	£300,000	£200,000
garage	no garage	no garage
central heating	central heating	no central heating
four bedrooms	two bedrooms	three bedrooms
good repair	poor repair	good repair
large garden	small garden	no garden
Victoria 15 mins	Victoria 20 mins	Victoria 15 mins

The subjects were presented with two conditions. Details of 56 dwellings were presented in either iconic (see Figure 3.63) or textual (see Figure 3.64) form, the layout in both cases being seven rows of eight dwellings (Figure 3.65). The 56 dwellings were so designed that there was a unique solution to all the tasks. Overall it was found that the time taken to identify the appropriate house using icons was about half what it was when using textual description. Observation of the subjects while they carried out the tasks strongly suggested that, if the display had been an interactive one rather than printed on paper, some means of tagging individual dwellings – either to 'discard' them or 'include' them – would have simplified the task. With the paper display, Post-it stickers were employed for tagging.

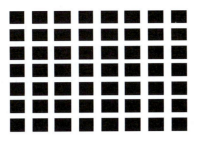

FIGURE 3.65
Layout employed in the experiment carried out to compare the relative merits of iconic and textual descriptions of dwellings

We have discussed two examples of metaphorical icons: in one there is a direct relation between icon and object (the house icon) while in the other there is no direct relation between facial features and the geological attributes they represent. Siirtola (2005) has observed that experiments support the idea that a data-related '**glyph**' (icon) is more favoured by users and, with respect to the task of information acquisition, leads to about 13 per cent more accuracy. Direct metaphorical icons find wide application (see, for example, Miller and Stasko, 2001).

Object and attribute visibility

We return briefly to the concept of visibility, discussed earlier in the context of different encoding techniques (Teoh and Ma, 2005).[4]

We can say that the property of object visibility is such that each object is represented as a single and coherent visual entity such as a point. Object visibility is desirable when a user is interested in knowing an object's attribute values in many different dimensions and how different objects relate to one another. Examples include Chernoff Faces, multidimensional icons and star plots (Figure 3.66). We do not include static parallel coordinate plots in this set because an object is then represented by a collection of points complemented by a polyline joining those points and it is extremely difficult either to discern a single object's attribute values or to see how objects relate to each other. The same comment applies to the Attribute Explorer.

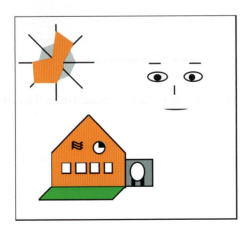

FIGURE 3.66
Representations of multi-attribute objects supportive of object visibility

---

4 We use the term 'visibility' in place of 'coherence' used by Teoh and Ma.

A similar form of description applies to attribute visibility, also known as dimension visibility. In a representation with attribute visibility the distribution of objects' attribute values in each dimension is clear. Attribute visibility is desirable when the user wants a clear picture of how objects are distributed in an attribute dimension – for example when there are clusters present. Attribute visibility is associated with the Attribute Explorer and parallel coordinate plots (Figure 3.67), but not with Chernoff Faces, multidimensional icons and star Plots. Teoh and Ma (2005) also introduced the concepts of *object correlation* and *attribute (dimension) correlation*. An example of the latter is provided by a parallel coordinate plot in which points on adjacent axes are connected by lines which clearly indicate a trade-off or correlation. Object correlation may be facilitated by representations such as star plots.

FIGURE 3.67

Representations of multi-attribute objects supportive of attribute visibility

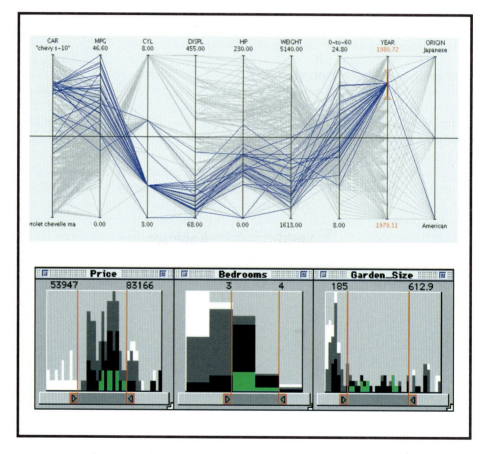

Although the emergence of visibility and correlation as useful characterizations of a representation is quite recent and remains to be validated, it already appears subjectively to be useful and, in addition, seems to have some relation to the 'popping out' property discussed earlier.

3.2 The encoding of relation

In our earlier discussion of data it was established that two types of data exist: *values* and *relations*. We have examined many ways of encoding values; we now ask, 'What do we mean by a relation?' and 'How do we represent it?'.

The dictionary definition says:

> **relation** (n): a logical or natural association between two or more things; relevance of one to another; connection.

A relation between two or more things can be represented in many different ways. A simple straight line or lines can be used to show that John Smith married Mary Robinson (Figure 3.68) or that John borrows money from the Stingy Bank to purchase a 1930 Bentley (Figure 3.69). The relation could be mathematical, of the form y = f(x), and, in turn, could be represented by a node and directed link diagram (Figure 3.70). As shown earlier in Chapter 2, the relation between a car and its price can be represented by a common colour (Figure 3.71). Figure 3.72 summarizes aspects of the warfare in Anglo-Saxon England between 550 AD and 700 AD far more effectively (for me) than an equivalent area of text – the warlike nature of the West Saxons immediately stands out (Arnold, 1997), as does the fact that the Britons continually took quite a beating. Colour and line thickness provide additional scope for encoding aspects of a relation.

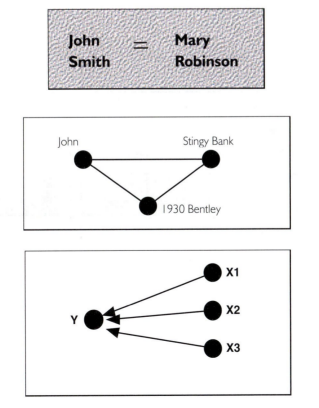

FIGURE 3.68
A simple symbol indicates the relationship of marriage

FIGURE 3.69
Lines indicate relationship

FIGURE 3.70
Arrows indicate unique unilateral functional relations

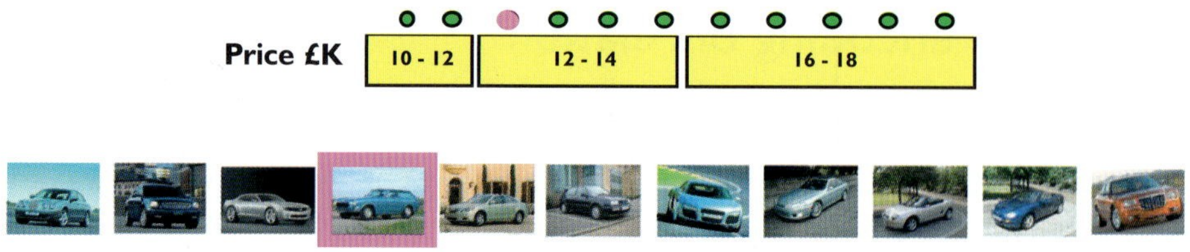

FIGURE 3.71
Colour indicates a relation

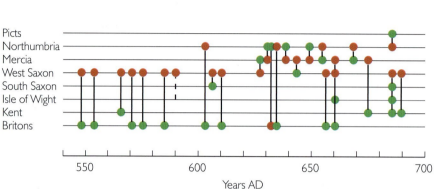

FIGURE 3.72

The incidence of warfare in early Anglo-Saxon England between 550 AD and 700 AD. Red indicates the aggressor, green the attacked

Source: *After Arnold (1997)*

With a relation there is the implication that we are dealing with *discrete* rather than continuous attributes. Whereas a car can have any price, an hotel either has or has not got a swimming pool. To buy my Bentley I apply to Bank A rather than Bank B. The suspect in a fraud case is either in Los Angeles conferring with a colleague or he is not. We are speaking about binary properties. It is therefore not surprising that different techniques may be appropriate to the representation of relations rather than values, since the latter can usually assume more than two conditions. However, the prime consideration in the choice of such a representation is identical to that which applied to value representation: an understanding of the task that is being undertaken, the insight that is sought and what questions might therefore be asked of the relation.

Some representations of relations are very simple, but nevertheless extremely powerful. We begin by examining some of these simple representations and the insights they can provide. As the definition above emphasizes, a relation exists between two or more *things*, so in discussing the representation of relation we must inevitably be concerned with representing the 'things' that are related. 'Thing representation' and 'relation representation' must be considered together.

3.2.1 Lines

Perhaps the simplest way of representing a relation between two entities is to draw a straight line between representations of those two entities. Even a short record of telephone calls (Figure 3.73(a)) is easier to comprehend if represented by a node-link diagram (Figure 3.73(b)), especially if disconnected subsets are present (Figure 3.73(c)). A node-link representation was in fact valuable in the mortgage fraud example mentioned in Chapter 1. If a large number of house purchases take place, involving relations between various lenders of money, solicitors, surveyors, etc., then a representation such as that shown in Figure

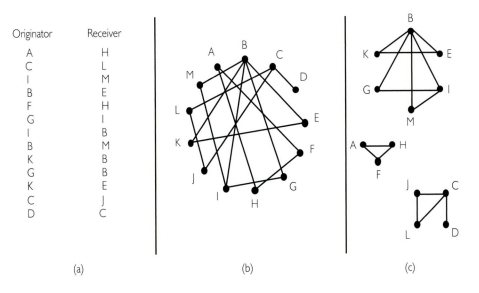

Originator	Receiver
A	H
C	L
I	M
B	E
F	H
G	I
I	B
B	M
K	B
G	B
K	E
C	J
D	C

(a)

(b)

(c)

FIGURE 3.73
Insight into even a short list of telephone calls, (a), is enhanced by their node-link representation, (b), especially if disconnected subsets can be identified, (c)

3.74(a) might emerge, where each person or institution involved is represented by a small segment of an annulus, as shown in Figure 3.74(b). By itself the pattern within the inner circle might provide little insight, but if a threshold is now imposed that excludes normal house purchases, a pattern begins to emerge (Figure 3.75) that can provide an investigator with evidence that leads to the arrest of a person perpetrating mortgage fraud (Davidson, 1993; Westphal and Blaxton, 1998).

(a)

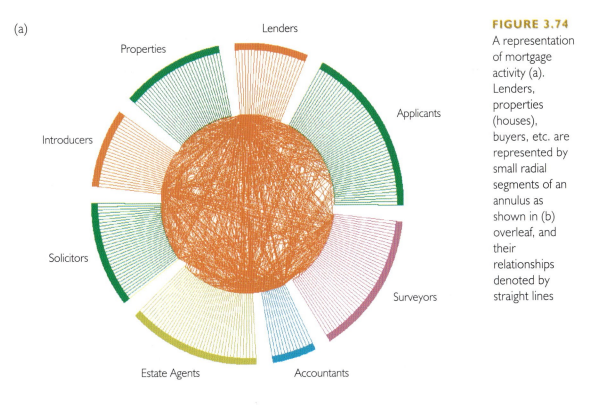

FIGURE 3.74
A representation of mortgage activity (a). Lenders, properties (houses), buyers, etc. are represented by small radial segments of an annulus as shown in (b) overleaf, and their relationships denoted by straight lines

FIGURE 3.74
(b) The representation of applicants by small radial segments within the representation of mortgage activity shown in (a) overleaf

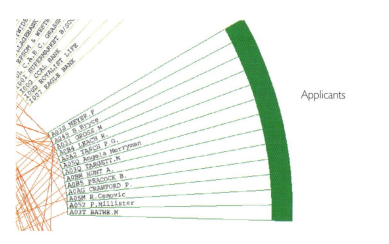

Applicants

FIGURE 3.75
For the data displayed in Figure 3.74 a threshold has been imposed to suppress the display of normal behaviour. As a result, unusual behaviour is revealed by the patterns formed by the lines

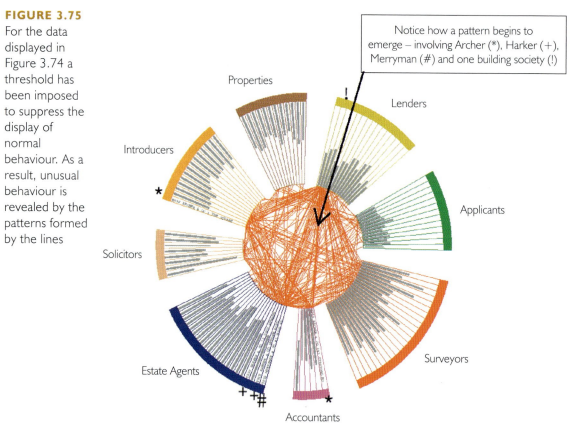

Notice how a pattern begins to emerge – involving Archer (*), Harker (+), Merryman (#) and one building society (!)

Properties

Lenders

Introducers

Applicants

Solicitors

Estate Agents

Surveyors

Accountants

Over the last decade the value of representing connections between people, things and institutions has been fully recognized, and exploited by means of powerful visualization tools which support tasks falling under the umbrella heading of intelligence analysis. A good example is provided by Analyst's Notebook (i2, 2006) which is used widely in such areas as law enforcement and forensic investigations. Visualization software of this kind allows the interrogation of data in complex scenarios, the analysis of volumes of seemingly unrelated data and, not least, the communication of actionable intelligence in a visual format. For some investigations the principal interest may lie in the connection between people, social networks, locations and property, for which an 'association' style chart such as that shown in Figure 3.76 would be appropriate. If – alternatively or additionally – a comprehensive chronology of events over time is of interest in view of the potential for highlighting temporal coincidence which may not be evident in an association style chart, then a 'timeline' style chart such as that in Figure 3.77 may be useful.

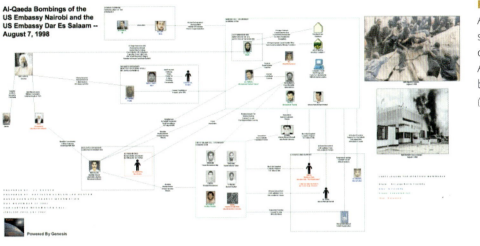

FIGURE 3.76

An 'association' style chart depicting the African bombings

(Courtesy i2 Ltd.)

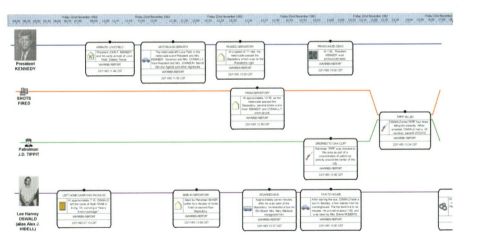

FIGURE 3.77

Part of a 'timeline' style chart depicting the Kennedy assassination

(Courtesy i2 Ltd.)

Perhaps the most familiar use of lines to represent relations, reflecting the term 'connection' in the definition above, is the map of the London Underground (Figure 3.78), a form of representation judged to be so effective that it is now employed by virtually every transportation authority in the world (Ovenden, 2003). It undoubtedly benefits from the shapes into which the lines connecting stations are arranged (indeed, Harry Beck was supposedly influenced by electrical circuit diagrams), as well as from the use of colour to denote differ-

FIGURE 3.78

Harry Beck's original London Underground map

(© Transport for London)

FIGURE 3.79

The Underground map in use prior to the introduction of Harry Beck's version

(© Transport for London)

ent underground lines and symbols to denote both ordinary and interchange stations (Garland, 1994). Often, coloured regions having implications for fares
payable can be provided as background. Another influence on the nature of the
map is its general – though not necessarily accurate – geographical veracity: it
would not matter if the separation between stations was not proportional to
their geographical separation but it would significantly reduce the value of the
map if, for example, Wembley (of football fame) in North London were placed
towards the bottom and Wimbledon (known for tennis) in South London were
placed towards the top. Although I know of no relevant usability study, the current map would appear at first sight to be easier to comprehend than the one in
use immediately before Harry Beck's design was introduced (Figure 3.79).

The term *relation* often carries the connotation of interactions between human
beings. We are familiar, for example, with the conventional family tree, but that
focuses principally on formal relationships cemented by marriage, including the
birth and death of children. The use of simple lines can, however, be broadened to
usefully represent what Freeman (2000, 2005) has termed 'the consequences of
the social nature of social animals'. Social network analysis is concerned with the
structural patterning of the ties that link social actors. Two kinds of patterns are of
particular concern: (1) those that reveal cohesive social groups, and (2) those that
reveal the social positions, or roles, of individual actors.

The representation of social relations by a network is not new: over 70 years
ago Moreno (1934) presented a network (Figure 3.80) showing the social choices
made by fourth graders in a school, from which it is clear that, overwhelmingly,
boys chose boys and girls chose girls (a more recent comparative study would be
interesting!). More recently Marbella Canales, a colleague of Freeman (2005),
collected data on the recreational social connections among the employees in
the cosmetics department of an upmarket department store. Her data revealed
the more or less linear pattern of connections shown in Figure 3.81(a) from
which it is clear that the interaction was not random but rather patterned

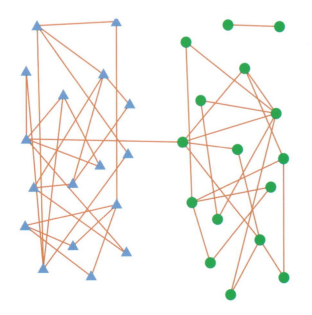

FIGURE 3.80
The social
choices of
fourth-grade
students (after
Moreno, 1934)

(Freeman, 2005). She then sought to discover the underlying basis of that pattern by colouring the nodes in the network according to various characteristics of the individuals involved. She tried sex, ethnicity, marital status and other traits that might lead to individuals choosing one another as recreational partners. Most did not work: Figure 3.81(b), for example, shows the individuals coloured in terms of their marital status: married individuals are yellow, singles are red. Because both red and yellow are spread throughout the image it is clear that these individuals did not choose others according to their marital status. When the investigator explored the age of the individuals, however, a very different picture emerged (Figure 3.81(c)). Blue points represent people who are 30 or younger, those between 30 and 40 are yellow and those 40 and older are red. Their connectivity shows that the individuals chose recreational partners on the basis of similarity in age.

FIGURE 3.81(a)
Social choices among department store employees
Source: *L.C. Freeman*

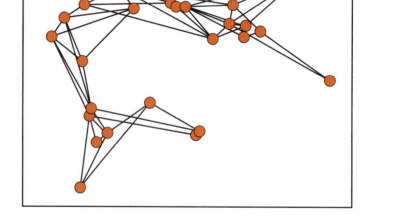

FIGURE 3.81(b)
Social choices among department store employees, with marital status encoded
Source: *L.C. Freeman*

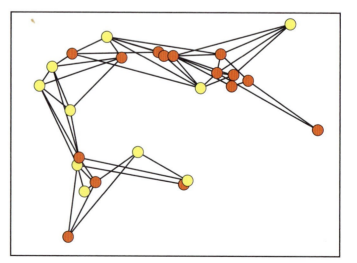

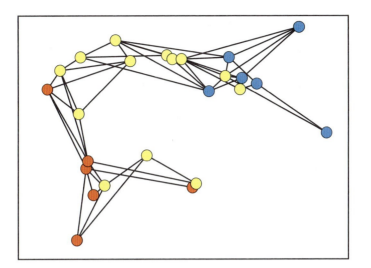

FIGURE 3.81(c)
Social choices among department store employees, with age range encoded (blue <30, 30<yellow <40, red >40)

Source: *L.C. Freeman*

3.2.2 Maps and diagrams

Venn diagrams

The definition of relation refers to 'logical association'. A very simple set of logical relations is contained in Table 3.2 which indicates, for example, that hotel B has a swimming pool *and* a golf course but *not* a restaurant. A search for a desirable hotel within a much larger table would be tedious and time consuming and could be much easier through the use of a familiar Venn diagram. The Venn dia-

TABLE 3.2 Facilities offered by eight hotels

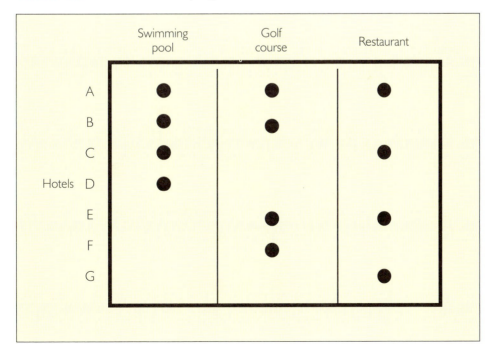

gram pertinent to the hotel information in Table 3.2 is shown in Figure 3.82: for a much larger collection of 24 hotels the corresponding Venn diagram (Figure 3.83) *might* quickly allow a traveller to identify the hotels which satisfy his or her needs. For example, it can be seen that if all facilities are required (swimming pool + golf + restaurant) then four hotels are candidates. Interaction can add considerable value to a Venn diagram.

FIGURE 3.82
A Venn diagram representation of the hotels listed in Table 3.2

FIGURE 3.83
A Venn diagram representation of the attributes of 24 hotels

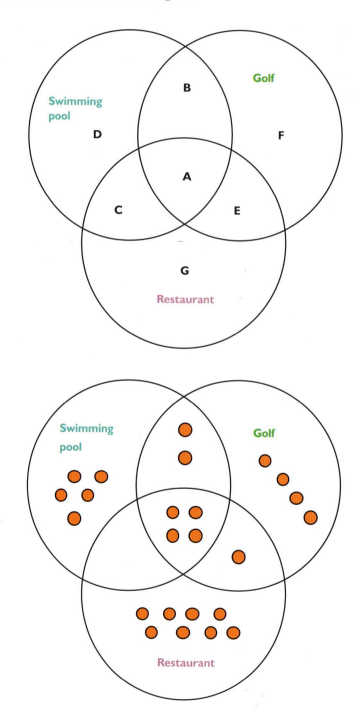

InfoCrystal

An improvement on the Venn diagram for the representation of logical relations was proposed by Spoerri (1993). Figure 3.84 shows a progression from a three-attribute Venn diagram to a three-attribute InfoCrystal. All possible logical relations between the three attributes are represented by regions within the crystal. The same colours are used to represent groups of houses as are used in the Attribute Explorer example of Figure 3.58. Thus, the region indicated by an asterisk in Figure 3.84 corresponds to, and can be used as a means of selecting (i.e. as a visual query), those houses which satisfy requirements on price and garden size, but not the number of bedrooms. Spoerri, however, complemented the simple representation of Figure 3.84 by adding interior icons (Figure 3.85) which indicate, by their shape, the number of criteria satisfied (circle = 1, rectangle = 2, triangle = 3) and, by an inscribed number, the number of items in that class. Thus, for the 24 hotels represented in Figure 3.83, four offer all facili-

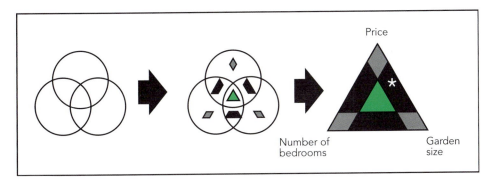

FIGURE 3.84 The development leading from a Venn diagram to an InfoCrystal. The InfoCrystal illustrated allows visual queries to be made concerning price, garden size and number of bedrooms (see the Attribute Explorer of Figure 3.58) The asterisk represents houses satisfying criteria on price and garden size but not number of bedrooms

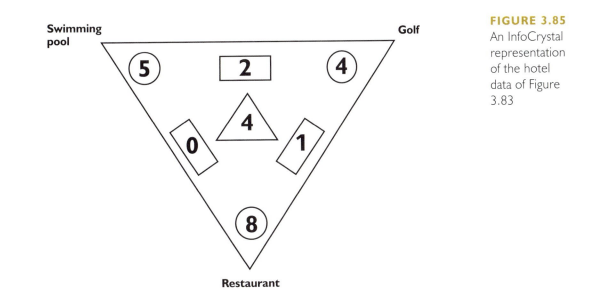

FIGURE 3.85 An InfoCrystal representation of the hotel data of Figure 3.83

ties and the number which offer both golf and a restaurant but no swimming pool is one. Spoerri's InfoCrystal can be extended to more than three attributes, but above four the effort needed to comprehend the representation and to readily formulate a query is probably such that only the specialist user would be able to do so.

Cluster maps

Figure 3.86 shows a cluster map (Fluit *et al.*, 2003) relevant to the hotel data represented by the Venn diagram of Figure 3.83 and the InfoCrystal of Figure 3.85. The labeled nodes represent the three attributes and carry a label identifying that attribute (e.g. 'restaurant') followed by a number indicating how many hotels possess that attribute. Note that the three numbers do not add up to 24, the number of hotels, because a hotel with a restaurant and a gym, for example, will contribute to the count on both those nodes. Associated with each node are one or more circles containing a number of yellow circles, each representing a

FIGURE 3.86
A cluster map
representation
of the 24 hotels
represented in
the Venn
diagram of
Figure 3.83 and
the InfoCrystal
of Figure 3.85
*(Courtesy Christiaan
Fluit, Aduna)*

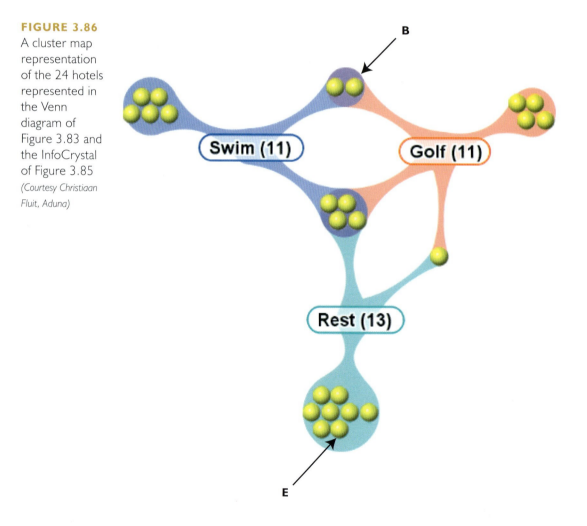

hotel. Each hotel is placed in a circle connected to all the attributes that the hotel possesses. Thus, hotel E has only a restaurant, so is placed in the circle associated only with the restaurant node, but hotel B appears in a circle attached to both the swimming pool node and the golf node because it possesses those two, and only those two, facilities. It is therefore reasonably obvious from the cluster map of Figure 3.86 that there are no hotels which possess both a swimming pool and a restaurant but no golf course. Mouse-over action can disclose more details of each hotel.

The test of any technique which represents logical data is how well it scales to many classes. Some impression of the cluster map's capability in this respect can be gained from an example representing 24 hotels each characterized by *four* attributes (Figure 3.87). The absence of any circular area connected solely to the gym node means, for example, that any hotel that has a gym will always possess at least one of the other three facilities. A cluster map can support many different kinds of interaction including the highlighting of all circles associated with a class node and the animated modification of a map following the inclusion of a new class (Fluit *et al.*, 2003).

3.2.3   Tree representations

In all the examples of relation representation we have discussed so far there has been no restriction upon what is connected to what other than it be meaningful.

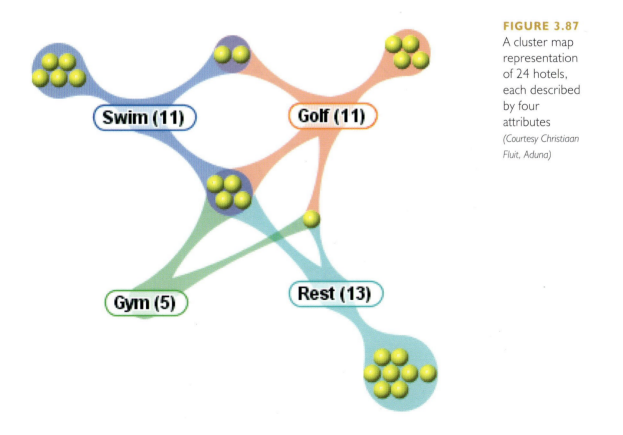

FIGURE 3.87
A cluster map representation of 24 hotels, each described by four attributes
(Courtesy Christiaan Fluit, Aduna)

The term 'network' is often applied to a node-and-link type of relation to which no topological restrictions apply. Examples include the simple network of Figure 3.73 representing telephone calls and the far more complex network of lines representing mortgage arrangements in Figure 3.74. There is, however, a class of networks having significant practical application in which the topological restrictions that apply allow a new family of representations to be derived. The restriction is that the network be a **tree**.

The mathematical definition of a tree is a network of nodes and links so connected that no loops are present. In other words you cannot start at a node and trace a path which arrives back at the same node without a direct retrace of steps. The reason for the considerable interest in trees is that many situations are described by hierarchical relations. To introduce relevant terminology we examine the simple tree of Figure 3.88. One node has been designated the root node: we use the term 'designated' because you can take hold of *any* node of a tree and call it the root node. In practice, however, a tree often refers to a hierarchy in which the designated root node is the president of a company or perhaps a department store comprising a number of product lines. If there is indeed a hierarchy, then all nodes except the root node are associated with a superordinate node and, if associated with subordinate nodes, these are often referred to as 'children'. If a node has no subordinate node it is called a 'leaf node'.

FIGURE 3.88
A tree

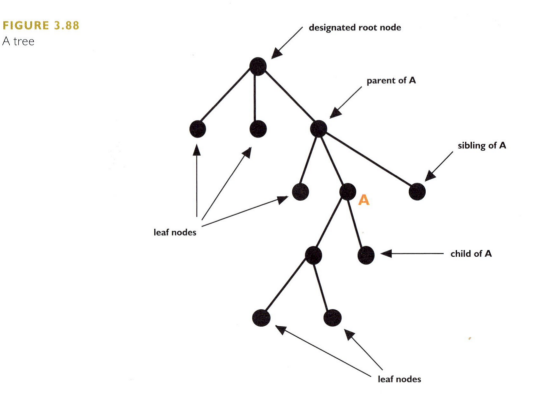

If some data describes a tree, the immediate question is how such data can usefully be represented and explored. What is wrong, however, with the representation shown in Figure 3.88? If it is satisfactory we need look no further!

Cone tree

The problem with the tree representation of Figure 3.88 is that in most practical cases the tree has many levels: even with an average fan-out (i.e. the number of subordinate nodes associated with a node) as small as three, the space needed to display a tree can become huge, mainly in the horizontal direction. A solution is to imagine the original tree (Figure 3.89(a)) to be rearranged into a 3D structure such that all nodes subordinate to a given node are arranged in a horizontal circle which, together with the superordinate node, forms a cone, as shown in Figure 3.89(b). The resulting 2D view of that structure, called a cone tree (Robertson *et al.*, 1991), is now more compact than the original representation of Figure 3.89(a) and, notwithstanding some occlusion, is easier to handle. The user of a cone tree may, for example, wish to see the reporting path of an employee within the organization represented by the cone tree, in which case entry of the employee's name by some means will bring about any cone rotations needed to position that employee and his reporting path to the foreground. A horizontal orientation of the cone tree, called the cam tree, may be more convenient for the display of node names (Figure 3.90). No record is available of any evaluation of the usability of the cone tree concept.

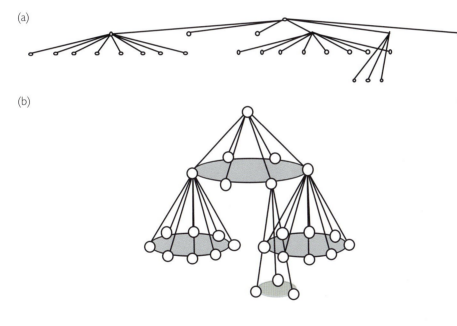

(a)

(b)

FIGURE 3.89
(a) A tree,
(b) the corresponding cone tree

Tree maps

An alternative representation of a tree is the tree map (Johnson and Shneiderman, 1991). Its derivation from the original tree representation is straightforward and is illustrated in Figure 3.91. Starting with the designated root node one draws a rectangle passing through that node. Usually, to make efficient use of display area, the rectangle will be made as large as conveniently possible. Within that rectangle are smaller rectangles, one for each of the nodes that are immediately subordinate to the root node. This construction is repeated until all nodes are accounted for. There is no constraint (except the resolution of

FIGURE 3.90
A reorientation of the cone tree, more convenient for the textual labelling of nodes

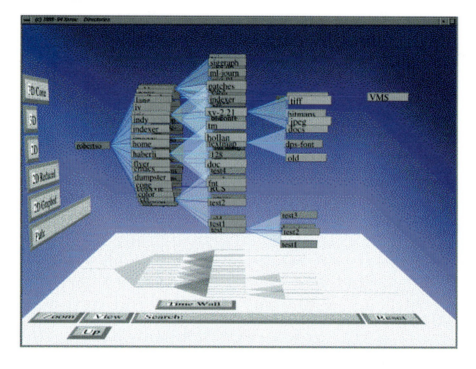

the display) on the depth of the tree and no requirement that all leaf nodes are at the same level or that the fan-out of every node is the same. Once the tree map is derived, colour coding, for example, can be employed to characterize different parts of the tree according to the use to which it will be put.

The main disadvantage of the tree map construction illustrated in Figure 3.91, but one which is easily overcome, is that for typical trees the result is a large number of very thin rectangles in which it is difficult, for example, to display text. The simple solution, illustrated in Figure 3.92, is a 'slice-and-dice'

FIGURE 3.91
The construction of a Tree Map

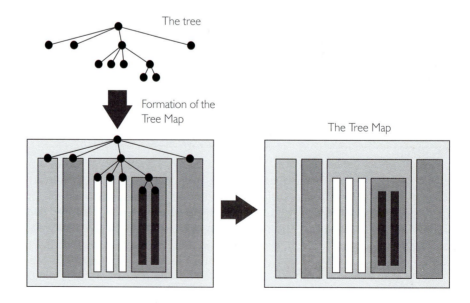

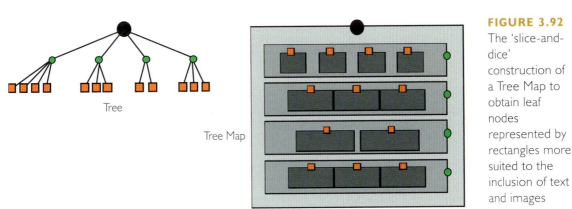

FIGURE 3.92
The 'slice-and-dice' construction of a Tree Map to obtain leaf nodes represented by rectangles more suited to the inclusion of text and images

approach in which the generated rectangles are drawn, alternately, vertically and horizontally from the nodes at successive levels. A typical result is shown in Figure 3.93 which is an author's collection of reports. An advantage of a tree map is that, as in Figure 3.93, it supports an awareness of leaf nodes: a disadvantage is that the hierarchy is not easy to discern.

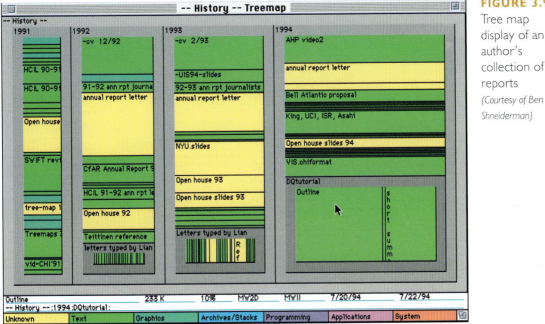

FIGURE 3.93
Tree map display of an author's collection of reports
(Courtesy of Ben Shneiderman)

The tree map technique has found a variety of applications. One is the representation to be found on the website Smartmoney.com (Figure 3.94). Major industrial sectors (e.g. energy, healthcare) are each represented by an area which, in turn, contains other areas representing relevant companies. As illustrated, there are many opportunities for encoding by colour and area, as well as for interaction by mouse-over and the selection of further detail by mouse click.

FIGURE 3.94
The Smartmoney.com website showing the status of companies within a number of sectors

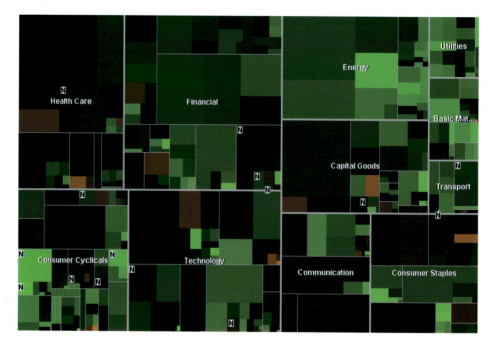

Distortion and suppression techniques to be discussed in Chapter 4 may also be appropriate. Figure 3.95 provides an example showing how the selection of attribute limits can control the view provided by a tree map, and illustrates once

FIGURE 3.95
A tree map presentation of economic information, allowing filtering according to attributes
(Permission from HIVE)

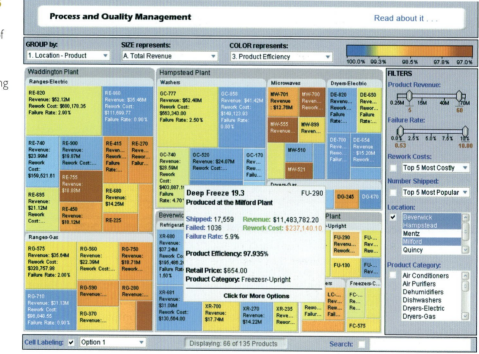

again the potential offered by combinations of techniques (see, for example, Csallner *et al.*, 2003).

Hyperbolic browser

An ingenious technique whereby an entire tree can be kept within the confines of a circular area on a conventional display screen was invented in 1994. Without going into the sophisticated mathematical detail involved (Lamping *et al.*, 1995; Lamping and Rao, 1994, 1996), the method is based on a hyperbolic geometric transformation which leads to all nodes of the tree being located within a specified area: the resulting appearance is the form shown in Figure 3.96. The designated root node is initially in the centre of the display, its immediate subordinate nodes are distributed around it at a particular distance, but as the number of levels separating a node from the root increases, the separation between a node and its parent decreases and the size of the node also decreases, in such a way that all nodes fall within the circular display area. A practical limit to the display of all nodes is imposed by the resolution of the display: drawing of the tree stops below one-pixel resolution.

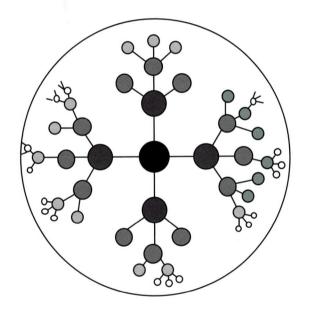

FIGURE 3.96
A sketch illustration of the hyperbolic browser representation of a tree. The further away a node is from the root node, the closer it is to its superordinate node, and the area it occupies decreases

It is the interactive nature of the hyperbolic browser that is its principal advantage. Any node of interest can be moved smoothly towards and into the central position, whereupon its subordinate nodes follow in roughly the same direction. Thus, by *smooth* movements of the tree within the available display area, relevant regions of interest can easily be explored. Figure 3.97(a) shows a hyperbolic display for the employees in an imaginary department: interactive movement of Rachel Anderson towards the centre pushes her superior away from the centre and reveals the employees who report to Rachel (Figure 3.97(b)). In turn, the movement of Eliza Doolittle towards the centre would reveal details of the people who report to her. As with the cone tree (but in contrast to the tree map), the hyperbolic browser places the hierarchical structure

FIGURE 3.97
(a) The reporting structure of the employees of a company.
(b) One employee of interest, Rachel Anderson, has been moved towards the centre, revealing her subordinates

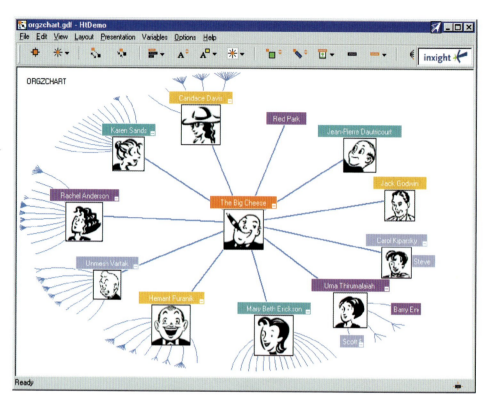

(a)

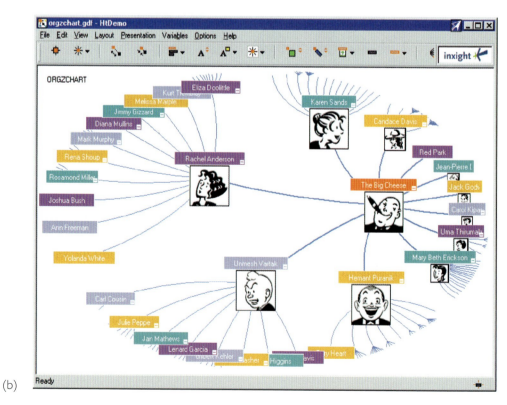

(b)

in evidence. But again in contrast to the tree map, the leaf nodes are not primarily in evidence unless dragged towards the centre. The application of the hyperbolic browser to the Library of Congress is illustrated in Figure 3.98.

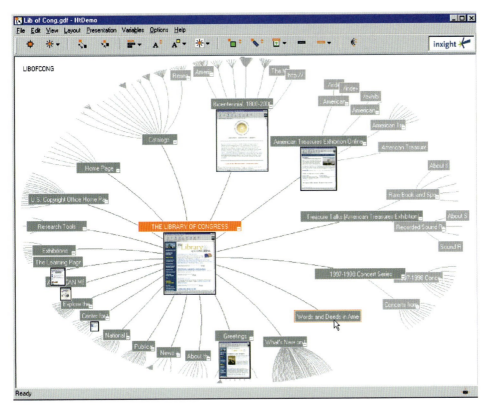

FIGURE 3.98
Representation of the Library of Congress by the hyperbolic browser

3.3 Support for design

The design of even the simplest visualization tool involves creativity. And, like the conventional artist who works in oils, the interaction designer has a number of palettes available. On one (Figure 3.99(a)) are some techniques drawn from an extensive collection that can be used for the representation of values and relations, each having its own advantages and disadvantages. On another (Figure 3.99(b)) is a collection of concepts of potential value when selecting a representation technique appropriate for a given application.

But two other palettes are needed before effective interaction design can occur. One, to be discussed in the following chapter, has to do with *presentation*, concerning the manner in which representations can be presented within the constraints of limited display area and time. The other, the subject of Chapter 5, concerns *interaction* – again, concepts and techniques are available for selection by the interaction designer to complement the benefits to information visualization offered by representation and presentation.

FIGURE 3.99
'Palettes'
available for the
interaction
designer:
(a) techniques,
(b) concepts

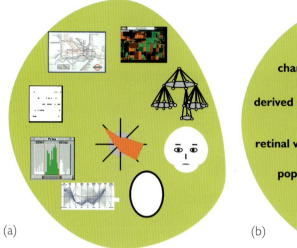

(a)

change blindness

derived structure

visibility

retinal variables

derived values

popping out

brushing

(b)

Exercises

The value of many of these exercises can be enhanced by discussing the results in open class.

Exercise 3.1 (Review)

Make a list of all the methods you can recall for encoding data visually and write brief comments about the circumstances in which they are particularly valuable. Comment upon whether, in their static form (i.e. without interaction), they support object and/or attribute visibility and correlation.

Exercise 3.2

Five students have taken exams in eight subjects and for each subject a mark out of ten has been assigned. Make a list of the questions that might be asked of this data by (a) a student, (b) a parent, (c) a subject teacher and (d) the headteacher. Aim for a total of at least ten questions. Write the questions on Post-its and stick them on the wall for reference during Exercise 3.3.

Exercise 3.3

The performance of the students mentioned in Exercise 3.2 is as follows:

**5 STUDENTS (A, B, C, D AND E) SIT 8 EXAMS.
THE MARKS OUT OF 10 ARE AS FOLLOWS:**

	A	B	C	D	E
Art	10	1	5	3	2
Science	1	10	5	4	8
History	8	5	7	1	1
Sport	2	9	5	10	4
Physics	–	1	2	3	1
English	2	8	6	8	5
Chemistry	4	1	1	1	4
Mathematics	10	1	5	4	2

Without using a computer, sketch one static representation of this data: no interaction with the representation is to be considered. Then see whether it answers any of the questions identified in Exercise 3.2.

For the questions identified in Exercise 3.2, and whose answer cannot easily be found, see whether you can make a useful modification to the representation, still without employing interaction.

■ Exercise 3.4

Compose a mosaic plot representation of the Titanic data (Table 3.1) but using a different sequence of steps (for example: survival -> gender -> class -> adult/child). List the observations that can readily be made from these representations. Are they different from those triggered by the representations derived in Figure 3.61?

■ Exercise 3.5

The London Underground map contains no distance or journey-time encoding. With sketches, suggest how this data can be represented. Would it be useful? What other data could usefully be encoded?

■ Exercise 3.6

At first sight, Florence Nightingale's 'rose plot' appears to have much in common with a star plot. Distinguish between the two, commenting upon the significance that can, or cannot, be associated with the enclosed area of a star plot.

■ Exercise 3.7

By means of sketches, suggest alternative ways in which the 'hits' returned by Google could be represented.

■ Exercise 3.8

For your school or university or department (real or imaginary), design a representation of scholastic achievements (e.g. marks in 12 subjects in five year groups) that will show not only the general level obtained but also (1) the way in which the achievements are changing (i.e. first derivatives), (2) the proportion of students obtaining better than a pass mark and (3) the number of students taking a particular subject. Design the representation so that it can be printed on a card that slides easily into the pocket (e.g. one-third of A4).

Exercise 3.9

Study and understand one of the following representation techniques that have not been discussed in this chapter, and prepare a ten-minute presentation in which its features are described and critically evaluated:

(1) Keim, D.A., Hao, M.C., Dayal, U. and Hsu, M. (2002) Pixel bar charts: a visualization technique for very large multi-attribute data sets, Information Visualization, 1, 1, pp. 20–34.

(2) Havre, S., Hetzler, E., Perrine, K., Jurrus, E. and Miller, N. (2001) Interactive visualization of multiple query results, IEEE, Proceedings Information Visualization, pp. 105–112.

(3) Yang, J., Ward, M.O. and Rundensteiner, E.A. (2002) InterRing: an interactive tool for visually navigating and manipulating hierarchical structures, IEEE, Proceedings Information Visualization, pp. 77–84.

(4) Havre, S., Hetzler, B. and Nowell, L. (2000) Theme river: visualizing theme changes over time, IEEE, Proceedings Information Visualization 2000, pp. 145–154.

(5) Geons, as described in Colin Ware's book *Information Visualization: Perception for Design* (2004).

Exercise 3.10

Suggest possible static (not interactive) representations for human relationships (including marriage, births, deaths), test them on real examples and identify the advantages and disadvantages of each.

Exercise 3.11

Bus, metro and train routes are typically represented by lines between nodes. However, with some large cities (London, for example) there are so many routes that it is not easy to plan a journey, especially if it involves intermediate changes. Explore the potential of adding, to the node-link route representation, some overall directional indicators to give a 'first glance' suggestion as to which route might be appropriate.

Exercise 3.12

Select one of the folders on your laptop which contains at least two levels and draw a tree map representation of its contents.

■ Exercise 3.13

Select one of the folders on your laptop which contains at least three levels and draw a hyperbolic browser representation. Comment on benefits it may or may not offer when seeking an item which is a leaf node.

■ Exercise 3.14

For a local shop, department store, book collection, recipe collection or photo collection, draw a tree descriptive of the contents, but stop at the third level. From this data generate a tree map. Comment on any difficulties you encounter.

CHAPTER 4

Presentation

A problem

Many of us have found ourselves with a report that has to be completed by a deadline, with the result (Figure 4.1) that the dining room table, extended to its 12-guest state, is covered in piles of paper as well as reports, books, clippings and even old slides, perhaps with more arranged on the floor and a couple of chairs. There may even be piles on top of piles. Such a presentation of vital information makes a lot of sense: everything relevant is to hand (we hope!), its visibility acts as a reminder (Bolt, 1984; Malone, 1983), and spatial memory (Czerwinski *et al.*, 1999) reminds us where we put something. Indeed, with so much on view, ideas may emerge opportunistically. In this environment I can concentrate on creative tasks rather than on organization, at which I do not excel.

FIGURE 4.1
Support for report preparation. Many sources of content are visible and ready to hand

Despite the availability of high-resolution displays and powerful workstations, I still draft most of my reports this way. Why? Not because of any Luddite tendency, but because the display area provided by typical workstations is far too small to support, visibly, all the sources that are relevant to my composition.

I am not alone in having too much data and too small a screen. A very large and expensive screen, for example, would be needed to display, in full detail, the London Underground map or the organization tree of a large company. And the problem is worse if only a PDA or a mobile is available: standing in a London street, with no map in sight, how can I effectively view the London Underground map in order to plan a journey?

The presentation issue

We identified the problems of inadequate screen real estate in Chapter 2 under the generic heading of '**Presentation**', for which it is now appropriate to offer a definition. Reference to a dictionary provides, among a number of definitions,

> **present** (tr.v): *to offer to view; display.*

Thus, irrespective of how data may be *represented*, a decision has to be made about how that representation is to be *displayed* – to be offered for view by a user – and even *whether* it is to be displayed. Necessarily, in view of limited display area, the issue of layout arises. Also, there will inevitably be an interdependence between representation and presentation. Even if represented data is chosen to be displayed there remains the question as to whether its display should be under interactive control. Such decisions are, of course, heavily influenced by the task that a visualization tool is designed to support. There is a pressing need for an understanding of the problems involved in presentation and related concepts that will correspondingly inform interaction design.

4.1   Space limitations

4.1.1   Scrolling

An obvious solution to the problem posed by a document that is larger than the display area is that of scrolling, in which a long document can be moved past a 'window' until something relevant is noticed (Figure 4.2). Sometimes this is a satisfactory approach but in many cases it is not. For example, I'm composing Chapter 2, working on Section 2.3 (I think – I can't see the last section heading) and I want to remind myself of a figure placed in the previous section. Where is it? I must scroll – but to where? Tedious and often time-consuming search may be needed during which memory for current tasks begins to fade, leading to the 'Now, where was I?' problem exacerbated by the need to scroll back to where I was. Users of microfilm readers will readily recognize this scenario. The main problem with scrolling is that most content is *hidden from view*.

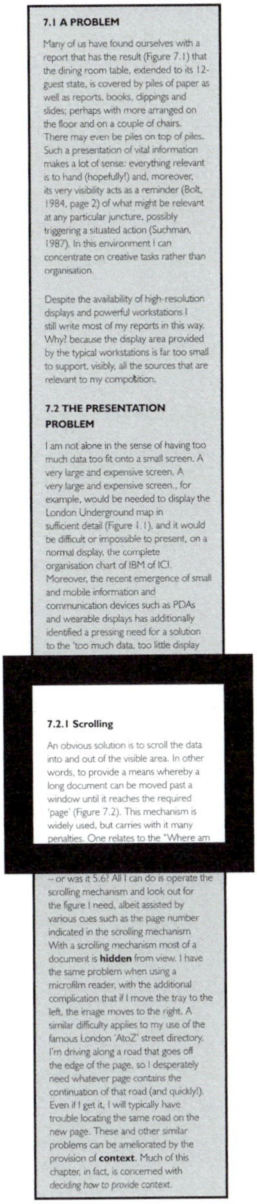

FIGURE 4.2
Scrolling hides most of a document

7.1 A PROBLEM

Many of us have found ourselves with a report that has the result (Figure 7.1) that the dining room table, extended to its 12-guest state, is covered by piles of paper as well as reports, books, clippings and slides; perhaps with more arranged on the floor and on a couple of chairs. There may even be piles on top of piles. Such a presentation of vital information makes a lot of sense: everything relevant is to hand (hopefully!) and, moreover, its very visibility acts as a reminder (Bolt, 1984, page 2) of what might be relevant at any particular juncture, possibly triggering a situated action (Suchman, 1987). In this environment I can concentrate on creative tasks rather than organisation.

Despite the availability of high-resolution displays and powerful workstations I still write most of my reports in this way. Why? because the display area provided by the typical workstations is far too small to support, visibly, all the sources that are relevant to my composition.

7.2 THE PRESENTATION PROBLEM

I am not alone in the sense of having too much data too fit onto a small screen. A very large and expensive screen. A very large and expensive screen., for example, would be needed to display the London Underground map in sufficient detail (Figure 1.1), and it would be difficult or impossible to present, on a normal display, the complete organisation chart of IBM of ICI. Moreover, the recent emergence of small and mobile information and communication devices such as PDAs and wearable displays has additionally identified a pressing need for a solution to the 'too much data, too little display

7.2.1 Scrolling

An obvious solution is to scroll the data into and out of the visible area. In other words, to provide a means whereby a long document can be moved past a window until it reaches the required 'page' (Figure 7.2). This mechanism is widely used, but carries with it many penalties. One relates to the "Where am

– or was it 5.6? All I can do is operate the scrolling mechanism and look out for the figure I need, albeit assisted by various cues such as the page number indicated in the scrolling mechanism. With a scrolling mechanism most of a document is **hidden** from view. I have the same problem when using a microfilm reader, with the additional complication that if I move the tray to the left, the image moves to the right. A similar difficulty applies to my use of the famous London 'AtoZ' street directory. I'm driving along a road that goes off the edge of the page, so I desperately need whatever page contains the continuation of that road (and quickly!). Even if I get it, I will typically have trouble locating the same road on the new page. These and other similar problems can be ameliorated by the provision of **context**. Much of this chapter, in fact, is concerned with deciding how to provide context.

4.1.2   Overview + detail

One disadvantage of scrolling – that one cannot have a view of context as well as detail – can be overcome by presenting views of both. But usually there is not enough space to achieve this in a *linear* fashion, with context presented at the same resolution as detail. Instead, and with greater benefit, two separate views, one of detail and the other of context, can be designed to present what is termed an *overview+detail* view. A familiar example (Figure 4.3) is the facility to see an overview comprising miniature pages of a document ranged vertically alongside one particular page from which detail is discernible. The user is afforded the

FIGURE 4.3
Overview + detail. Miniatures of pages of a pdf document provide useful context while attention is paid to detail of one page

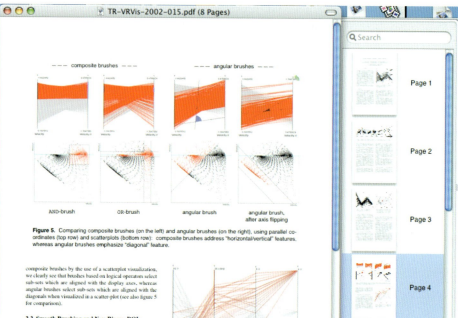

FIGURE 4.4
Use of a video editing suite is supported by the presentation of overview + detail. Eight available video clips (at top) provide an overview of available material; the one currently in use is highlighted. Lower left shows an overview representation of the portion of the complete video being edited, while the image at right provides detail of the image associated with the selected moment in the time domain

Source: *Courtesy of Colin Grimshaw*

opportunity, at their own pace and discretion, to drill down into detail but retain an awareness of context, iterating their attention easily between the two views. The highlighted miniature provides a 'you are here' sign. Another example is provided by a video editing suite (Figure 4.4) which presents the editor with a reminder of the context of the few seconds that are currently subject to careful and detailed attention. Overview+detail separates content into comprehensible pieces, at the same time clarifying their interrelationships.

The concurrent need for overview and detail is frequently present during travel, particularly by car. For example, a person from the South of England is

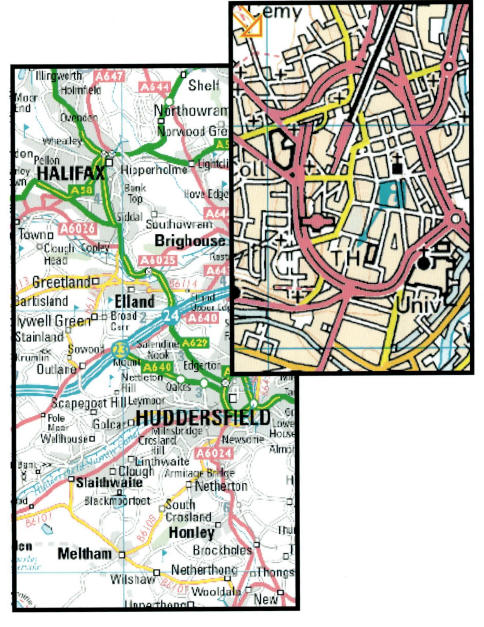

FIGURE 4.5

A journey north towards Halifax requires detail of the town (Huddersfield) through which the traveller passes

travelling north to visit his Aunt Mabel in Halifax and, on the way, must travel through Huddersfield. Negotiating the streets of Huddersfield is no mean achievement and requires a detailed map, but he must not lose sight of the over-all purpose of the journey, which is to reach Halifax. For this reason the (typically stressed) human navigator is usually to be found clutching two paper-based maps, one of detail and the other providing an overview (Figure 4.5). Possible improvements include a real or simulated magnifying glass (Figure 4.6) and the DragMag (Ware and Lewis, 1995) in which a small region of interest within the context map can be flexibly positioned to provide a magnified view, often with added detail (Figure 4.7). While DragMag avoids the drawback of masking inherently present with the real or simulated magnifying glass, both of

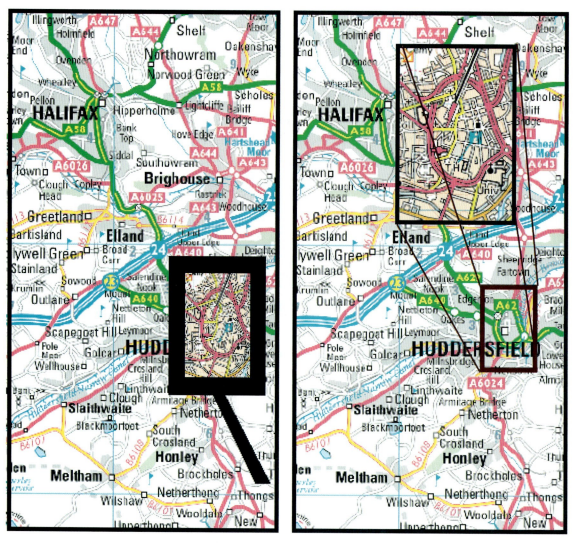

FIGURE 4.6

The use of a real or digitally simulated magnifying glass masks detail around the magnified region

FIGURE 4.7

The DragMag technique allows flexible positioning of the region to be magnified these presentations have the same drawback as two separate maps, a drawback which, in fact, is immediately apparent to the navigator who is trying to guide the driver through the streets of Huddersfield on to the main highway going north to Halifax. The drawback is typically articulated by the question, 'Does the High Street or Market Street take us to the main highway north?' What is missing is the *connection* between the detail and overview presentations. What the navigator needs is some presentation in which a road in the detailed map flows smoothly into a road in the context map. This need, which is extremely general and not confined to maps, is referred to as the *focus+context* problem, a solution to which is now presented.

4.1.3 Distortion

The technique called *distortion*, first suggested in 1980, offers a way of solving the focus+context problem. The bifocal display (Imperial College Television Studio, 1980; Spence and Apperley, 1982) is based on the very simple metaphor illustrated in Figure 4.8. An information space in the form of a long strip of paper (a) too large to be viewed in detail within a normal display area is wrapped around two uprights (b) in such a way that, when viewed from an appropriate direction, part of that space can be viewed in detail while a 'bird's eye view' is provided of the remainder (c). Thus, in the digital embodiment of

(a) An information space containing documents, emails, etc.

FIGURE 4.8
Metaphor illustrating the principle of the bifocal display

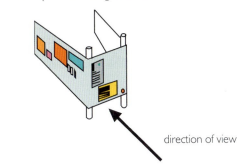

direction of view

(b) The same space wrapped around two uprights

(c) Appearance of the information space when viewed from an appropriate direction

the bifocal display a user can be reading or composing a letter displayed in the central region, yet be aware of the appearance in an outer region of a message from his or her boss, perhaps because of its distinctive colour or vertical position. That message cannot of course be deciphered in the distorted region, but that is not the point: the user has *noticed* the important message (necessarily in the form of a thin rectangle) and has the option to scroll the information space so that the message moves smoothly and continuously into the central, non-distorted region, expanding as it does so and becoming readable. An early illustration of the bifocal display technique is shown in Figure 4.9.

FIGURE 4.9
An early illustration of the bifocal display principle

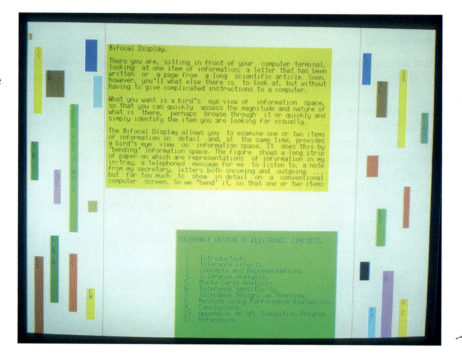

The bifocal display embodies a number of important features. A principal one is *distortion*, allowing available display area to be allocated to two different regions we may call the focus (undistorted) and context (distorted) regions. Another is the fact that an information item moves smoothly and *continuously* from context to focus during the scrolling action and, even without scrolling, embodies both geometric and (to some degree) encoding continuity between the regions. A third feature is the opportunity that the display affords for representation. Since the original information space (Figure 4.8) was two-dimensional, there is the opportunity to use those two dimensions to encode two attributes of the information items. Time or date of receipt might be assigned to the horizontal axis and type of item (e.g. in-email, out-email, manuscript, timetable) to the Y-axis. There is also an opportunity for further encoding, for example by colour or shape, to additionally distinguish the information items. The issue of representation also arises from the fact that an item can usefully be represented in a different way in the two regions. In the focus region the premium is on readability and interaction; in the distorted regions readability is not the main purpose –

the essential feature is that of *awareness and identification*. In a distorted region, text and other detail would normally be *suppressed* and a representation chosen for the information item which, while supporting awareness and identification, will nevertheless not be so different from the representation in the focal region that transition from one region to another is disruptive.

Another important feature of the bifocal display is its *manual control* by a user. As originally proposed, the scrolling action would be achieved via a touch screen, making use of the visio-motor ability of the human being: in other words, the user can continuously monitor, simply by visual observation, how close the desired item is to the focus region and adjust finger movement and hence the associated scrolling action accordingly.

Application

Applications of the distortion technique are to be found in many domains. An example is provided by the field of bioinformatics which, broadly speaking, is the application of information technology to the analysis of biological data. Of primary importance are sequences, for example the nucleic acids in the familiar DNA molecule, and the amino acids comprising a protein molecule which encode life. One such sequence of amino acids is shown in Figure 4.10: each letter refers to an amino acid and the background colours denote what might loosely be termed the 'charge' on the amino acid. Because the one-dimensional sequences encode three-dimensional information, the sequences are long. Therefore, because an investigator needs to be aware of the complete sequence when associating it with other representations of a protein, some distortion may have to be introduced, as shown in Figure 4.10. Note, however, that the distortion is generated without any discontinuities – in other words, there is no point at which the sequence suddenly 'bends' as it does in Figure 4.8 – since a discontinuity would be an artifact of the display itself and would detract from the real information about the protein.

MIEIKDKQLTGLRFIDLFAGLGGFRLALESCGAEC

FIGURE 4.10
A sequence of amino acids within a protein *(Courtesy of Tom Oldfield)*

Another example, and one which demonstrates the possibility of multiple focus regions, is provided by the table lens (Figure 4.11), a means of presenting information which has the advantage that many people are familiar with tables (Rao and Card, 1994). The table of Figure 4.11(a) contains details of around 300 baseball players, each normally assigned to such a thin row that their name cannot be discerned, though associated thin bars (providing a histogram) usefully encode attributes such as a player's position in the field and his or her number of 'hits'. A powerful feature is that rows can be reordered according to a selected attribute simply by a mouse movement down the corresponding column. The table lens supports a focus+context view in that one or more rows can be expanded to reveal names, as shown in Figure 4.11(b).

Generalization

The simple but powerful distortion concept can usefully be generalized (Leung and Apperley, 1994). For example, whereas the distortion illustrated in Figure 4.8 might be called X-distortion (Figure 4.12), it is possible to introduce

FIGURE 4.11
The table lens,
(a) without
distortion, (b)
with distortion
(expansion) to
show names

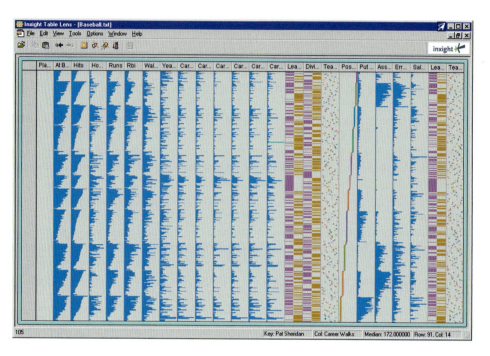

(a)

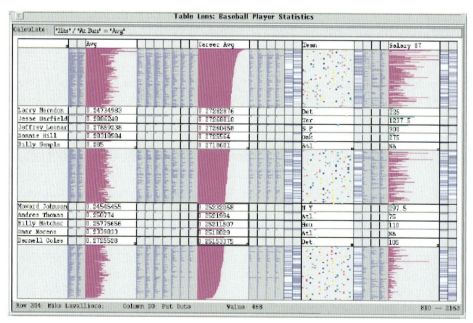

(b)

distortion in both X and Y directions (Figure 4.13). The latter combination of distortions is well suited to the display of the London Underground map (Leung *et al.*, 1995). Outside a movable focus region (Figure 4.14), station names are suppressed in view of the limited space available, but there is valuable *continuity* of railway lines at the boundary of the focus region, allowing easy comprehension.

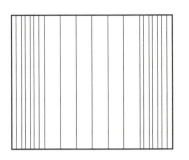

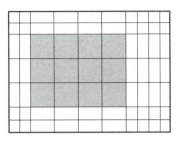

FIGURE 4.12 Schematic representation of X-distortion

FIGURE 4.13 Schematic representation of combined X- and Y-distortion

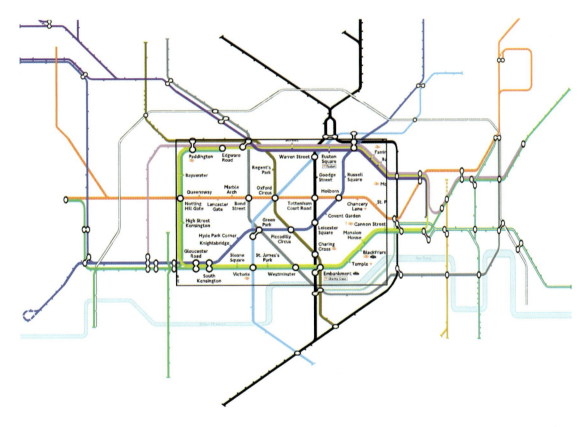

FIGURE 4.14 Distorted presentation of the London Underground map, illustrating continuity across the boundary of the distorted region

A different combination of X- and Y-distortion finds useful application to calendars (Figure 4.15). Whereas in 1980 the implementation of such a calendar was impracticable (Spence and Apperley, 1982; Apperley *et al.*, 1982), the bifocal display principle underpins a modern PDA-based calendar (Bederson *et al.*, 2003, 2004), described in detail in a case study in Chapter 6. One advantage of simultaneous X- and Y- distortion is, of course, when the distortion factors are equal, whereupon recognizable miniatures can result. This advantage was exploited

FIGURE 4.15
Combined X-
and Y-distortion
provides a
convenient
calendar
interface

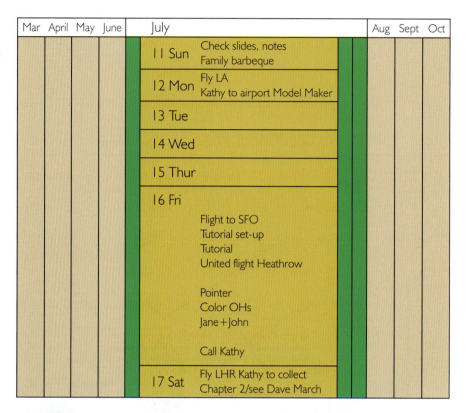

Mar	April	May	June	July			Aug	Sept	Oct

11 Sun	Check slides, notes Family barbeque
12 Mon	Fly LA Kathy to airport Model Maker
13 Tue	
14 Wed	
15 Thur	
16 Fri	
	Flight to SFO Tutorial set-up Tutorial United flight Heathrow Pointer Color OHs Jane+John Call Kathy
17 Sat	Fly LHR Kathy to collect Chapter 2/see Dave March

FIGURE 4.16
Visual
designer's
sketch of the
application of
the flip-zoom
technique
to the
presentation of
photographs on
a Nokia mobile
phone
(Courtesy Ron Bird)

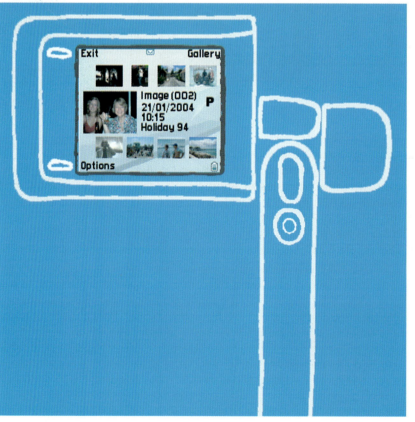

(Figure 4.16) in the flip-zoom technique (Holmquist, 1997). Originally demonstrated on a PDA where space is at a premium (Bjork *et al.*, 1999), it has recently been adopted to facilitate the browsing of photographs on a mobile phone: Figure 4.16 shows the original designer's sketch for this facility. Other recent exploitations of both X- and Y-distortion are to be found both in the presentation of route information in the small area of a PDA display (Figure 4.17) and, by contrast (Figure 4.18), in the presentation of geographical information for collaborative use on an interactive table of conventional size (Ryall *et al.*, 2005).

FIGURE 4.17
Distorted map on a PDA, showing the continuity of transportation links
(Courtesy David Baar, IDELIX Software Inc.)

Equal distortion factors are employed in the distortion exhibited by the 'dock' of the MacOSX system (Figure 4.19), a technique that has also found application in the rapid browsing of photographs (see Section 4.2) (McGuffin and Balakrishnan, 2002). In 1991, Mackinlay *et al.* (1991) showed an implementation of the bifocal display technique in which a 3D effect was introduced (Figure 4.20) and features such as the stretching of the focal region were made possible; the result was called the perspective wall. Distortion can also be applied to hierarchical data (Stasko and Zhang, 2000).

4.1.4 Suppression

Another presentation technique having a similar goal to that of distortion is **suppression**. Furnas (1981, 1986) made the point that it is often necessary to provide a balance of local detail and global context, and identified the useful analogy of the famous Steinberg poster entitled 'View of the World from 9th

FIGURE 4.18
Distorted map
on a table
(*Courtesy IDELIX*
Software Inc. and
Mitsubishi)

FIGURE 4.19
Equal X- and
Y-distortion
centred around
a manually
chosen location
in the
Macintosh OSX
'dock'

FIGURE 4.20
The perspective
wall applies a
3D effect to the
bifocal display

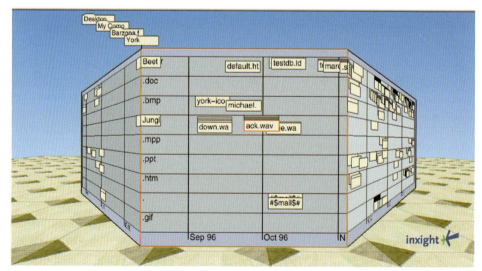

Avenue'. For the centre of Manhattan the poster shows the postbox, the subway entrance and the corner shop which are of far greater interest to a local resident than the entire landmass of Australia, which is therefore given token display as a mound somewhere out to sea. Furnas found it useful to identify a *degree of interest* to determine which data should be represented and presented and which should not. Like the bifocal display, Steinberg's poster map of the USA is distorted as well as modifed to suppress details considered irrelevant.

Furnas placed the concept of suppression on an intuitively attractive formal basis. The *degree of interest* (DoI) of any item of data is expressed as a function of two quantities. One is that item's *a priori importance* (API) and the other is some measure of the *'distance'* (D) between that item and whichever item is currently the *focus* of a user's interest.

Both concepts – API and D – can be illustrated by reference to the organization tree of a company (Figure 4.21). We first consider the concept of distance D. Let us suppose that we have a query about the production activities of that company and therefore wish to focus our attention on the person P who is in charge of production. We could, of course, simply click on some representation of P and be presented with information about that person. However, in view of the general nature of our enquiry it may be useful, while *focusing* on P, to be aware of the *context* in which he operates. His immediate superior S might well be relevant, as might the three people K, M and N responsible to P for day-to-day activity. It is less likely that we need concern ourselves with F and G who report to N; it is also unlikely – at least initially – that the president of the company will be relevant to our concerns. We can formalize these considerations through the concept of the *distance* between the focus (P) and any other person, by assigning a value of unity to the distance between two directly connected nodes. In that way each node in Figure 4.21 is assigned a value indicating its distance from the focus (P) (Figure 4.22). In view of the nature of our enquiry we might first place an upper threshold of unity to define the scope of interest (Figure 4.23) and, thereby, the nature of any display of the information we require (Figure 4.24).

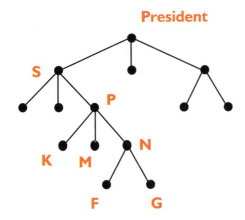

FIGURE 4.21 The organization tree of a company

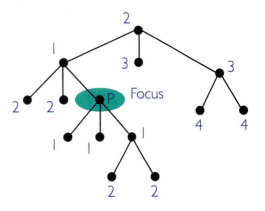

FIGURE 4.22 Showing the 'distance' of each node from the focus of attention

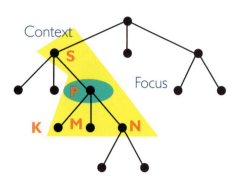

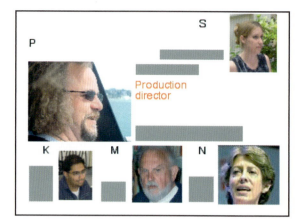

FIGURE 4.23 The context defined by setting an upper threshold of unity for distance from a focus

FIGURE 4.24 Example of a display that might be associated with the focus and context defined in Figure 4.23

The second concept, that of API, can be introduced by assigning an API value – representing intrinsic importance – to every node in the tree quite independently of the intended focus. It would be appropriate to assign the highest value of (say) 10 to the president, with values of API decreasing by unity as one goes down the company hierarchy (Figure 4.25). The difference between the API value for any node and its distance D from the focus (see Figure 4.26) is called the degree of interest of that node: the values of DoI for our example are shown in Figure 4.26. Now, if a lower threshold of 6 is imposed to define relevance, the focus and context are defined as shown in Figure 4.26 and the display of information will be composed accordingly. Clearly the implication, inherent in the assigned API values, that the president is the most important in the organization has biased the context towards the more senior people in the organization.

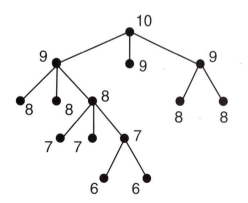

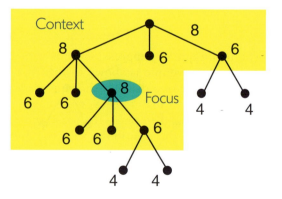

FIGURE 4.25 Each node in the organization tree has been assigned an *a priori* importance (API)

FIGURE 4.26 Nodal values of degree of interest (=API – D). Setting a lower limit of 6 for DoI identifies the nodes within the shaded region

The DoI concept enunciated by Furnas has wide application. Many examples arise from situations in which an understanding has to be acquired of the function of a small component part within a large structure. The location and correction of a fault in a mechanical system, for example, typically requires an expert to examine a very large diagram to see what (usually small) part of it might be relevant to the fault that has developed and hence to its repair. Such is the case with aircraft maintenance, a fact that prompted the US Air Force to develop a system in which, for example, the engineering drawing of Figure 4.27 is automatically replaced by that of Figure 4.28 once the function of interest has been defined (Mitta, 1990).

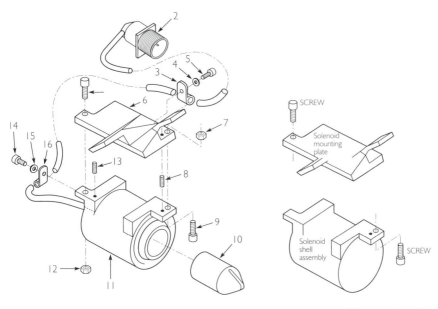

FIGURE 4.27 Part of an engineering drawing

FIGURE 4.28 The engineering drawing simplified in the context of a suspected fault

The technique of suppression finds valuable application in the magic lens technique. An example is shown in Figure 4.29. In (a) we see a conventional geographical map of a district, showing roads, streets, a church, a railway line and a station. But a maintenance crew concerned with a fault in the gas supply to the area will need to know the location of underground gas pipes and their interconnections, the position of valves and other buried systems such as electrical and telephone cables that may affect digging to reveal a gas pipe (Figure 4.29(b)). But Figure 4.29(b) is of limited value since no geographical context is shown: what is far more valuable (c) is the display of gas pipes and electricity and telephone cables in a small area of interest within the geographical map, not least because the maintenance crew have got to get themselves and their equipment, as far as conveniently along available roads, as close to the problem as possible. The ability to examine a different 'layer' of data, and especially to do so

FIGURE 4.29
Illustrating the
concept of a
magic lens.
(a) shows a
conventional
map of an area,
(b) shows the
location of
services (gas,
water and
electricity
pipes) in the
same area, and
(c) a (movable)
magic lens
shows services
in an area of
interest, in
context

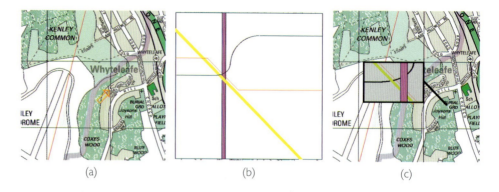

(a)   (b)   (c)

interactively – by 'bringing the tool to the data' – is a valuable facility and is
called a *magic lens* (Stone *et al.*, 1994). Part of its attraction might lie in the
metaphor of the familiar magnifying glass. Again, generalization is possible, for
example to the effect of two superimposed lenses and to the class of so-called
'see-through' tools (Bier *et al.*, 1994). An illuminating example of the magic lens
technique is provided by the field of bioinformatics. Figure 4.30 illustrates the
use of a movable magic lens to view the atomic structure within the molecular
surface of a protein.

FIGURE 4.30
A molecular
surface of the
protein
transferase
coloured by
electrostatic
potential bound
to DNA shown
as a schematic
(ID = 10mh).
The magic lens
window allows
a view of the
atomic
structure
bonding to be
shown, with
the bound
ligand structure
highlighted as
cylinders,
thereby
providing a
view inside
the protein
*(By kind permission of
Tom Oldfield and
Michael Hartshorn)*

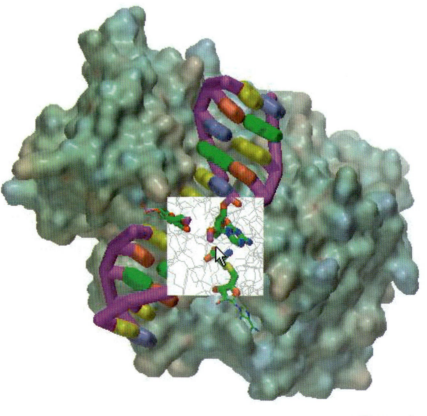

Combined distortion and suppression

When to focus and when to filter is a common design challenge. In some applications a combination of distortion and suppression can be beneficial. The bifocal display, of course, combines the two, since information items in the distorted regions usually benefit by not being displayed in full detail. It may be possible to use Furnas's DoI concept to automatically determine item representation in the distorted region, though it is more likely that a visual designer will create rules particular to a given application.

An example of combined distortion and suppression is shown in Figure 4.31 and employs the concept of rubber sheet distortion (Kadmon and Shlomi, 1978) illustrated in Figure 4.32. The task for which the application was proposed arose from a scenario in which a user is staying in a hotel in Manchester and wants to visit his Aunty Mabel in Huddersfield about 40 miles away. To support this task we first imagine a map of Northern England to be printed on a rubber sheet which is then pushed from behind to display Manchester and Huddersfield in sufficient detail (Figure 4.31) to allow street-by-street navigation in both cities, to and from the termination of the motorway. In addition to this distortion, we recognize that, once on the motorway, detail is not important to the user, for whom just the occasional landmark can provide comforting reassurance that the journey is proceeding as planned. For this reason only landmarks are retained along the motorway, all other details being suppressed.

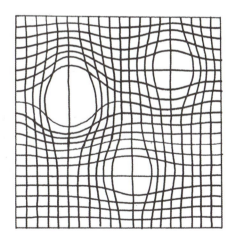

FIGURE 4.31 A combination of rubber-sheet distortion and suppression leads to a map appropriate to a journey from one city to another

FIGURE 4.32 The rubber-sheet distortion technique employed in the map of Figure 4.31

A reminder of the fact that representation and presentation are usually inextricably linked, and of the consequent danger of focusing on one to the exclusion of the other, is provided by a recent solution to the 'keyhole' problem presented by PDAs and mobiles. With the halo technique (Baudisch and Rosenholtz, 2003), circular arcs on a map (Figure 4.33) are associated with unseen locations of points of interest. The short arcs appearing on the PDA are representations of the unseen locations and adopted as such in view of the human user's ability to form a mental model of the complete circle and hence the unseen location at its centre.

FIGURE 4.33
The use of representation (by a 'halo') to provide context for a small display
(By kind permission of Patrick Baudisch)

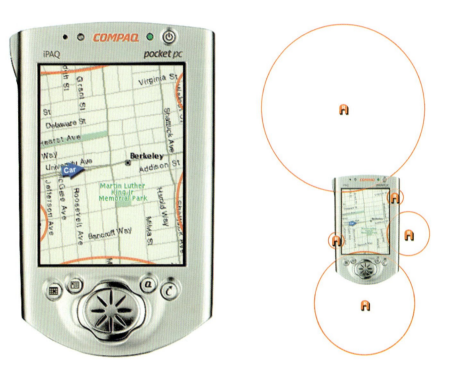

Historical note

While the introduction of distortion and suppression occurred during the early 1980s, it is not surprising that the need to maintain a balanced view of focus and context was identified even earlier. For example, in 1973 we find Farrand (1973) remarking, on the basis of his extensive industrial experience in engineering design, that

> *windowing . . . forces man to remember 'what part the viewed portion plays with respect to the total scene'*

where 'windowing' means 'scrolling', and that

> *an effective transformation must somehow maintain global awareness while providing detail*

where the transformation referred to is that from an existing large diagram to a more useful one in a limited display area. In the same thesis Farrand coins the popular term 'fisheye' (which nowadays appears to refer both to distortion and suppression) and quotes an even earlier (1971, unreferenced) comment that

> ... there is a need for presenting a display with 1. sufficient detail for interaction, while 2. maintaining global vision of the entire scene.

4.1.5 Zoom and pan

The presentation techniques discussed so far – scrolling, overview+detail, distortion and suppression – have all been concerned with the most effective use of available display area. To these we must now add the processes of zooming and panning. *Panning* is the smooth, continuous movement of a viewing frame over a two-dimensional image of greater size (Figure 4.34), whereas *zooming* is the smooth and continuously increasing magnification of a decreasing fraction (or *vice versa*) of a two-dimensional image under the constraint of a viewing frame of constant size (Figure 4.35). The choice of view location afforded by panning, and the ability of zooming to allow a continuous transition between overview and detail by variable magnification, render panning and zooming valuable processes.

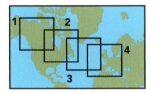

FIGURE 4.34 Panning is the smooth movement of a viewing frame over a 2D image

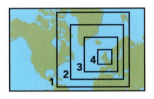

FIGURE 4.35 Zooming is the increasing magnification of a decreasing fraction of an image (or *vice versa*)

In a conventional 'geometric' zooming action no change in the data or its representation is involved, only the activity of filtering caused by the inevitable discarding of context when zooming in. In this sense zooming-in is very different from distortion (e.g. the bifocal display) whose purpose is to *retain* context in order to permit a *focusing* rather than a *filtering* action. Cairns and Craft (2005) usefully point out that zooming facilitates two different cognitive tasks. With zooming-in, extraneous information is removed from the visual field, perhaps resulting in a more manageable view, whereas zooming-out reveals hidden information, often context that is already known but perhaps cannot be recalled. It often allows a user to rediscover their location in an information space and to integrate new context within a mental model.

An analytic framework supporting the discussion of panning and zooming is provided by the concept of *space-scale diagrams* (Furnas and Bederson, 1995). In three-dimensional space (Figure 4.36) there are two dimensions of space and one (vertical) of scale (hence, a space-scale diagram). Four copies of a map are shown, each magnified by an amount proportional to its position along the scale

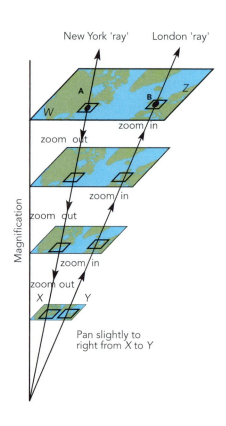

axis. Note that a *point* in the map becomes a *ray* in the space-scale diagram. The user's viewing window is represented by a rectangle of *fixed* size which when moved horizontally in the diagram corresponds to panning and to zooming when it moves along a ray.

The nature of a space-scale diagram can be illustrated by a familiar combination of pan and zoom that can help maintain a user's mental model of data. With reference to Figure 4.36 we assume that a user has been looking at New York City and now wishes to view London. A horizontal movement of the viewing frame (from W to Z) – i.e. a pan – might seem the obvious move, but most of the rapid transition would mainly show only the Atlantic Ocean. A better transition will be one involving a gradual zoom-out to X (perhaps to include the Eastern Seaboard of the USA and the map of the United Kingdom), a pan across the Atlantic to Y but with both the USA and England in view for most of the time, and then a zoom-in to London (Z) once the United Kingdom begins to fill the picture. A similar combination of pan and zoom is employed very effectively by Google Earth, and the automatic combination of zoom and pan has been studied extensively by Cockburn and Savage (2003).

As pointed out, the zooming action illustrated above is often referred to as *geometric zoom*. It is continuous and, when zooming in, results in filtering and the loss of context, but with the advantage that magnified detail is available. In many situations, however, it is inappropriate for a change of view to be continuous: a more useful change may be a *discrete* one in which *additional detail* as well as pure magnification is provided. An example would be a change from the overview of the North of England (Figure 4.5, left) to the detail of Huddersfield

(Figure 4.5, right). Another example was shown earlier in Figure 3.21 where car prices were supplemented by details of make in view of the extra space made available by the restriction to fewer cars. Another example based on the Spatial Data Management System (SDMS) (Herot, 1980; Herot *et al.,* 1981) is shown in Figure 4.37 (A to C). In certain circumstances a ship's captain needs to be aware of a collection of available ships (View A), but may then require details of a particular ship (View B). The transition from View A to View B is not solely a geometrical zoom: if it was, the text describing the ship would have appeared in A and would have been unreadable and probably distracting. The transition is also discrete and we use the term *semantic zoom* because the meaning conveyed by the new view differs from that conveyed by the old one. While View B may be satisfactory for a while, additional detail – and even a pictorial rather than an iconic image of the ship – may be required: here, a purely semantic zoom to View C is needed. We have, in fact, already seen an example of semantic zoom within the bifocal display, where the representation of an object differs between the focal and distorted regions (Figure 4.8).

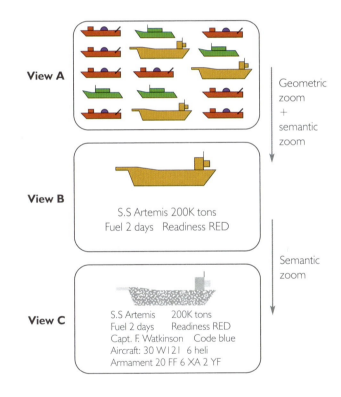

FIGURE 4.37
A combination of geometric and semantic zoom

All the examples of semantic zoom shown above stress the way in which it differs from geometric: with the latter an entirely automatic process (magnification) is involved, whereas with semantic zoom a *new representation* is involved. The design of the selective suppression associated with semantic zoom is far from being automatic; the interaction designer must understand the task that is being performed and the way it is carried out to be able effectively to design the sequence of data representations that will constitute semantic zoom. Such design is far from straightforward: there could well be a trade-off between content needed as a reminder of the previous view, content required for an overview and content to impart new understanding. An example illustrating these and other design issues is provided by a case study (Section 6.5).

4.2 Time limitations

4.2.1 *Rapid serial visual presentation*

Bringing selected data to the visual attention of a user can involve more than just a choice of layout within a given display area. Another design freedom available to the interaction designer is the opportunity to present data *sequentially* (and often quite rapidly) rather than *concurrently*. An example from the physical world is the familiar activity of quickly riffling through the pages of a new book in order to gain, in the space of a few seconds, some idea of its content. That activity can correctly be described as *rapid serial visual presentation* (RSVP). In its digital form a collection of images is presented (Figure 4.38) by showing each one separately, and in the same location, for a short period of time, typically 100 milliseconds. Even at such a rapid presentation rate there is a very good chance that a user will be able to correctly identify the presence or absence of a sought-after image. With the availability of the RSVP mode we now begin to see alternatives to the use of display area: the RSVP mode shown in Figure 4.38 (the 'slide-show mode') is now an alternative, for example, to the concurrent and therefore non-sequential presentation of the images at reduced size (Figure 4.39) in what we shall refer to as the 'tile mode'.

Perhaps surprisingly, the RSVP technique offers a potential solution for a very wide range of everyday tasks (Spence, 2002). There are, for example, many occasions on which it would be beneficial to 'riffle' rapidly through an unsuitably labelled folder ('New') to 'see what's there' or to see whether that folder contains a diagram whose location has been forgotten ('is it here?'). In a meeting where

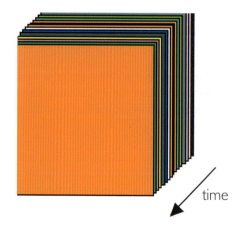

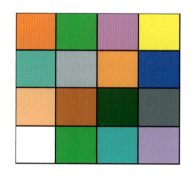

FIGURE 4.38 Rapid serial visual presentation (RSVP). A collection of images is presented, one at a time, at a rapid rate (e.g. ten per second)

FIGURE 4.39 The concurrent presentation of a collection of images

participants have all their reports on their laptops, the task of finding a page of interest in a report is often approached in an RSVP manner, the rapid search enhanced by the user's memory of the appearance and location of that page ('the page with the greenish diagram bottom left, about half-way through'). On arriving home in the evening to watch television the question 'what's on?' might usefully be answered by some sort of riffling action through images taken from the many television channels. Searching among your photo collection for a known image to show to a friend is often achieved by riffling through a collection in a shoebox and can now be achieved by digital RSVP (e.g. iPhoto).

Even if a problem is ill-defined ('What can I buy Mum for Mother's Day?'), a rapid sequential view of items in either a paper-based or online catalogue can serve the user well and has much in common with a brisk walk around a department store. To address this problem, Wittenburg *et al.* (1998, 2000) demonstrated 'floating RSVP' in which images appear to start 'a long way away' and then 'move towards' the viewer, in a manner similar to that in which motorway signs appear to move towards you when you are driving. Figure 4.40 is a snapshot of the use of such an online department store; cursor position over the two arrows on the right-hand side permits manual control of the direction and speed of movement. Another variant of RSVP, called 'collage RSVP', was proposed by Wittenburg *et al.* (1998, 2000) again in the context of online buying and employs the metaphor (Figure 4.41) of depositing images (book covers in the illustration) on to a table top. Even though previous images will thereby eventually be masked, there is opportunity to identify one of interest and also to reverse the presentation. Lam and Spence (1997) combined manually controlled RSVP with the bifocal principle to provide convenient access to a library of films (Figure 4.42). RSVP also offers valuable potential to ameliorate the limitations of small display area in what might be termed a 'space-time trade-off'. This was explored in the context of Web browsing from a mobile by de Bruijn and Tong (2003) (see Section 6.3).

A very different application of RSVP was investigated by Tse *et al.* (1998) and Komlodi and Marchionini (1998). The task addressed was that of discovering whether you want to watch a particular video or film, but without the need to start watching it at the normal speed of presentation. Tse and his colleagues arranged for the potential film viewer to see a rapidly presented sequence of 'key frames' so chosen that some gist of the film could thereby be gained. It was found that successful interpretation of gist could be maintained up to a key-frame presentation rate of ten per second. Some trailers for TV movies have similar properties, so that a second or two of viewing will often lead to a decision whether or not to view the entire movie. The page-flipping metaphor used to introduce the RSVP technique was also recently employed as the basis for Flipper, a system facilitating the visual search of digital documents (Sun and Guimbretiere, 2005).

To exploit the many potential applications of RSVP the interaction designer needs to possess some fundamental knowledge about how human beings perform when presented with a rapid sequence of images. Fortunately, cognitive psychologists began studying such performance long before the digital implementation of RSVP was a realistic proposition.

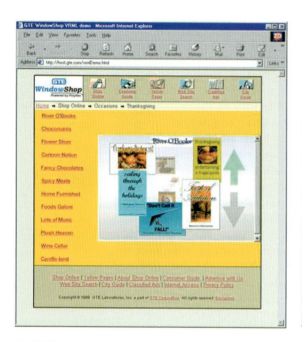

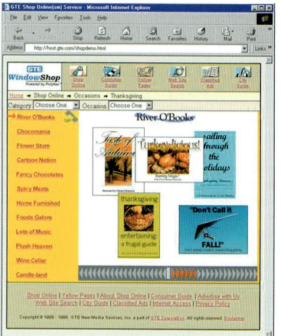

FIGURE 4.40 'Floating RSVP' in which images appear to approach the viewer from a distance. Sensitive arrows allow the speed and direction of 'movement' to be controlled by a user
(Courtesy Kent Wittenburg)

FIGURE 4.41 The contents of an online bookstore are presented in 'collage mode' RSVP, simulating the placing of book covers on a table in sequence. The set of arrows just under the presentation allows control of the speed and direction of presentation
(Courtesy Kent Wittenburg)

FIGURE 4.42
An interface facilitating the browsing of posters advertising videos. Cursor movement along the stacks causes posters to briefly 'pop out' sideways and the whole bifocal structure can be scrolled to bring a video of interest to the central region, where a mouse click will cause a clip from a video to be played

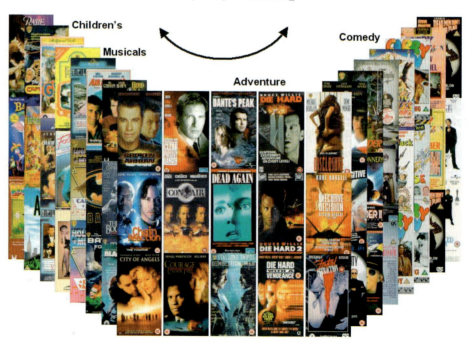

Briefly glimpsed images

An obvious question is, 'How fast can images be presented while allowing a sought-after (target) image to be identified?' In other words, how rapid is the 'rapid' in RSVP? The faster a collection of photographs can be presented while allowing the single one of interest to be identified, the more attractive is RSVP as a presentation technique for that task. Relevant experimental evidence is available (Potter and Levy, 1969) and is summarized in Figure 4.43. In this experiment, a subject is first shown an image. They are then asked to say whether that image appears in a sequence of images presented, one after the other, in quick succession. It is found that even if the rate of image presentation is as high as ten per second, so that each image is presented for only 100 ms, there is about a 90 per cent chance that the presence or absence of the image in the collection will be correctly reported. The experiment summarized in Figure 4.43, although probably the most pertinent to the application of RSVP, is nevertheless only one source of experimental evidence that has been accumulated over the years and, indeed, continues to be accumulated. For the reader who wishes to 'dig deeper', the book *Fleeting Memories* (Coltheart, 1999b) is highly recommended.

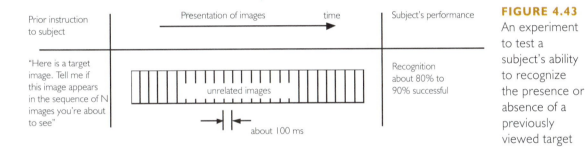

FIGURE 4.43 An experiment to test a subject's ability to recognize the presence or absence of a previously viewed target image within a collection presented sequentially at a rate of around ten per second

4.2.2 Space and time resources

It is easy, but dangerous, to argue intuitively about the merits of different presentation modes, some of which have already been encountered. What is needed is some basis for comparison. One such basis is that of *resource*. One could argue that the interaction designer concerned with the presentation of a collection of images to support a task is limited by two resources. One is *display area*, a resource whose exploitation we have just discussed in Section 4.1. Another is *total presentation time*, in the sense that tasks usually have to be performed within a given time limit. We have all had the experience of systems in which the difficulty and frustration of performing a task have been exacerbated by the excessive time required for relevant information to be presented.

We can represent concurrent limits to display area and total presentation time by the 'resource box' shown in Figure 4.44. The interesting question now is, 'Given that a collection of images needs to be presented to a user, how should those images be arranged in the resource box?' There are many known possibilities, some of which we have already met, and others will no doubt be invented, but to present information of value to an interaction designer we select, for illustration, the six presentation modes shown in Figure 4.45. Commensurate with our use of the resource box for comparison, the available display area is assumed to be the same for all modes, as is the total presentation time.

FIGURE 4.44
Representation
of limits on
display area
and total
presentation
time by a
'resource box'

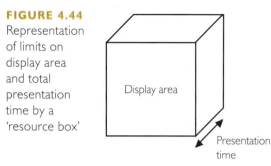

The modes shown in Figure 4.45 have been arranged into two groups based
on a simple criterion: whether any given image appears in a unique position on
a display (the 'static' group) or can appear to move by occupying a number of
positions in a sequence (the 'moving' group). Of the three static modes we have
already encountered slide-show mode (A) and tile mode (C). In the remaining
static mode – 'mixed mode' (B) – each image has the possible advantage of being
displayed for four times as long as in slide-show mode but the possible disadvantage of occupying one-quarter the display area. It is included in Figure 4.45
because, in early experiments (Fawcett *et al.,* 2004), it was the most preferred
static mode and often led to the most efficient identification of the presence or
absence of a target image in the presented collection.

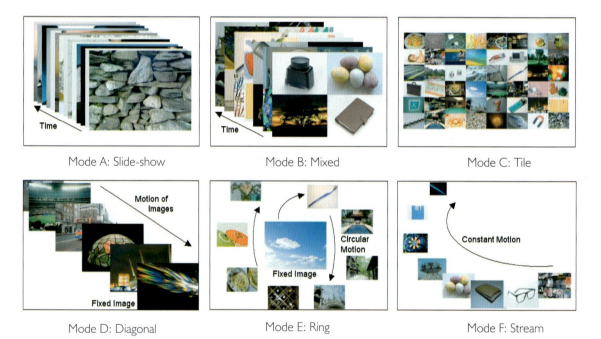

FIGURE 4.45 Three 'static' image presentation modes (A, B, C) and three 'moving' image presentation
modes (D, E, F)

Source: *Courtesy of Katy Cooper*

Of the three moving modes shown in Figure 4.45 the first (D), called the diagonal mode – also known as the 'time-tunnel' mode (Wittenburg *et al.*, 2003) – involves movement of each image from top left to bottom right: the interaction designer might choose to let images increase in size as they proceed along the diagonal trajectory and/or have adjacent images overlap to some degree, hoping that the advantage of more images will not be offset by the reduced fraction of each that is visible. With this mode it turns out – as we shall see later – that a crucial design decision concerns the manner in which an image disappears from the display. It could move in a continuous fashion so that less and less of it appears, or it could be 'captured' (Wittenburg *et al.*, 2003) full-size at the lower right-hand corner for about 100 ms before removal from the display. The latter option turns out to be a wise choice, as we shall see. In the ring mode (E), an image first appears at maximum size in the centre of the display, remains there for a short time and then moves in a roughly circular trajectory, exiting top left. In the stream mode (F), images are in constant motion, entering from lower right and exiting towards upper left.

Since the relative benefits of the six modes illustrated in Figure 4.45 appear to be closely associated with the eye-gaze behaviour adopted by a user, we anticipate later discussion by briefly examining this aspect of human visual performance.

Eye-gaze

When we look at a display with the intention of gaining insight, we constantly move our eyes with the result that our eye-gaze travels over the displayed image (Ware, 2004). The eye-gaze of a human being is primarily characterized by **saccades** and **fixations** (Figure 4.46). Saccades are movements of gaze: they are rapid – lasting between about 20 and 100 ms – but also ballistic in the sense that, once initiated, the movement cannot be modified mid-saccade. Fixation refers to a dwelling of gaze at a fixed point: a fixation generally lasts between about 200 and 600 ms. Indeed, we are all familiar with saccades and fixations

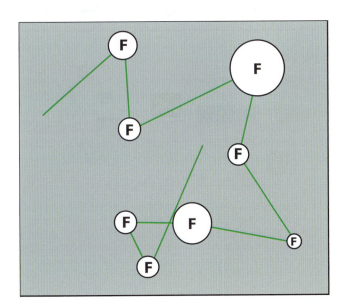

FIGURE 4.46

A simple representation of eye-gaze behaviour. The rapid saccades are shown green, the fixations (F) of varying duration by circles of proportionate size

from the activity of reading text. Gaze can also move slowly in a 'smooth pursuit' manner in which the eyes 'lock on' to a moving image and track it.

When our gaze is directed to a particular location within a display the greatest detail is registered on the fovea, which is a small area in the centre of the retina. It is here, within a subtended angle of about two degrees, that vision is sharpest; at the periphery of vision we can discern only large objects. Another aspect of human visual performance is pupil diameter. It is widely believed that this measure is strongly influenced by various aspects of cognitive and perceptual behaviour.

Investigations of eye-gaze performance during the search for a target image among a collection of images is made possible by gaze detectors such as the one shown in Figure 4.47. An infra-red laser beam is (safely) directed towards each eye and the resulting reflections from retina and cornea are detected by a video camera and processed to identify the location of eye-gaze.

FIGURE 4.47
A piece of equipment for the recording of eye-gaze. An infra-red laser beam is aimed at the user's eye and reflections from the retina and cornea are detected by a television camera. It also records pupil diameter

4.2.3 Presentation modes

Cooper *et al.* (2006) investigated the relative advantages of the three static modes and three moving modes shown in Figure 4.45. Subjects were asked to say whether a target image[1] was present or not in a given presentation of 48 images and also to identify their most liked and least liked modes. The results were revealing. Figure 4.48 shows that all static modes were better than all moving modes with respect to the accuracy with which the presence or absence

---

[1] Three types of target image description were employed. For a given presentation of a collection of images, subjects (1) were shown the target image for a few seconds, or (2) had the target image described in specific terms (e.g. 'a cat'), or (3) had the target described in general terms (e.g. 'an animal'). Three total presentation times were also employed to see how this influenced the outcome of the experiment. The usual precautions were also taken to avoid well-known effects such as attentional blink (Raymond *et al.*, 1992). For more detail see Cooper *et al.* (2006).

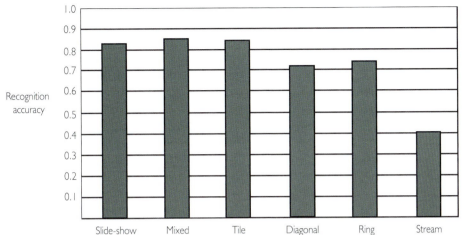

FIGURE 4.48
The accuracy with which the presence or absence of a target image was reported for the six presentation modes of Figure 4.45, averaged over all tasks and presentation times

of target images was identified, the stream mode being noticeably worst. Figure 4.49 also shows that the static modes (slide-show, mixed and tile) accounted for 75 per cent of preferred modes and only 25 per cent of subjects preferred a moving mode (though none preferred the stream mode). When asked to identify their least preferred mode (Figure 4.50), most identified a moving mode, and of those the stream mode accounted for many of the least preferred moving modes.

Eye-gaze data recorded during this and an earlier (Fawcett *et al.*, 2004) experiment is particularly revealing. Figure 4.51 shows some representative trajectories (saccades are green and fixations are denoted by 'F'). In a slide-show presentation (a) it is not surprising to find that gaze appears to be concentrated around the centre of the image. However, while eye-gaze behaviour for the tile mode (b) is again as expected due to the need to search for a target image, relatively little movement is recorded for the mixed mode (c): in some way the user appears to be able to assess all four images without undue movement, a fact that may account for that mode being highly preferred and characterized by high

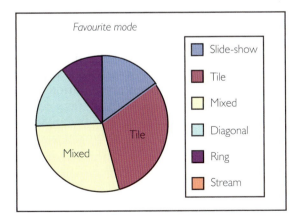

FIGURE 4.49 The (static) slide-show mixed and tile image presentation modes account for three-quarters of the preferred modes

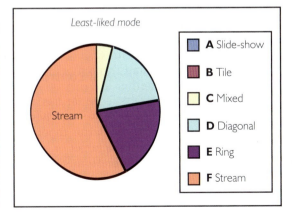

FIGURE 4.50 Almost all the least preferred image presentation modes were moving modes and the stream mode accounted for over half

accuracy of target identification. We turn now to the moving modes. Figure 4.51(d) shows the eye-gaze trace for a subject who disliked the diagonal (moving) mode, whereas (e) shows the trace for a subject who preferred it. The difference is striking and suggests that eye-gaze strategies adopted by subjects may underlie not only preferences but also target identification performance. Notable is the concentration of gaze at the 'capture' location (bottom right) in Figure 4.51(e) where, for a short while, an image is static. The subject is essentially viewing the image in slide-show (static) mode. It will not be surprising to learn that the trajectory shown in Figure 4.51(f) is that of a subject who disliked the stream mode.

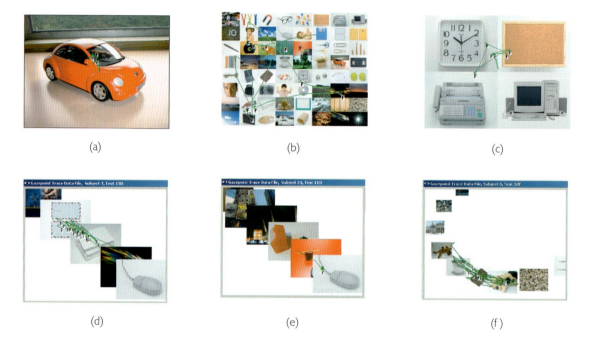

(a)　　　　　　　　　　(b)　　　　　　　　　　(c)

(d)　　　　　　　　　　(e)　　　　　　　　　　(f)

FIGURE 4.51 Representative eye-gaze trajectories recorded for selected image-collection presentation modes: (a) slide-show, (b) tile,(c) mixed, (d) diagonal, for a subject who disliked that mode, (e) diagonal, for a subject who liked that mode, (f) stream, for a subject who disliked that mode

4.2.4 *Manual control*

The discussion so far has assumed a fixed image presentation rate. There are circumstances, however, when a user might wish to exert control over both rate and direction, the latter to allow, for example, retreat to an image thought likely to have been the target or one that could now be defined as the target (e.g. a box of chocolates for Mother's Day). Not surprisingly many schemes for manual control have been proposed. We have already encountered manual control within 'floating RSVP', illustrated in Figure 4.40, and within 'collage RSVP', shown in Figure 4.41. The Nokia mobile photo library illustrated in Figure 4.16 can be controlled manually, as can the conventional 'scrolled tile' mode typified by iPhoto.

　　　Another manually controlled presentation mode can be based on expanding images, a feature incorporated in the MacOSX tool bar and illustrated in Figure 4.52. In its dormant state the collection of images can be quite compact, with

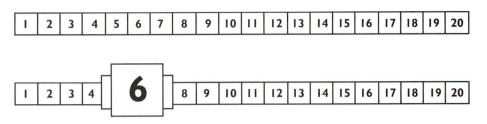

FIGURE 4.52
The acquisition
of an expanding
target. (a) The
dormant
appearance
of
the image
collection, and
(b) its
appearance
when the
cursor rests
over image 6

each image displayed in miniature so that the collection occupies little display area. Compaction may also be achieved by overlap. However, when a cursor is moved along the collection, individual images are considerably magnified, allowing a user to decide whether that image is a target. This 'expanding target' presentation mode has the potential advantage that little display area is needed to accommodate either the dormant or sampled image collection. In the extreme, this presentation technique closely resembles a manually controlled slide-show presentation. Indeed, recalling the experimental results reported for static and moving modes, one wonders if a 'snap-to-maximum-size' action, rather than a continuous expansion of image size, might lead to improved image recognition and enhanced preference. The acquisition of expanding targets has been investigated in depth by McGuffin and Balakrishnan (2002).

It is certainly the case that the design of any scheme allowing either the manually controlled or automated presentation of a set of images is a complex undertaking. The results concerning eye-gaze discussed above may be useful in both these circumstances. The presentation of image collections to support a variety of tasks continues to be the subject of intensive research (see, for example, Cockburn *et al.,* 2006).

4.2.5 Models of human visual performance

Though much experience has been accumulated regarding image presentation modes, our common understanding of human visual performance – which has a much wider relevance to information visualization as a whole – often lags behind. Nevertheless, it is pertinent to add some brief remarks here. For example, the experiment (Potter and Levy, 1969) illustrated in Figure 4.43 might suggest that, without seeing an initial target image, a user might still remember the general nature of ten or more rapidly presented images sufficiently to be

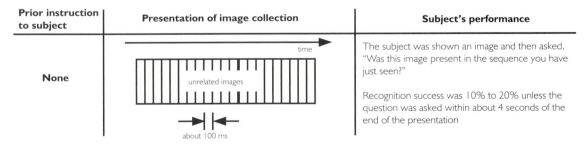

FIGURE 4.53 An experiment in which a subject first views the rapid (e.g. 10 per second) presentation of a collection of images, is then shown a single image and then asked to say whether that image was part of the collection. Identification success is highly dependent upon the time elapsing between the end of the presentation and the questioning of the subject

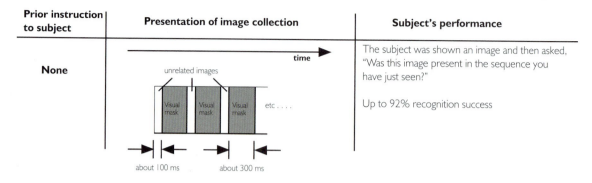

Prior instruction to subject	Presentation of image collection	Subject's performance

FIGURE 4.54 An experiment in which a collection of images is presented to a subject. Each image is presented briefly (e.g. for 100 ms) and followed by a 'visual mask' lasting about 300 ms. Subjects were able to say, with a considerable degree of success, whether an image shown afterwards had been part of the presentation

able to say with accuracy whether a target image shown *after* the presentation was present or not (Figure 4.53). This is not the case unless the user is questioned *within a few seconds* of the termination of the presentation (Potter, 1976; Potter *et al.*, 2002). Perhaps surprisingly, this inability to recall after a few seconds have elapsed is *not* a consequence of the brevity (e.g. 100 ms) of an image's presentation; another experiment (Figure 4.54) showed (Potter, 1976; Intraub, 1980) that if each brief image presentation is followed, for about 300 ms, by a 'visual mask', then a user's confirmation of the presence or absence of a target image (presented afterwards) is considerably enhanced.

Another effect of which an experimenter or interaction designer should be aware is attentional blink (Raymond *et al.*, 1992). If, prior to a slide-show presentation containing a previously viewed target image, the user is told that 'the target comes just after the red square with the yellow circle', then if those two identified images occur within about 300 ms of each other, the target will not be noticed.

Within the vast amount of literature concerning human visual performance, to which a good introduction is offered by Coltheart (1999a), there is one concept that may well be of immediate value to our understanding of information visualization and which justifies mention here. Potter (1993, 1999) has proposed the notion of **conceptual short-term memory** (CSTM) to account for those aspects of human visual and aural performance occurring between the moment an image or sound is received and about a second later, a time frame which is highly relevant to the activity of information visualization and which precedes the familiar short-term memory (STM) and long-term memory (LTM).

4.2.6 Interaction design

The material in this chapter provides one of the interaction designer's missing palettes identified in the previous chapter (Figure 4.55), containing techniques and concepts related to presentation. As examples have shown, however, there can be considerable influence between design decisions related to presentation and representation. The next chapter provides the designer with a fourth palette relevant to interaction.

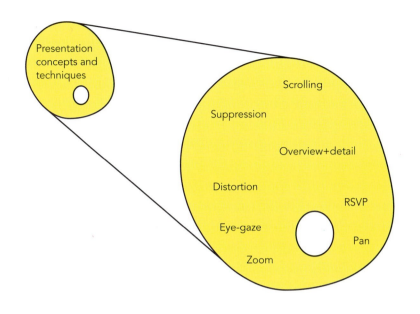

FIGURE 4.55
A third palette for the interaction designer, addressing issues of presentation

Exercises

The value of many of these exercises can be enhanced by discussing the results in open class.

■ Exercise 4.1 (Review)

For each of the following approaches to presentation write one sentence summarizing its essential features: (1) scrolling, (2) overview+detail, (3) distortion, (4) suppression and (5) zoom and pan.

■ Exercise 4.2 (Review)

What is the point of using a bifocal display? What are the principal features that make it potentially attractive? What problems might be encountered in using it within an application?

■ Exercise 4.3

Your PDA is fitted with a GPS facility and therefore 'knows where it is'. Sketch a design for a street map, with street names, which will draw attention to, and suggest the approximate location of, places of interest (restaurants, petrol stations, etc.) over an area equal to nine times the area covered by the PDA.

■ Exercise 4.4

Explore the potential offered by the distortion principle for a person using a mobile to text messages and, at the same time, be aware of other items of interest (e.g. recorded calls and text messages). Show how colour and position and any other encoding mechanism can be used to advantage. Justify the minimum size of icon used in the distorted region.

■ Exercise 4.5

Identify a city of modest size that tourists or professionals may have to visit (examples: Eindhoven in The Netherlands, York in England, Konstanz in Germany, Oslo in Norway, Boston and Seattle in the USA). The local Visitors' Bureau wishes to make available, for travel and sightseeing planning, a (printed) representation of local transport and places of interest as well as major transportation links to destinations from 50 to 200 miles away. Sketch a possible design using the overview+detail approach. Identify advantages and disadvantages of your design.

■ Exercise 4.6

Repeat Exercise 4.5, but employ the distortion technique to provide continuity between local and global detail.

■ Exercise 4.7

Figure 4.E.1 shows, in incomplete detail, one possible approach to answering Exercise 4.5. Here, geographical veracity has been sacrificed to allow a focus on possible individual activities classified as 'culture', 'transportation' and 'entertainment'. Walking distance has been indicated qualitatively by short cross-streets. Complete the design for the city you have selected in Exercise 4.5 and identify its advantages and disadvantages. (Courtesy Roel Vossen)

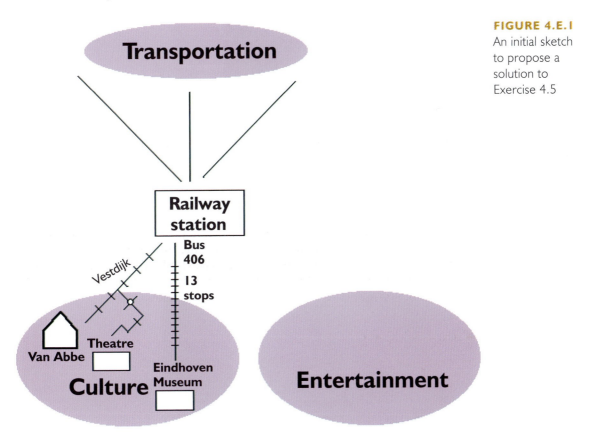

FIGURE 4.E.1
An initial sketch to propose a solution to Exercise 4.5

■ Exercise 4.8

Figure 4.E.2 provides a partial view of an answer to Exercise 4.5 in which 'continuity' between overview and detail is a single entity, here the central railway station. Complete the design for your selected city and comment on its advantages and disadvantages. (Courtesy Oliver Moran)

FIGURE 4.E.2
An 'overview+ detail' exploratory design relevant to Exercise 4.5

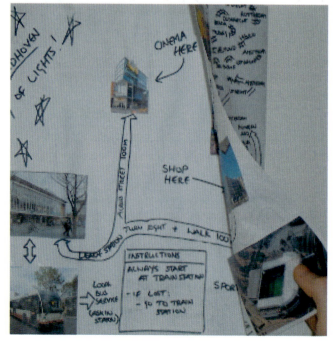

Exercise 4.9

Figure 4.E.3 illustrates one approach in response to Exercise 4.6. The visitor is provided with the means of simply constructing a 'visitor's cube' in which one side provides local detail of the city while other sides provide context. Decide how continuity can be achieved along the edges of the cube and complete the design for the city you selected in Exercise 4.5. Comment on the advantages and disadvantages of your design. (Courtesy Maurits Kaptein)

FIGURE 4.E.3 A suggested design in reponse to Exercise 4.6 (see Exercise 4.9)

Exercise 4.10

Propose a design for a facility which will enable a user to review up to 500 photographs with a view to selecting one to show to a friend.

Exercise 4.11

A particular tree map is so extensive that it cannot usefully be presented in its totality on the display of a PDA. Suggest possible solutions to the problem of examining the tree map using a PDA.

CHAPTER 5

Interaction

Interaction between human and computer is at the heart of modern information visualization and for a single overriding reason: the enormous benefit that can accrue from being able to *change* one's view of a corpus of data. Usually that corpus is so large that no single all-inclusive view is likely to lead to insight. Those who wish to acquire insight must explore, interactively, subsets of that corpus to find their way towards the view that triggers an 'ah ha!' experience.

Having acknowledged that interaction is vital to much – though not all – of information visualization, many questions remain. Interaction, for example, involves work: not just the physical work of clicking a mouse but the cognitive effort of interpreting what is then seen in order to enhance a mental model. Is that work useful? Is it justified? Are there different types of interaction? If so, do different guidelines apply to their design? What is it about a data set that makes one type of interaction more appropriate than another? What is it about a task that makes one type of interaction more suited than another?

Answers to these and many other questions about interaction are perhaps best discovered by first looking at a variety of scenarios in which the interaction between a human being and a system takes on different and representative forms. We can then attempt some classification that will enable us to examine essential issues.

Scenarios

In one form of interaction a person simply walks up to Minard's map (Figure 5.1) and quite readily forms a mental model of most of the data encoded in that display. No physical action is required of the user; the encoded data is *immediately*

136

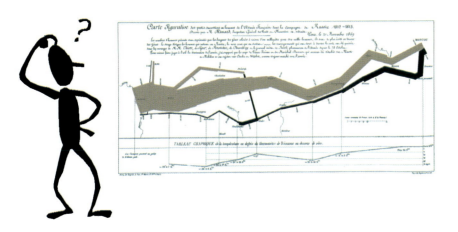

FIGURE 5.1
Static display.
No physical
interaction.
Encoded data
immediately
viewable

available because the display is *static*. With Minard's map the information will mostly 'pop out', though in other cases training might well be required to make sense of encoded data.

In another scenario a couple are **searching for** entertainment in London. They go to the top page of an online entertainment guide (Figure 5.2), a page which offers a choice of different types of entertainment. A selection of one type (Films) then allows the query to be gradually refined via a sequence of displays. Eventually, and possibly after retracing some steps in order to explore the entertainment available, a decision is made. Here, interaction of a 'mouse click' kind is needed to cause movement in a *discrete* information space from one page to another, *interpretation* and a *decision* are required at each page, and the entire process might be called '*stepped interaction*'.

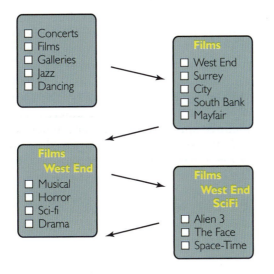

FIGURE 5.2
Discrete
information
space.
Stepped
interaction

In our third scenario a professional estate agent is employing an Attribute Explorer (Figure 5.3) to find a house, or a small collection of houses, that might be of interest to a client. In the course of the dialogue between professional and client, a number of limits to various house attributes will be explored. At one point

FIGURE 5.3
Discrete
information
space.
Continuous
interaction.
Responsive
system

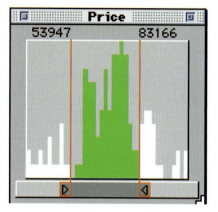

the client may say, 'If I could afford to pay more, what then?' The professional may then *manually* explore the effect, on houses that satisfy all limits, of changes in the upper price limit. Such exploration is beneficial because the effect of a limit change is displayed essentially immediately. He may even move the *Price* range rapidly up and down to see its overall effect on other house attributes.

In a fourth scenario people are sitting around a table drinking coffee, eating donuts and discussing the latest film. But the coffee table is no ordinary table (Living Memory, 2000; Stathis *et al.*, 2002). Its surface is an LCD display (Figure 5.4) and moving slowly around the curved periphery are small images containing perhaps a single picture and very few words and advertising local interests such as a chess tournament or a lost cat. It may happen that the gaze of one person in the group alights on an image which is relevant to their interests whereupon, with minimal interruption to the flow of conversation, the image can be moved by finger action away from the periphery; the consequently enlarged and more detailed image (see Figure 5.4) can then be assessed and, if the topic is of interest, the image can be 'placed' on that user's token which is seen in the cup in the centre of the table. Conversation then resumes after only a minimal pause (de Bruijn and Spence, 2001).

FIGURE 5.4
Discrete
information
space.
Moving images.
No physical
interaction

In this coffee table scenario, and until the small image is moved by finger action towards the centre of the table, there is no physical interaction whatsoever: the people around the coffee table do not have to do anything. If an image attracts attention, visualization begins. The collection of images slowly circumnavigating the table top constitutes a discrete information space. Sight of a potentially interesting image is often opportunistic rather than planned.

A fifth, and for the moment last, scenario finds an electronic circuit designer exploring the effect on the performance of a circuit of the value of one component (Spence and Apperley, 1974, 1977). The designer has signalled to the software that he wishes to examine the effect, on the amplification of an amplifier between bass and treble limits, of changes in a particular component. Following a computation which may take some time, the designer is then able (Figure 5.5) to manually and smoothly vary the component value by mouse-drag along a slider, whereupon the plot of amplification versus frequency *immediately* takes on values corresponding to the current value of the component. As a result of that interaction the designer will hopefully have a better mental model of the relation being explored and, indeed, may well leave the component at a value that leads to improved circuit performance. Here, the designer is exploring a *continuous* space and benefiting from a very *responsive* system.

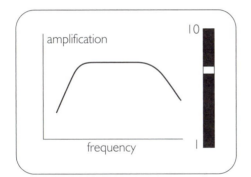

FIGURE 5.5
Continuous interaction. Continuous relation. Immediate response. Preliminary calculation may be needed

Spaces, interactions and balance of control

What can we learn from these scenarios, all of which involve the activity of information visualization? Despite their variety, there are some common features which form the basis for useful classification and which, in turn, can lead to concepts and techniques of value to the interaction designer.

Information spaces

First, we observe two different types of *information space* (Figure 5.6). In the entertainment guide (Figure 5.2) the information has been intentionally arranged as a collection of *discrete* entities; so have the images moving around the coffee table (Figure 5.4). The histograms of the Attribute Explorer are composed of discrete elements, each associated with a given house. The World Wide Web, of course, is another example of a discrete information space. In distinct contrast, *continuous* information spaces are in evidence in the electronic circuit example (Figure 5.5): there is a continuous mathematical relation between a circuit property and the value of the component that is being varied. Minard's map

FIGURE 5.6
Two classes of
information
space

Continuous   Discrete
Information spaces

(Figure 5.1) would be regarded as a special case of a discrete information space containing one item: its classification as a continuous space – except in a pathological sense – would imply that it was part of a larger representation.

Interaction modes

Quite separately from the nature of the information *space*, we have seen considerable variety in the ways in which users can *interact* with a space. With the examples discussed there is considerable variation in what might be termed the balance of control between the computer and the user. As always, it helps to have some classification that identifies the essential nature of the forms that interaction can take (Tweedie, 1997). We shall identify three modes of interaction[1].

One we shall call *continuous interaction* was exemplified (Figure 5.5) by a designer exploring a continuous functional relationship between a component within a circuit and some property of that circuit, but there are many other examples from a range of disciplines in which such continuous mathematical relationships are to be found. The classification can also be extended to examples typified by the Attribute Explorer (Figure 5.3) which, while representing a discrete information space, can nevertheless be interacted with in an essentially continuous movement: the granularity of the input device (the limit indicators) and the representation of the data (histograms) are such that the result of interaction can be modelled, in the user's mind, as a continuous function (Figure 5.7). Even if the responsiveness of the system is degraded to introduce a delay of about one second, it appears that users may still regard the exploration as continuous (Goodman and Spence, 1978).

We can also identify, through the example of the entertainment guide (Figure 5.2) as well as our own experience of the World Wide Web, a *stepped mode* of interaction. Here, a minimal action such as a mouse click causes movement in discrete information space from one location to another (Figure 5.7).

It is a challenge to classify the sort of interaction – almost 'non-interaction' – employed by the person viewing Minard's map (Figure 5.1) or the coffee drinker happening to catch sight of an apparently interesting image (Figure 5.4). The term

---

[1] Many different terms have been used to characterize the variety of ways in which a user can interact with a visual display. The terms 'manual', 'direct manipulation' and 'direct engagement' are virtually synonymous in describing the sort of interaction in which, for example, a mouse is clicked or dragged over a display to reposition an object. Norman (1988) has used the term 'first person' or 'do it yourself' in this context. As Dix *et al.* (1998) have remarked about this form of interaction, 'there is [apparently] no intermediary between user and world'.

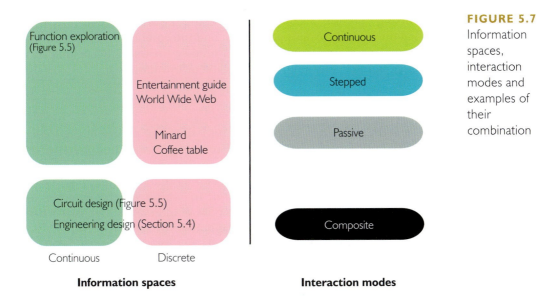

FIGURE 5.7
Information spaces, interaction modes and examples of their combination

passive interaction, perhaps at first sight rather contradictory, comes to mind. There should be no problem with this term. The prefix 'inter' means 'between or among' and 'act' is defined as the process of doing or performing something. We speak, for example, of social interaction, an exceedingly complex process in which there is no need for any physical act to take place, and therefore it is appropriate to speak of passive interaction to describe the considerably complex visual and cognitive performance on the part of the person viewing Minard's map. As we shall see, the term passive does *not* imply a static display such as Minard's map: a display can usefully be dynamic and designed in such a way that a user can derive considerable insight by watching it (Section 5.4). A preferred alternative to 'passive interaction' might be 'visual interaction' or 'sensory interaction'.

Although there is considerable merit in identifying the three interaction modes we have labelled *continuous*, *stepped* and *passive*, most useful visualization tools employ a mixture of these modes. We have therefore coined the term *composite interaction* (Figure 5.7) to describe such frequently occurring examples.

Intention

Quite separate from the nature of the information space and the interaction mode is the *intention* of the user. The circuit designer (Figure 5.5), for example, may at any given moment be exploring simply to form a mental model of the relation that is being simulated. He or she is *learning* about a relation or information space: the interaction is prompted and guided by a need to *explore*. By contrast, the user may be involved in a search for a specific target, in which case the intention is to *seek* or find, even though the target may be reformulated from time to time as the user learns more about the space. Yet another situation occurs when the user has no particular target in mind and simply surveys an information space to 'see what's there', an intentional activity which might be described as *opportunistic*. Finally, as in the case of the coffee table (Figure 5.4), the direction of eye-gaze towards a particular image on the table might be *involuntary* simply as a result of the continuous movement of eye-gaze that occurs all the time and which, if absent for more than a few seconds, would probably cause concern in an observer!

Browsing ('perusal' according to one source) has been defined as an activity involving the (usually visual) perception and interpretation of content, including navigational cues. It is convenient to qualify browsing according to intent, whether exploratory, seeking, opportunistic or involuntary.

This chapter

We have addressed three aspects of interaction: the nature of the information *space*, the interaction *mode* provided to the user and the *intent* behind that interaction. Intent and the associated cognitive processes lie outside the scope of this book and will receive little detailed mention. Also, because an information space is usually presented as a *fait accompli*, in this chapter we shall concentrate on the different available modes of interaction, the issues they raise and the potential they offer to the interaction designer.

A major unanswered question is, 'Is there some *framework for interaction* that will provide a tool for organized thought about all interaction modes?' Happily there is: Norman's Action Cycle is presented in the following section (5.1) and is, perhaps surprisingly, relevant even to the non-interactive 'passive interaction' scenarios we have encountered. Following the introduction of the framework for interaction the scene is set for the remainder of this chapter by our classification of modes of interaction. The three principal modes of interaction, continuous, stepped and passive, are examined respectively in sections 5.2, 5.3 and 5.4. In view of its considerable potential, the interaction mode we have called *composite* is then illustrated in Section 5.5. Section 5.6 returns to consider the *dynamic nature* of the 'change of view' that is so central to information visualization: in essence we ask the question, 'How fast or slow must that change be? and 'Can we usefully design the *nature* of that change?' Finally, in the last section, we address the difficult question of design for interaction.

5.1 Interaction framework

Many interface designs supporting human–computer interaction have benefited from the Action Cycle, a concept proposed by Donald Norman (1988). Norman identified two 'gulfs' existing between the human who has a goal to achieve and the 'world' – typically but not necessarily a computer – that must be changed for there to be a chance that the goal can be achieved. The concept is of direct relevance to information visualization since its goal is a useful mental model and the 'world' that must be changed is some representation – visual or aural – of data.

The Gulf of Execution (Figure 5.8) reflects the problem of knowing what to do to bring about a change in the world (in information visualization, a new view of data) while the Gulf of Evaluation reflects the problem of interpreting and evaluating the change in the world. Each gulf comprises three activities (Figure 5.8). By referring to a very simple and familiar interface, that of a camera, we shall illustrate the dire consequences that can ensue if the interaction designer fails to support those activities.

In the camera example the user's *goal* may be to obtain a pictorial record of an event. To that end the user *forms an intention*, in this case to use a camera

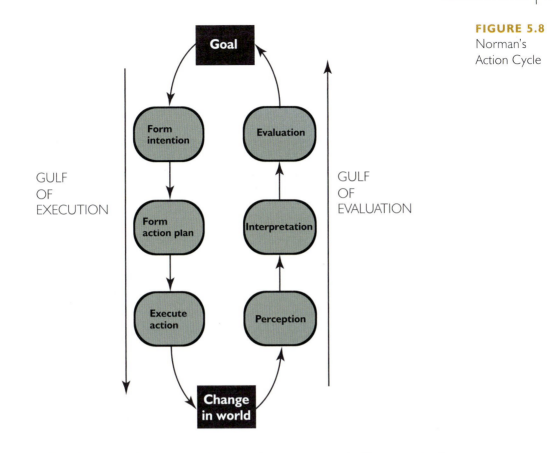

FIGURE 5.8
Norman's
Action Cycle

(rather than, for example, hiring a photographer or an artist). This step involves only cognitive effort. So does the following step, which requires an *action plan* to be formulated. With a camera this involves, at the very least, deciding which part of the camera to point at the subject and deciding which button to press. These decisions are not always easy for the user. For example, a camera manufactured some time ago had a viewfinder and a camera lens that were difficult to tell apart, with the result that many developed films showed, exclusively, an out-of-focus portrait of the person attempting to take a picture. The last step in the Gulf of Execution is physical and involves the *execution* of the formulated action plan. Shutter release mechanisms must be designed to support this action. With at least one make of camera, 'execution' (of the shutter release) could take place whether or not the camera contained a film.

The executed action may or may not change the world. If it does, the sequence now follows the Gulf of Evaluation, the first step of which is *perception* of the change. With a camera, what is perceived is usually an audible 'click' and possibly a blanking of any view in the viewfinder. What is perceived is now *interpreted*. Whereas an audible click might suggest that the film has been appropriately exposed, it may indicate only that the shutter has been opened and closed: there are examples where the same click is heard whether or not there is a film in the camera. The last step within the Gulf of Evaluation is the *evaluation* itself of what has taken place. With a digital camera the evaluation can take place immediately, with the huge advantage that any corrective action needed can take place without delay. The person who 'photographed' a wedding with an empty camera had to wait some time before the mistake was discovered.

The camera example illustrates the valuable guidance that the Action Cycle can offer to an interaction designer, acting as a checklist and a basis for organized thought. We now employ the same Action Cycle framework as a basis for discussing continuous and stepped interaction in Sections 5.2 and 5.3. In Section 5.4 we see how part of the Action Cycle – in fact the part that involves only the Gulf of Evaluation – is pertinent to passive interaction. A discussion of composite interaction follows in Section 5.5, and Section 5.6 discusses that part of the Action Cycle concerned with the 'change in the world'.

5.2 Continuous interaction

Continuous interaction is not new. It wasn't very long after Sutherland's (1963) pioneering work with SKETCHPAD had established the field of interactive graphics that examples of continuous interaction began to appear in the literature. Early examples of the use of graphical methods in statistics (Fowlkes, 1969) involved the turning of a knob to cause a continuous change in a shape parameter associated with a probability plot. Contemporary examples associated with electronic circuit design have already been described. Researchers such as Newton (1978) and Becker and Cleveland (1987) also provided early examples. Eventually, the increasing power and affordability of computational resources and display technology led to a striking demonstration by Williamson and Shneiderman (1992) of the potential of continuous interaction.

To establish the issues associated with continuous interaction we select a specific example to show how Norman's Action Cycle can provide useful guidance. It is the Attribute Explorer familiar from Chapter 3, employed to search for a house to buy.

The first stage encountered in Norman's Action Cycle is the *formulation of an intention*. Depending on the strategy being adopted and the mental model already formed, many different intentions could be appropriate, and it is the task of the interaction designer to ensure that a user is aware of what is possible. Such awareness can be enhanced if, for example, each histogram is clearly labelled and the current limits are clearly shown. One intention might be to understand the general consequences of changing *Price* limits; another might be to undertake exploration to see 'how much the houses near that lake cost'.

The second stage in the Gulf of Execution, that of *forming an action plan*, can often be challenging. Here, for example, the interaction designer must strive to ensure that it is intuitively clear to a user how to adjust the upper and lower limits to *Price* in order to explore their ramifications. An early design of the Attribute Explorer (Figure 5.9) was found wanting in this respect: one subject assumed that to move the (say) upper limit, a mouse-down on the arrow (Figure 5.9) was all that was required, whereas the actual procedure was a mouse-down-and-drag action. There are many ways of hopefully making this apparent to a user: one whose appearance occurs in response to mouse-over is shown in Figure 5.10.

The third stage, that of *execution*, must also be supported by the interface. In many situations in which continuous interaction is exploited there will be a series of executions, each moving a limit along a scale by a small amount: it may

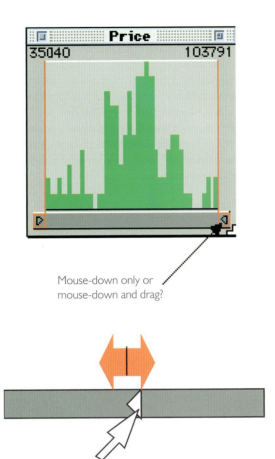

FIGURE 5.9
Ambiguity
concerning the
means of
placing a limit

Mouse-down only or
mouse-down and drag?

FIGURE 5.10
One way of
reducing the
ambiguity
illustrated in
Figure 5.9.
Mouse-over
indicates
possible
movement

involve, for example, the adjustment of a *Price* limit. It may seem a trivial matter to facilitate execution, but it is not always the case. For example, the user should not be required to exercise great accuracy in this movement because, whereas a limit must move along a horizontal or vertical slider, the user will almost certainly be paying attention to another part of the display and the cursor movement may therefore depart from the ideal trajectory. Nevertheless, that movement should be *interpreted* as being along the slider. Another example of well-designed support for execution is to be found in situations where selectable parts of a histogram are located in close proximity, apparently requiring very accurate positioning of the cursor. An alternative which can overcome this difficulty ensures that successive mouse clicks, all at the same location, will sequence through the selectable parts.

In many examples of continuous interaction the user is endeavouring to form a *mental mapping* of the relation between the independent parameter being adjusted (e.g. the *Price* limit) and some dependent quantity such as an impression of the total area of green on the histograms or the existence of houses with more than two bedrooms. It is possible that only one adjustment of a limit is explored, in which case the resulting change in one or more histograms will be perceived and interpreted and the result evaluated to see whether the original intention has been satisfied. Alternatively the user may decide to explore a fairly rapid sequence of executions – perhaps gradually increasing the *Price* limit – in order to see the effect on other histograms. Here, as mentioned earlier, the user is exploring a discrete information space whose granularity, combined with speed of exploration, allows interpolation from discrete to continuous in the user's mind. For such interaction the trajectory on the Action Cycle might be represented as in Figure 5.11 and as a function of time as in Figure 5.12. The resulting interpretation may well be of the form 'it's well worth thinking about paying more in view of the extra bedrooms that become available'. When the interpretation is judged to be satisfactory in the *evaluation* stage, or for other reasons, the series of interactions/executions may be terminated.

FIGURE 5.11
Stages of the Action Cycle involved in the dynamic exploration of an effect

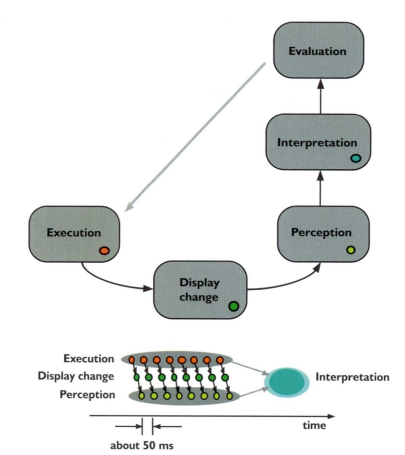

FIGURE 5.12
A sequence of interactions and the corresponding view changes are interpreted to form a mental mapping

Two further comments can usefully be made about the above cycle. First, from what we know about change blindness (Rensink *et al.*, 2000; Rensink, 2002; Rensink URL) as well as the foveal angle (Ware, 2004) within which most detail is discerned, it is dangerous to assume automatically that a user will be aware of every change in the display: a small decrease in the upper *Price* limit might, for example, lead to a significant change in a histogram well outside the foveal angle. Measures may need to be put in place to ameliorate such effects – one possibility is a brief background 'flash' where a possibly unexpected change may be missed. Second, although this has been conveyed implicitly above, mapping is immensely enhanced by the concurrent visibility of input (from the user) and associated output.

5.2.1 Dynamically triggered 'pop-out'

A user employing continuous interaction will quickly realize that it can lead to a phenomenon similar to pop-out (see Chapter 3) and equally welcome. This effect is not unconnected with the concepts, also introduced in Chapter 3, of the visibility and correlation of objects and attributes. Below we provide two examples to show how object and attribute correlations which are not evident from a static display can be made obvious through the use of continuous interaction.

We need look no further than the sensitivity circles of Figure 3.31, repeated here as Figure 5.13, to see how continuous interaction can reveal object correlation. As the position along the frequency scale at the right is moved either manually or automatically, the circles superimposed on components vary in size (Spence and Drew, 1971). If two circles suddenly expand together, for example, object correlation is immediately apparent and, in most cases, would warrant further investigation in order to gain insight into the implications for design.

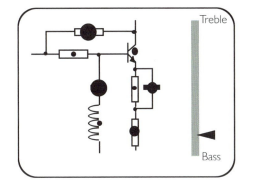

FIGURE 5.13
Circles indicate the qualitative effect, on some overall circuit property, of variation in the corresponding component

Our second example concerns attribute correlation and is illustrated by the Attribute Explorer discussed in Chapter 3. Figure 5.14 shows four histograms which are the result of calculating the stresses S1 to S4 at four locations in a structure[2] for a randomly chosen set of designs of that structure. Thus, each design – like each house in the original Attribute Explorer example – contributes to each of the histograms. Movement of the upper limit of S4 from its maximum to a much lower value (Figure 5.15(a)) suggests that there might be a trade-off between the stress S4 and the stress S3. This suggestion is confirmed if the range of S4 is slowly moved between limits as shown in Figures 5.15(b) and (c). Attribute correlation can also be revealed without the need to view histograms by placing, on each attribute slider (Figure 5.16), a circle indicating the average, for that attribute, of selected objects. Movements of those average values are easy to discern.

---

[2] The structure in question supports the filament inside an electric light bulb. Its design is defined by four parameters whose values are chosen by the structure's designer. Within the structure, four stresses are of particular interest (Su *et al.*, 1996).

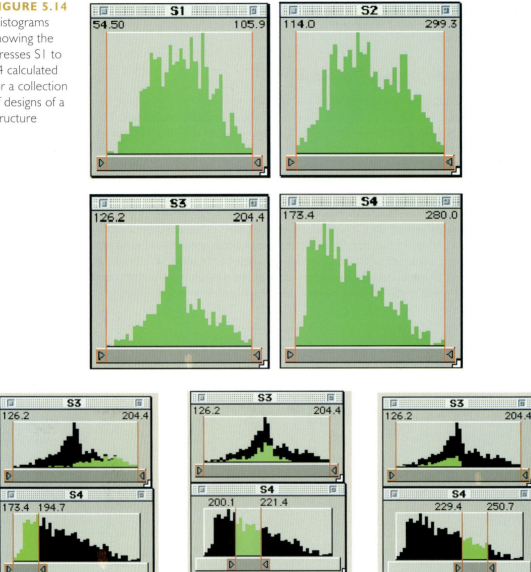

(a)   (b)   (c)

FIGURE 5.15 As the range of S4 is moved to higher values, the corresponding values of S3 move to lower values, indicating a trade-off

FIGURE 5.16
Yellow circles
indicate the
average attribute
values of objects
satisfying all
limits

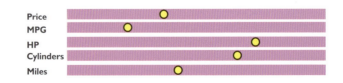

Both the above examples are reflected in the comment of Teoh and Ma (2005) that:

> *. . . in animated visualizations (sic) the correlation among the objects/ dimensions [attributes] shown between two adjacent frames is more obvious than between two frames separated by a long period of time.*

5.3 Stepped interaction

5.3.1 Discrete information spaces

There are many examples of stepped interaction in which movement occurs between locations in a discrete information space. The simple example shown in Figure 5.2 and repeated as Figure 5.17 recorded the successive pages visited by a couple seeking an evening's entertainment: they stepped through a sequence of discrete locations in order both to explore what was available and, hopefully, arrive at an acceptable choice. No continuous interaction is involved and, although the information space cannot be classified as 'responsive', the success of task performance obviously benefits if movement from one location to another is as fast as possible (but not *too* fast – see Section 5.6).

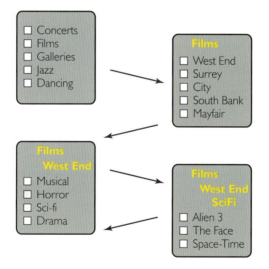

FIGURE 5.17
Stepped interaction involved in a search for entertainment

Another – and contrasting – example of stepped interaction is provided by a typical computer-aided design system supporting engineering design. Even a modest chip-based electronic circuit such as an operational amplifier will have at least 100 components whose value can be chosen by the designer, and at least 200 aspects of performance upon which limits are placed by the customer. There is no doubt that information visualization can benefit the engineering designer, but there is no possibility whatsoever of the interaction designer anticipating which views of this data will be helpful, simply because the number of alternative views is huge. Nevertheless we still have a discrete information space and somehow we have to support the designer's stepped progress from one view to another – that is, navigation – as best we can.

Both examples bring to mind Bertin's (1981) remark:

A graphic is never an end in itself: it is a moment in the process of decision making.

His comment will resonate with anyone who has attempted to solve a problem by accessing a sequence of pages from the Web, itself an extensive and unstructured discrete information space.

Stages of action

The problems associated with stepped interaction can be illustrated by reference to Norman's stages of action. As with continuous interaction, the goal of enhancing a mental model of some data triggers the formulation of an intention to explore a change of view – but now a *discrete* one – of the data. It is the second step, that of forming an action plan, that again poses a distinct challenge for the interaction designer. With stepped interaction the user must decide which is the *single* most beneficial movement in information space and to this end asks questions such as, 'Where [in discrete information space] can I go from here?' and 'How do I get there?' We say that the user must *navigate* from one location in discrete information space to another. Having decided upon and executed the required interaction, resulting in a discrete change of view, that change is perceived and interpreted. To support interpretation the techniques and concepts of representation discussed in Chapter 3 are relevant and, in view of limitations on space and time, so is the issue of presentation.

5.3.2 Navigation

To support navigation we need to know what sort of question the user is asking. In fact, the user of a digital information space that may be unknown, unstructured and extensive is asking the same questions that occur to a person in a *physical* space that is unknown, unstructured and extensive, especially if, as is often the case, the problem being solved is initially not formulated with precision. Although Wittenburg (1997) has rightly cautioned that 'the concept of navigation in cyberspace has a completely different physics from navigation in the physical world', the questions asked are identical:

Where am I?

Where can I go?

How do I get there?

What lies beyond?

Where can I usefully go?

When considering these questions we must bear in mind the fact that movement in information space is not always 'forward' to as yet unvisited locations – it can be 'backward' along a path already taken. Thus, another frequently posed question is:

Where have I been? (I want to go back.)

Since movement in a discrete information space is what we term **navigation** we must identify the concepts underlying this movement and see how navigation can be facilitated (Jul and Furnas, 1997; Woods and Watts, 1997). We must be aware, however, of the many reasons why users move through information space. They may, for example, have a single, specific and known destination, such as information about the mating call of the Tasmanian Devil. Or they may be using an online department store to find a present for Mother's Day and spend a great deal of time and movement in learning about what is on offer before making up their mind. Or the user may be an engineering designer or financial advisor using many movements to gradually make a number of decisions to finalize a product. In all these examples we may talk about *navigation*, which is simply a sequence of movements in information space. If there is a specific known unique goal, the term **wayfinding** may be appropriate. By contrast, the term **exploration** is used to denote movement having the aim of allowing the user to *learn* about information space (i.e. enhance their mental model of that space). The term **pursuit** may be used to describe movements in information space undertaken with the sole aim of achieving, in the most direct manner, a specific target, and with minimal reference to an accumulated mental model of the information space.

Anyone who has tried to locate useful information on the Web or who has used a poorly designed information system will realize the importance of providing answers to the six questions listed above. We shall address all of them in this section, beginning with the second and third which are closely related.

5.3.3 Sensitivity

An example of navigation in a *physical* space is provided by a Polynesian seafarer (Lewis, 1994) who is close to an island which he cannot see beyond the horizon. However, the seafarer notices a cloud (Figure 5.18) which is almost certainly positioned over an island. That cloud is a navigational *cue* and suggests what is there and how to get to it. In contrast, we are now concerned with an electronic space rather than a physical space; nevertheless, we still look for cues that will answer the questions:

Where can I go from here?

How do I get there?

now in the context of *semantic* rather than physical relationships (Dourish and Chalmers, 1994).

It transpires that the concept of **sensitivity** can help. Reflecting the fact that the above questions refer directly and respectively to a movement in informa-

FIGURE 5.18
The cloud formed above an island invisible beyond the horizon provides a navigational cue

tion space and the interaction required to achieve that movement, we define sensitivity as:

sensitivity: a movement in information space and the interaction required to achieve it.

For convenience we express sensitivity S as a 2-tuple:

S = SM, SI

where SM denotes a single movement in information space and SI denotes the interaction needed to achieve that movement. Two examples, one from a physical space and the other from an information space, will illustrate the concept of sensitivity and its two components.

Figure 5.19 shows a door through which a person may need to pass. The label on the door encodes SM in the sense that when interpreted it tells the user that passage through the door leads to a cafe. The interaction (SI) needed to achieve that movement (i.e. passage through the door) is encoded by the appearance of the door: there is no way of pulling it open, and the appearance of a flat plate is conventionally understood[3] to indicate that pushing is required to achieve passage through the door. SI is, in fact, what we know as an *affordance* (Gibson, 1977; Norman, 2004)[4] and any designer of a physical space will know

---

[3] In some countries this convention does not exist: there is a handle on both sides of the door, with instructions to 'push' or 'pull'. In the absence of such instruction, complex strategies have been adopted to identify the affordance.

[4] The concept of affordance was first introduced by Gibson (1977) and refers to interaction between a human being and 'the world'. We can say that the door shown in Figure 5.19 *affords opening by pushing*. That is the *actual* affordance. Clearly, to help people who wish to pass through the door, it is essential that the *perceived* affordance is also that the door affords opening by pushing. Norman (2004) provides a discussion of affordance.

FIGURE 5.19
The label 'cafe' and the flat plate provide navigational cues by showing where the user can go (the cafe) and how they can get there (push the door)

how important it is for the perceived affordance to be identical to the actual affordance. Designers of hotel shower controls, in particular, come to mind.

Figure 5.20 shows part of a web page labelled 'Holidays-to-go'. Five areas distinct from their surroundings, together with informative labels (Britain, Europe, etc.), indicate that movement (SM) is possible to other pages concerned with different types of holiday and that a mouse click (SI) on the appropriate area will lead to movement to the corresponding page. Thus, the same cues encode both SM and SI. In some cases such cues are easy to interpret whereas in badly designed cases the identification and interpretation of a cue may be difficult. Much depends upon the ability of the interaction designer and their skill in visual design (Nielsen and Tahir, 2002; Wildbur and Burke, 1998). Potential difficulty of interpretation is sometimes ameliorated by the provision of clarification upon mouse-over.

FIGURE 5.20
Part of a web page. Each label and surrounding grey area indicate that a mouse click on the area (SI) will cause movement (SM) to another page concerned with the selected type of holiday

One example of the encoding of sensitivity information is provided by the Attribute Explorer, already discussed in Chapter 3. For the example of three house attributes Figure 5.21 shows the encoding, in black, of those houses which fail only one of the six limits placed on the attributes, the use of grey for houses failing

FIGURE 5.21
Black encoding
of houses that
fail one
attribute limit
provides
sensitivity
information

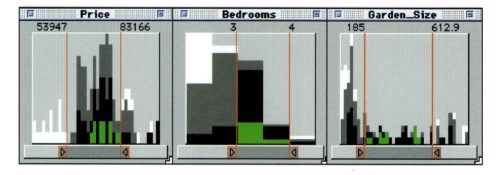

two limits and so on. In the Attribute Explorer we see that the interaction designer
has not chosen a separate cue to indicate movement (SM) to each house within a
huge collection. Rather, because a user will typically be trying to whittle down the
number of houses to be given more detailed consideration, and in view of the
importance of initially receiving guidance about possibly beneficial changes to
attribute limits, the houses failing only one limit have been aggregated and coded
black. Thus, many SMs are identically encoded but conveniently grouped. A major
advantage of the black encoding is that, even when limits are so stringent that no
green houses are visible, a black house just outside a limit provides a valuable
identification of a limit that might beneficially be relaxed.

Another example in which aggregate sensitivity is usefully and very simply
encoded is provided by the limit positioning mechanism (Ahlberg, 1996) shown
in Figure 5.22. It was originally employed in the **Dynamic Query** interface (see
below) and is currently used in the Spotfire™ visualization tool (Spotfire). The
white area of the slider shows limit positions which will lead to no effect whatsoever on the information displayed, whereas movement of a limit within the
yellow area will cause movement in information space. Such an encoding can be
immensely valuable in what have been termed 'what would happen if?' (or
simply 'what if?') situations: the encoding performs the useful function of indicating that, for some 'what if?' questions, the answer is 'nothing'.

FIGURE 5.22
In a limit
positioning tool
colour coding
indicates that
selection will be
unaffected
while the lower
limit stays
within the
white region.
When a limit
moves into the
yellow region,
selection will be
affected

The value of sensitivity information can be emphasized by an example in
which the relevant data is immediately available *but not exploited*. The
Dynamic Query interface (Williamson and Shneiderman, 1992; Ahlberg, 1996)
is illustrated by the Homefinding example in Figure 5.23. It is designed to facilitate the task of finding a house to buy. Within a geographical area shown on a
map, it identifies by dots those houses which satisfy limits set by a user on the
values of certain attributes. A major disadvantage, however, especially when
there are no houses that satisfy the limits, is that no sensitivity information is
provided – no guidance is given as to the variations in limit values that might
lead to an acceptable house being shown on the map. As a consequence, the formation of a mental model of the collection of available houses can be achieved

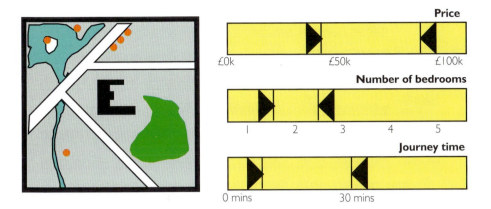

FIGURE 5.23

The Dynamic Queries interface. Limits placed on house attributes by a user lead to the display of houses satisfying those limits on the map

only, and with considerable difficulty, by the adjustment of each limit in turn, a time-consuming and tedious procedure if, as is typical, there are ten or more attributes. This disadvantage is especially cogent if a great deal of useful 'non-directed' exploration precedes a more directed movement to a desirable house. Where the Dynamic Queries interface *filters* (and necessarily hides) available data, the Attribute Explorer encodes *all* the data according to the user's interests. As it happens, 'black house' sensitivity cues could easily be introduced to a Dynamic Queries interface, as illustrated in Figure 5.24. The introduction of sensitivity cues supports a 'see and go' approach, whereas without those cues a user is confined to the much more laborious 'go and see' approach.

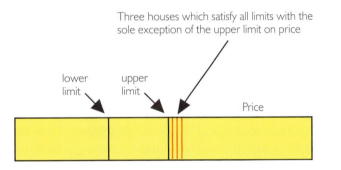

FIGURE 5.24

A possible modification to the Dynamic Queries interface. Houses violating only one limit are identified, so that sensitivity is explicit rather than having to be uncovered by manual movement of the limits

A commercial application of information visualization which exploits the concept of sensitivity to advantage has already been introduced in Chapter 2. It is the EZChooser (Wittenburg *et al.,* 2001), designed to support online sales in which one item must be selected from a collection on the basis of its attribute values: the example in Chapter 2 related to car sales and is repeated in Figure 5.25. The cars represented by outline icons only fail one requirement. A more detailed account of the development of EZChooser is to be found in Section 6.2.

In some situations sensitivity information may not be directly available, but nevertheless can readily be computed. Andrienko and Andrienko (2003) provide an example (see also Spence, 2004), while for some physical systems powerful algorithms are available for sensitivity computation (Brayton and Spence, 1980).

FIGURE 5.25
In the EZChooser outline cars are those which satisfy all requirements except one. Selection of the range immediately underneath an outline car ensures that the car then satisfies all requirements

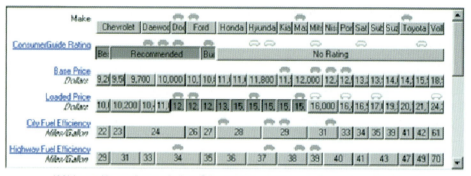

Vehicles matching your feature selections. (Color a vehicle in all rows by selecting a color over the picture.)

A form of navigation of emerging interest (Munro *et al.*, 1999; Hook *et al.*, 2003) is called *social navigation* in which cues influencing the choice of destination are created, not by an interaction designer but collectively by the actions of users. A familiar example is provided by the statement that 'customers who bought this book also bought . . .'. The term 'recommender systems' is current; the term '*recommender-generated sensitivity*' may be appropriate.

5.3.4 Residue

Our definition of sensitivity has assumed a single movement in information space, from one page to another. Normally, a succession of pages is visited before a problem is solved, so that the user is continually asking, 'What lies beyond?' Thus, the representation of a movement (SM) by a cue which additionally indicates what lies beyond that single movement could enhance the navigation process. It was for this reason that Furnas (1997) identified the valuable notion of residue. We define residue as:

residue: an indication of distant content in the SM encoding

where 'distant' implies content requiring more than one movement from the current location to reach it. While residue can be valuable for the user, it constitutes an additional requirement that the interaction designer has to keep in mind: he or she must design a cue which will not only correctly identify the outcome of a single movement in information space but will also suggest content that can be reached beyond that single movement. Thus, residue encodes distant content and, in this sense, can be considered to be a generalized form of sensitivity encoding if the definition of sensitivity is extended to multiple sequential movements. Since there is a tendency to regard 'distant content' as that which has not yet been visited it is vital to acknowledge that content already visited may be *revisited*, typically by use of a BACK control. Thus, design to support navigation should ensure that consideration is given to the provision of residue to support revisitation as well as visitation.

The notion of residue – as well as sensitivity – can be illustrated by the example of a hierarchical menu-based system providing information about animals: Figure 5.26 shows part of the top two levels of the menu system. A collection of animals has been arranged in a hierarchy to facilitate navigation towards information about a particular animal. At the top level of the menu system one of four available selectable options is labelled *Mammals* to indicate that a mouse click on it will lead to another menu in which options correspond to different kinds of mammal. Thus, the option label 'Mammals' encodes an SM and an SI. But the label 'Mammals' also provides residue for each of the mammals that can be accessed from the second level, as well as animals further down the hierarchy. For example, an Abyssinian cat, located at the level immediately below 'Cats', has, in the label 'Mammals', residue at the top level of the menu.

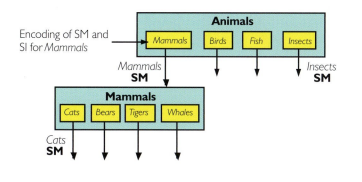

FIGURE 5.26
Representation of the top two levels of a hierarchically structured menu-based system providing information about animals

The ability of the label 'Mammals' to effectively provide residue as well as encode sensitivity is a result of the hierarchical structure adopted for the Animals information space. By contrast, in an unstructured information space such as the Web, the addition of an Abyssinian cat on one web page will not be associated with a residue on many – if any – other pages. Even with a hierarchical menu structure, of course, residue design may not be straightforward: for example, a user's incomplete knowledge might lead to the erroneous selection of 'Fish' in the search for information about whales.

If any doubt still lingers regarding the importance of residue in the context of design for navigation, a convincing answer is provided by the work of Snowberry and her colleagues (1983, 1985). Snowberry *et al.* (1983) studied the navigation of hierarchically structured menu-based systems. Subjects were asked to search for a target word within a hierarchically structured database of 64 common English words. Since the number 64 is equal to 8^2, 4^3 and 2^6 it was possible to compare shallow and broad menu structures with narrow and deep ones. That part of the 2^6 menu required to reach the target word 'Marlin' directly (i.e. without retreats) is shown in Figure 5.27.

Each subject was shown a target word and then asked to make successive menu selections, without any backtracking, to arrive at the target word. Figure 5.28 shows, for the 2^6 menu structure, the percentage of errors (i.e. incorrect selections) made at different levels of the menu structure. Not surprisingly, most errors occurred at the first and second encountered levels, emphasising the difficulty of providing residue at a distance from a target. In a separate experiment

FIGURE 5.27
That part of a 2^6 menu to be traversed in a successful search for the target word 'Marlin'

FIGURE 5.28
Errors made at different levels of a narrow and deep six-level menu in the search for a target at the lowest level

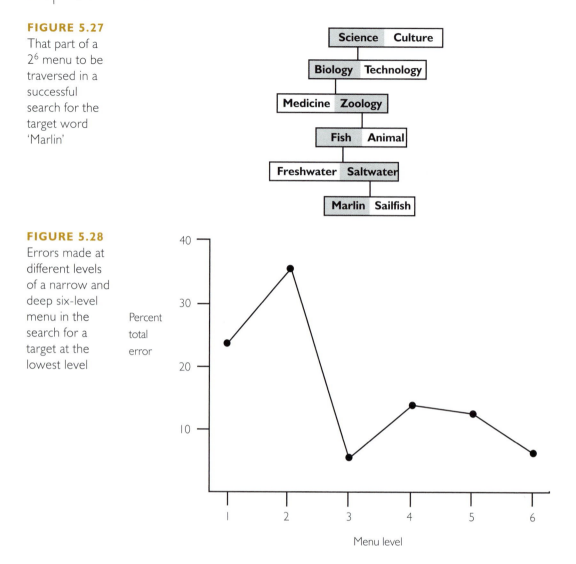

investigating the relative merits of, on the one hand, broad and shallow structures and, on the other, narrow and deep ones, the results shown in Figure 5.29 reveal that percentage error was significantly[5] (p<0.0001) affected by menu structure. There is, here, a clear suggestion that broad and shallow menu structures offer the possibility of a good residue of a target word at the top level(s). Hierarchical structures other than those investigated by Snowberry *et al.* are of course possible (Norman and Chin, 1988; Norman, 1991).

The same investigators (Snowberry *et al.*, 1985) also directed their attention to what they called *help fields*, of which an example is shown in Figure 5.30. Below each selectable option in the menu is displayed an unselectable sample subset of options that would appear next if that option were selected. The intention is that sight of these sample labels will clarify the meaning of their superordinate options

---

[5] A value of 0.0001 for p means that there is a 1 in 10,000 chance that the observed effect was chance.

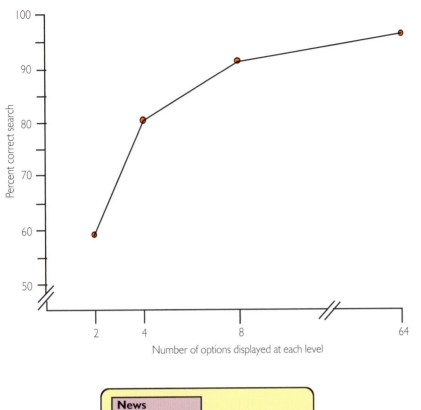

FIGURE 5.29
Percentage
correct search
as a function of
menu structure

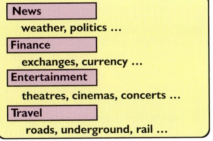

FIGURE 5.30
Example of the
provision of an
'Upcoming'
help field,
where samples
from the next
lower level help
to enhance
confidence
in the
interpretation
of the menu
options

and thereby provide residue. The question being posed, in effect, was whether the help field, together with the category labels, constituted useful residue. As with sensitivity cues, mouse-over can sometimes be used to provide additional residue.

It was found, using the 2^6 structure, that the presence of the upcoming help field led to only 8–10 per cent error as opposed to around 22–28 per cent error when no help field was displayed, a result that was found to be statistically very significant (p<0.001). It seems, therefore, that the upcoming help field was effective in providing residue at each level.

5.3.5 Scent

So far we have discussed the need to design cues that encode both sensitivity and distant content in such a way as to enhance the likelihood of correct interpretation. The need to interpret cues arises from the fact that this activity must be followed by *evaluation* if anything other than a random choice is to be made from available movements. Thus, the user must assess the *benefit* of each available movement (SM), in effect asking not only

> *Where can I go from here?*

but, crucially,

> *Where can I* most beneficially *go from here?*

It is for this reason that the concept of scent was introduced (Pirolli and Card, 1999). Scent can be defined as:

scent: the perceived benefit associated with a movement in information space, evaluated following interpretation of one or more cues.

The term 'scent' arises from the extension of foraging theory, originally developed in a biological context (Stephens and Krebs, 1986), to the search for information (Pirolli and Card, 1999). Implicit in the term 'benefit' is a consideration of the 'cost' of the movement in information space.

It is essential to recognize that the evaluation of scent, and hence a decision as to where next to go in information space, involves high-order cognitive processes, some of which were identified in Figure 2.17. It makes reference, for example, to the user's current (though usually ever-changing) internal model of the information space, as well as the strategy – again often subject to change – being adopted to carry out a task. The user may, for example, be exploring to enhance a mental model of information space and/or to refine a goal or they may be moving as directly as possible towards a temporary or final target. Quite often it is some combination of the two. Thus, scent calls upon higher-order cognitive processes – such as mental modelling and strategy formulation – of considerable complexity. While our understanding of these higher-order processes is certainly sufficient for the interaction designer to be aware of their profound importance, it is insufficient to provide anything other than the most general guidelines for that designer. Nevertheless, ongoing investigations (e.g. Chi *et al.,* 2001) attempt to employ the concept of scent to develop mathematical models relating user goals, interaction behaviour and visible cues, with potential application to web design. The relation between sensitivity, residue and scent is illustrated in Figure 5.31 (Spence, 2004).

FIGURE 5.31
The relation between sensitivity, residue and scent

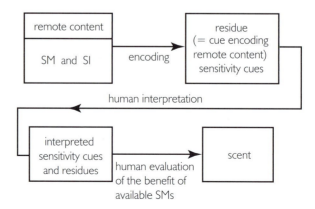

Despite the inherent cognitive complexity of scent evaluation, some simple encodings can nevertheless be very effective. A good illustration of an encoding supportive of scent evaluation is provided by the Model Maker (Smith *et al.*, 2001), a tool that supports the fitting of a polynomial to measured points. It is specifically developed for users inexperienced in statistics though expert in the domain of interest. The problem is illustrated in Figure 5.32. Six points show corresponding values of Y and X. However, a mathematical model of the relation between Y and X is sought, perhaps because the measurement of the six points is expensive and the value of Y for other values of X is required. Usually the dependent variable Y is a function of many independent variables, as illustrated in Figure 5.33.

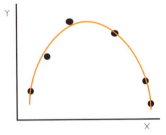

FIGURE 5.32 The value of Y has been measured or calculated for six different values of X. The task is to find a simple mathematical function that relates Y to X with acceptable accuracy

$$Y = a + bX_1 + cX_2 + dX_3 + eX_1X_2 + fX_2X_3 + gX_3X_1 + hX_1^2 + jX_2^2 + kX_3^2$$

FIGURE 5.33 A typical relation between dependent and independent variables

Software (e.g. the GENSTAT package) exists that will calculate the values of the coefficients (a, b, c, etc. in Figure 5.33) to achieve the best fit to the original points. However, the terms to be included in the model need to be chosen by an expert in the field to which the model relates. That expert may know, for example, that the term X_1X_2 is unlikely to be relevant, whereas the term involving X_1X_3 corresponds to his understanding of the effect being modelled. To support the choice of terms for inclusion in the model, the Model Maker is available (Figure 5.34). Every possible term in the polynomial model is represented by a small box: for the example of four independent variables and including up to third-order terms, the appearance of the Model Maker is shown in Figure 5.34. Within each box is a circle whose size indicates the extent to which that term is beneficial to the fitting process. If the circle is black the term is already included in the model, if white it is not. The aim of the circles is to support the evaluation of scent by showing the benefit of the terms which may subsequently be added or removed. SM and SI are simply encoded by the boxes: a click on a box will include the term if it is not already included or remove the term if it is already included.

Figure 5.35 provides another example in which the size of the selectable menu options might usefully indicate the extent of the data that each option will

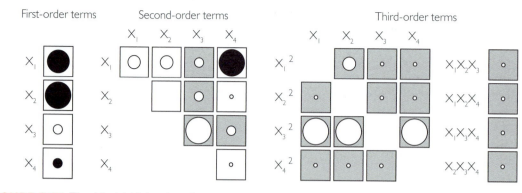

First-order terms Second-order terms Third-order terms

FIGURE 5.34 The Model Maker interface

FIGURE 5.35
Encoding to
support the
evaluation of
scent

reveal. Additionally, colour coding could represent the popularity of each option. Even such a simple example, however, may not be straightforward, since there is often a tendency for a user to make a decision regarding a movement before all the available SM cues have been interpreted (Nielsen, 2000) and the benefit of each movement has been evaluated.

For a third example of an interface that can support the evaluation of scent we return to the Attribute Explorer. The distance of a black house from the single limit it violates may well influence the choice of limit adjustment to be explored.

5.3.6 Where am I?

It may seem odd for the question 'Where am I?' (in information space) to be addressed last. On the contrary: if, by the design of appropriate cues, we have answered the other questions:

Where can I go from here?

How do I get there?

What lies beyond?

   and

*Where can I **usefully** go from here?*

then we have gone a long way towards informing the user about the nature of the information space they are currently inhabiting as well as their location within it. But more can be done.

The concept of *breadcrumbs* turns out to be useful in this context. It arises from the story of Hansel and Gretel who, in their progress through the forest, left a trail of breadcrumbs so that they could later retrace their path (a story whose impact is somewhat diminished by the fact that they never made use of the breadcrumb trail!). Essentially, breadcrumbs represent history, and to good effect. Why? Because another question that continually occurs to the user is:

Where have I been, because I may want to go back there?

There are two types of **breadcrumb trails**: path breadcrumbs and location breadcrumbs.

Path breadcrumbs

Path breadcrumbs represent the user's recent path through information space. They and the user's current location in information space are represented symbolically in Figure 5.36. As we have pointed out, retreat is a frequently adopted movement in information space, so it is useful not only to encode recent locations but also to use the same representations to encode SI so that selective retreat is easily achieved by interaction. Selective retreat is, in fact, a very common movement in information spaces. For example, about 60 per cent of all movements within the World Wide Web are *revisitations*, to pages already – and normally very recently – visited (Tauscher and Greenberg, 1997). There is, in fact, on average, a 39 per cent chance that the next URL visited will be found within a set containing the six previously visited pages. As Tauscher and Greenberg remark, 'the success of [the] Back [control] is in line with our observation that extreme recency is a good predictor of what page will be revisited'. Thus, in the context of interaction design to support navigation, an important conclusion is that the design of sensitivity cues and residue should fully acknowledge the likelihood of revisitations and support them through the provision of breadcrumbs.

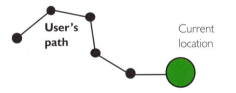

FIGURE 5.36

A representation of history leading to the current location

A simple example of support for selective retreat is the list of recently visited URLs (Figure 5.37) available on demand beside a BACK button ('one of the world's most heavily used interface components' (Cockburn *et al.*, 2002)). While a user's internal model of recently visited URLs may be poor (Cockburn and Jones, 1996), it is likely that the user will be able to recognize the appearance of recently visited pages (Kaasten *et al.*, 2002). Therefore, graphical breadcrumbs (Figure 5.38) within a pull-down menu, and particularly the ability to zoom in on a miniature before selection (Cockburn *et al.*, 2002, 2003), can facilitate revisitation. The design of support for revisitation – itself an exercise involving information visualization – is a challenging task on its own.

FIGURE 5.37
An ordered list
of recently
visited URLs

http://news.bbc.co.uk
http://news.bbc.co.uk/1/hi/education/default.stm
http://news.bbc.co.uk/1/hi/england/south_counties/4932646.stm
http://news.bbc.co.uk/1/hi/england/south_counties/4892000.stm

FIGURE 5.38
An ordered
collection of
miniatures of
recently visited
web pages may
provide useful
navigational
cues

To *some* extent a 'path breadcrumb' trail tells the user 'where they are in information space' – it provides a partial view of local details of that space. The current location will also normally be associated with available outlinks; their associated destinations are represented in blue in Figure 5.39 and they, too, can help the user to establish their location in space.

FIGURE 5.39
Available paths
from the
current location
in discrete
information
space

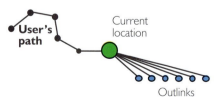

Location breadcrumbs

Once a user is located *within* a website (e.g. an organisation or company website) it is also useful not only to be able to see the *structure* of that space but also to move within that structure with ease. Thus, as indicated symbolically and encoded red in Figure 5.40, it is often useful to make the structure of a website explicit by providing representations of available locations within that structure. Furthermore, to facilitate access, many or all of these representations could be sensitive to interaction (i.e. they would encode SI). Outlinks coloured blue in Figure 5.40 represent access to destinations outside the location structure. The relevance of the term 'breadcrumb' can of course be questioned, since location breadcrumbs have not been 'scattered' by a user.

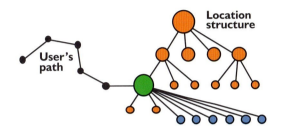

FIGURE 5.40
Location breadcrumbs (red) provide an awareness of the structure of a site within which the current location resides

It is frequently useful for path breadcrumbs *within a site* to be made explicit. An example taken from a website is shown in Figure 5.41: the site was entered at 'Poole', not 'Fine Hotels', providing the user with the ability to expand their horizon. The decision as to whether to make *all* location breadcrumbs interactive, thereby additionally encoding SIs, is not an easy one: it must be

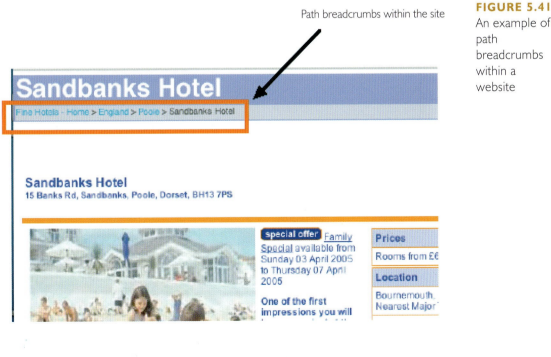

Path breadcrumbs within the site

FIGURE 5.41
An example of path breadcrumbs within a website

made by the interaction designer when taking into account all the many other requirements of a website. The need for the provision and careful design of location breadcrumbs is emphasized by the not infrequent and certainly frustrating occasions where use of a search engine has led to a useful page which nevertheless begins 'My view is that . . .' and fails to mention the identity of the author and/or the institution or company with which they are associated. Some interactive means of ascending any hierarchy would be most useful in such cases.

Experimental study

Probably the first example of path breadcrumbs, as well as a thorough and realistic evaluation of their effectiveness, was reported by Field and Apperley (1990). They removed many of the constraints inherent in the studies of Snowberry and her colleagues by addressing the more realistic task of navigating a reasonably large and non-uniform menu structure to solve a complex task capable of more than one acceptable solution. Added realism was acknowledged by permitting exploration, including retreat (facilitated by interactive breadcrumbs) specifically forbidden in the Snowberry experiments. Their information space was a 'videotex' database describing various aspects of the fictitious city of Carlton and the task given to subjects required the planning of an evening's entertainment with a friend involving travel, a cinema visit, a vegetarian meal and a return journey.

Field and Apperley compared the two menu systems illustrated in Figure 5.42. One, called Standard Menu (left), allowed normal selection from a menu but also selection, via short typed command, of either the 'home' page or the immediately previous page. The other, called Selective Retreat (right), not only displayed a 'trace' of previously selected options at each level (in other words, path breadcrumbs) but allowed retreat to any one of them via a typed number.

FIGURE 5.42
The two menu systems investigated by Field and Apperley (1990)

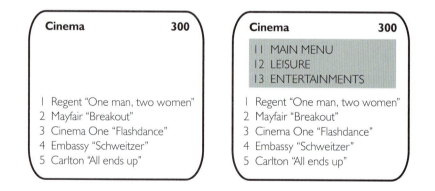

The result of this experiment was a rich collection of results and conclusions deserving more detailed study than can be offered here. There were, for example, significant differences in the number of pages accessed in the two conditions (means for Standard Menu and Selective Retreat were 50.3 and 39.7 respectively). If 'efficiency' is defined as 'the minimum number of frames to target divided by the actual number of frames to target', the Selective Retreat group were 63.3 per cent efficient and the Standard Menu group 51.3 per cent efficient.

In the context of our discussion perhaps the most relevant conclusion drawn by Field and Apperley is that subjects using the Selective Retreat structure gained a better understanding of the complexities of the database – that is, they seemed to acquire a better contextual map (i.e. internal model) of the city of Carlton. As Dahlback (1988) has reminded us, navigation is concerned with *learning* about an information space as well as *using* it.

5.3.7 Guidance regarding design to support navigation

We have introduced the concepts of sensitivity, residue and scent and illustrated their relevance with typical examples. The question remains, 'How does the inter-action designer make use of these concepts?' Briefly, the answer is that, while these concepts can *guide* interaction design to support navigation, they do not *prescribe* how that design should proceed. The reason is simple: the design of a web page, for example, is influenced by many considerations, of which navigation is just one, albeit an important one. Even when we focus on navigation, a wide range of expertise can be relevant to the design of navigational cues, an important one being visual/graphic design. Thus, the concepts of sensitivity, residue and scent are there to guide, to act as a checklist, to ensure that all that can be done to support navigation has at least been considered even if other factors are assigned priority.

The importance of interaction design to support navigation should be self-evident from the experience that many people have had with the Web and other information spaces. One measure of importance is suggested by the screen area ('real estate') assigned to navigation in typical home pages on the Web. In Nielsen and Tahir's (2002) critique of 50 home pages, the fraction of screen area devoted to navigation ranges from 3 per cent to 48 per cent, with 22 per cent being about average. The importance of navigation is further emphasized by the screen area devoted to 'content', which varies from zero (in eight cases) to 50 per cent, with two clusters, one between about 30 per cent and 50 per cent and the other between zero and about 14 per cent. Thus, perhaps contrary to expectation, the screen area devoted to navigation is, broadly speaking, of the same order as that devoted to the content of a home page.

5.4 Passive interaction

There are two aspects of passive interaction that must be appreciated. First, that during typical use of a visualization tool, most of a user's time is spent in this activity, often involving many eye movements and a great deal of higher-order cognitive processing. Second, that passive interaction does not imply a static representation. For many reasons the representation of data may be changing, often quite rapidly, with the user benefiting from observation of the representation. These aspects should be apparent in the examples which follow.

5.4.1 Static display

A static representation may be bespoke, designed to answer one question, as with Minard's map, or it may be 'authored' by the user, as with the EZChooser.

Regrettably there may be a great temptation to view static displays as somewhat 'low tech' in contrast to continuous and stepped interactions which may be regarded as more 'advanced' or 'cool'. Such temptation must be resisted. After all, each frame encountered in stepped interaction is static until a selection is made. The interaction designer should therefore be aware of the potential benefit of employing a static representation of data in view of the concomitant reduction in cognitive effort and the number of mouse clicks. The EZChooser introduced in Chapter 2 provides a simple but persuasive example. The question 'What is available if we choose to go into the next higher price range, or the next higher MPG range?' *could* be answered by clicking first on a *Price* range, observing the result, then cancelling that selection and choosing the next higher *MPG* range and observing that result. Instead, the designers chose to employ a static representation containing 'outline cars' which provide the same answers without the need for interaction and require much less cognitive effort. The static display engenders a 'see and go' approach (Rao, 1999) in contrast to the much more demanding 'go and see' (Dynamic Queries) approach which is disappointingly common. As Rao asks,

Would you go to India just to see if you wanted to be there?

5.4.2 Browsing

Visual interaction is typically characterized by a succession of many eye movements. And since the human visual system is so fundamental to information visualization it deserves further discussion, especially to define commonly used terms.

When conscious, a human's eye-gaze is constantly moving. Wherever the gaze is focused, Potter's (1999) notion of conceptual short-term memory tells us that a captured image is first perceived and fleetingly stored in sensory memory; it is then interpreted and later evaluated. This entire process can take up to about 500 milliseconds. It is this process, which can be described as the *assessment of content*, that we shall call *browsing*.

Unfortunately, the term browsing often carries the connotation, in many texts, of casual intent. On the contrary, although eye-gaze *can* be directed in a casual manner, it is more helpful to qualify browsing according to three categories:

- Exploratory browsing is eye-gaze activity undertaken to accumulate an internal model of part of the scene available to view. Thus, in a bookshop (Figure 5.43), I may visually scan a display and decide that the fourth case along has to do with psychology.

- Opportunistic browsing is eye-gaze activity undertaken to 'see what's there' rather than to model what is seen. An example would be my rapid glance, on entering a party, to see whether there are any familiar faces.

- Involuntary browsing is undirected and not associated with any conscious intent. It describes the normal pattern of eye movement undertaken by humans. An example would be a person using the coffee table of Figure 5.4 whose gaze happens to alight on an image on the table.

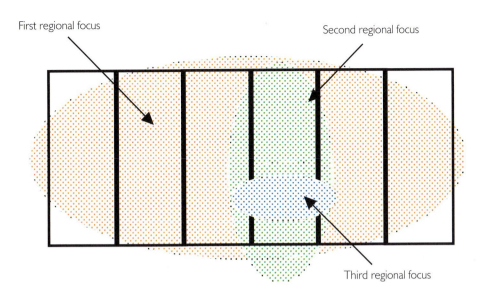

First regional focus

Second regional focus

Third regional focus

FIGURE 5.43
Depiction of the visual browsing undertaken by a person with an interest in books on cognitive psychology, on approaching a book display. The first regional focus (red) explores the entire collection to establish a new focus (green) associated with psychology. As a result of the exploration of the green region a new region of focus (blue) is established concerned with cognitive psychology

After establishing, by exploratory browsing, that the fourth bookcase has to do with psychology, I may undertake a new exercise of exploratory browsing but now with a focus on the region of the fourth bookcase (Figure 5.43) to establish a model of its content. Here, the regional focus of my attention has been moved in (continuous) information space, focusing on that particular bookcase to establish a model of its content. Exploratory browsing in this new region may well identify locations dedicated to cognitive, clinical and social psychology. This progression, in which attention is focused on a new user-defined region of continuous information space is very closely analogous to the progression in which attention is given to a succession of user-selected locations (e.g. web pages) during stepped interaction with a discrete information space, and the term *navigation* is therefore appropriate.

5.4.3 Moving displays

Much benefit can be gained through a moving representation which is 'data driven' in the sense that the user is not directly controlling the movement as would be the case with continuous or stepped interaction. A simple example is provided by a 'live stream' display presented to a currency dealer who is concerned with the buy and sell rates for conversion between US dollars and euros (Figure 5.44). The display changes about every four seconds according to the dynamics of bourses throughout the world. Here the interaction is passive; the dealer simply monitors the display and makes decisions based on experience. In passing we note that the figures normally regarded as least significant are here the most significant!

A second example of a moving display occurs when a human user must observe the progress of an algorithm in order better to understand it or its consequences (Pu and Lalanne, 2000; Wright *et al.*, 2000). Figure 5.45 shows the interface of a system (Colgan *et al.*, 1995) designed to facilitate the design of electronic circuits by combining two powerful resources. One resource is a so-called

FIGURE 5.44

A continuous
sequence of
representations
of the US dollar
– euro
exchange rate

time

etc.

'optimization algorithm' which, given a first design of a circuit, will automatically alter the values of its parameters with a view to minimizing the difference between the actual performance of the circuit and the desired performance. Notwithstanding the value of such algorithms, however,[6] their effectiveness can be enhanced considerably if the human designer can observe the algorithm's progress and, on the basis of their experience of circuit design, help to guide the algorithm to a satisfactory solution that it might not have achieved on its own. An extremely valuable additional outcome of such monitoring is the discovery of trade-offs and correlations encountered during the optimization process.

In view of the analogy of the behaviour just described to that of a pilot in command of an aircraft flying on automatic pilot, the interface of Figure 5.45 was referred to as 'the cockpit'. The hierarchical representation corresponds to the functional dependence of the artefact's quality, represented by the uppermost circle, on various primary properties represented by the second row of circles, which are in turn a function of other aspects of the design. The size of a red circle denotes the discrepancy between the desired performance of the artefact and that currently achieved. Thus, the smaller the circle, the better the

---

[6] On its own, the outcome of an optimization algorithm has sometimes been likened to the result '42' returned by the computer in Douglas Adam's *Hitchhiker's Guide to the Galaxy* in the sense that the process by which the answer was achieved is opaque.

Discrepancy between
desired and achieved
quality

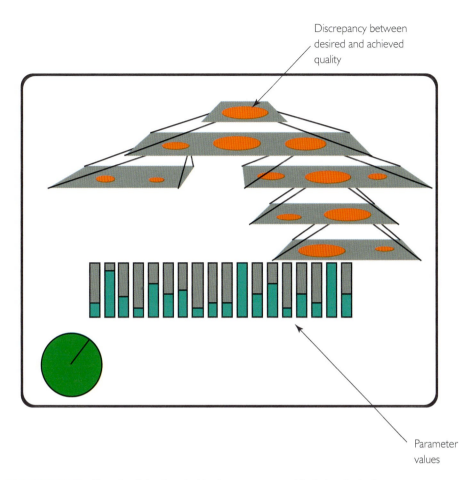

Parameter
values

FIGURE 5.45 Sketch of the 'cockpit' of a computer-aided circuit design system supporting the human guidance of automated design. The clock hand rotates in discrete steps to represent the iterative behaviour of the optimization algorithm. Simultaneously, the parameter values chosen by the algorithm and the various performances of the designed circuit are represented, respectively, by the size of the blue bars and red circles. At any time the designer can halt the algorithm and adjust either the details of the algorithm or certain allowed limits to circuit performance

artefact is.[7] The purpose of the algorithm is to iteratively adjust the parameters describing the artefact in order to achieve a design improvement: as it does so the designer observes the changing size of the circles as well as the parameter values (encoded by the bars) chosen by the algorithm and, on the basis of experience, intervenes to enhance the optimization process. As a reminder, the process just described – until any intervention by the designer – constitutes passive interaction.

---

[7] This relation between circle size and unwanted discrepancy leads to the intriguing consequence that a perfect circuit is represented by a circle of zero size!

A third example of passive interaction is provided by the coffee table scenario illustrated in Figure 5.4. Although there is no physical action on the part of the user (until his or her finger pushes an image towards the centre of the table to achieve semantic zoom), it is useful to understand what is happening by, yet again, referring to Norman's Action Cycle (Figure 5.46). We start at the top, with a person's goal. It is essential to realize that a person has many goals. They reside in long-term memory and for most of the time are not articulated as they would have to be, for example, in a scenario in which a user is thirsty and a cup of coffee is then sought from a machine. Thus, the person enjoying conversation around the table might be a keen chess player, but would not articulate this and many other interests during that conversation and would therefore avoid the often cognitively demanding stage of formulating an action plan. Nevertheless, when his gaze alights *involuntarily* on an image showing a chess piece, that view is automatically perceived and interpreted, and evaluated with reference to the general goal of an interest in chess. No cognitive effort is involved until an awareness of relevance occurs. If the viewed image is irrelevant to a person's interest, it is simply forgotten (Potter, 1999). People responsible for advertisements are, of course, familiar with the underlying behaviour described above.

FIGURE 5.46
Norman's
Action Cycle
for involuntary
browsing

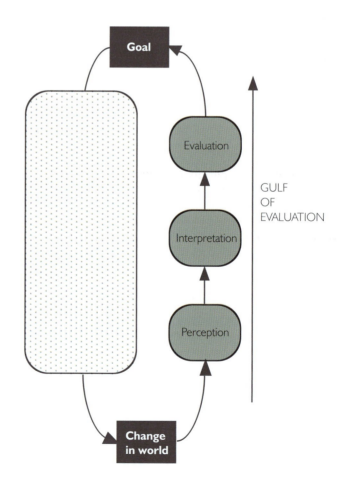

5.5 Composite interaction

There are many situations in which none of the individual interaction modes on their own can provide the most effective solution to a problem and where a combination – called *composite interaction* – is an appropriate choice. The volume of data involved might, for example, be so large that stepped interaction is required to define an appropriate subset in anticipation of future exploration by continuous and passive interaction. Another example is provided by the automated design system described in Section 5.4 and illustrated in Figure 5.45; the passive interaction involved in monitoring the progress of automated design frequently leads to stepped interaction in order to examine more detail 'behind' the red circles, and could also lead to continuous interaction to explore part of the hierarchical relation embodied in the tree of red circles.

We shall illustrate composite interaction with an example drawn from design. There are many design disciplines: financial, electronic, hydraulic and mechanical, to name a few. But whatever the discipline, the designer is always concerned with two sets of quantities. *Parameters* are those variables whose value the designer can choose. The mechanical designer can choose the diameters of shafts and the thickness of plates; the financial/investment designer selects shares and the amounts to be invested; and the electronic circuit designer chooses values for resistors and the dimensions on a silicon chip. In every case, the choice of parameter values affects the *performance* of something: for the mechanical designer the brake horsepower of an engine; for the financial designer the risk and profit of an investment; and for the circuit designer the amplification within an iPod.

5.5.1 *Influences*

There are many software packages which can predict the performance resulting from a particular choice of parameter values and provide the designer with an understanding of the *influence* of parameters on performances. While useful, this information is not directly relevant to the designer's task because it is the customer who will specify acceptable limits to performances and leave the designer to make a suitable choice of parameter values. So the designer would like to understand another influence, that of performance limits on possible parameter values. There is yet another influence of crucial interest to a designer: the influence of one performance on another. Thus, the financial designer is aware of a trade-off between risk and profit and the mechanical designer of a correlation between cylinder size and brake horsepower. As we shall see, information visualization can help the designer to explore these three influences (Tweedie *et al.,* 1995, 1996; Spence, 1999).

To simplify – though not trivialize – our discussion we shall assume that something being designed is completely described by two parameters (X1 and X2) and that two performances (S1 and S2) are of interest. We assume the realistic situation in which a customer has specified acceptable limits to S1 and S2. To investigate the influences discussed above, some data must be generated. Usually the designer will have some idea as to the region of parameter space in which a suitable design will lie and will arrange for a randomly distributed collection of points, each describing a design, to be generated (Figure 5.47(a)). A simulation package can then calculate, for each design, the corresponding values of the performances S1 and S2 (Figure 5.47(b)). For this unrealistically simple case it can be seen that points lying within an acceptable region of performance space (Figure 5.47(b)) could be traced back to find suitable values of the parameters X1 and X2 (Figure 5.47(a)). For the results shown in the figure it is also clear that some sort of trade-off exists between S1 and S2.

FIGURE 5.47

A number of randomly generated designs in parameter space (a) are simulated and the corresponding properties displayed in performance space (b). If acceptable performance is identified in performance space (b) the corresponding designs can be traced back to parameter space (a)

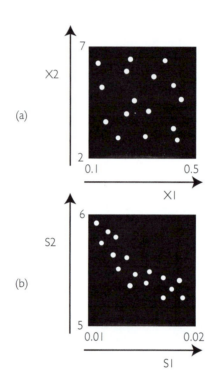

Real design involves many parameters and many performances for which limits must not be exceeded. The approach in this more realistic situation can, however, be essentially the same as with the two parameters and two performances considered in Figure 5.47: many possible designs within a region of parameter space are simulated to find the corresponding performances, with a result such as that shown in Figure 5.48. Here, a structure (a support for the filament inside a lamp) is described by four parameters X1 to X4, and four performances S1 to S4 (stresses within the structure) are of interest. A single design is defined by its contribution to eight histograms, four of which are shown in Figure 5.48, just as a single house contributed to each of the histograms of the Attribute Explorer.

The advantage of the display of performance histograms seen in Figure 5.48 is that limits can now be placed on any parameter or performance *and the effect brushed into all other histograms* in an activity characterized as *continuous interaction*. Thus, in Figure 5.49 we see that constraints placed by a customer on the stresses S1 to S4 have been brushed into the parameter histograms to identify, by the colour red, those parameter combinations leading to acceptable

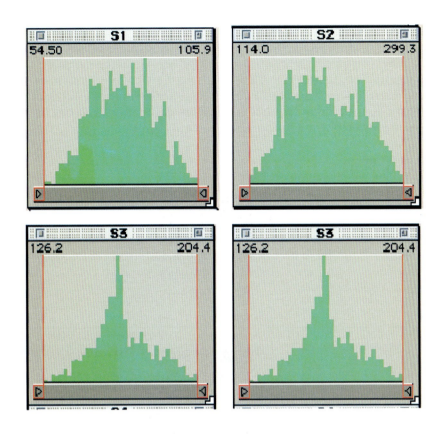

FIGURE 5.48
The four stresses occurring in each of a randomly generated set of designs of a structure are displayed in the form of histograms

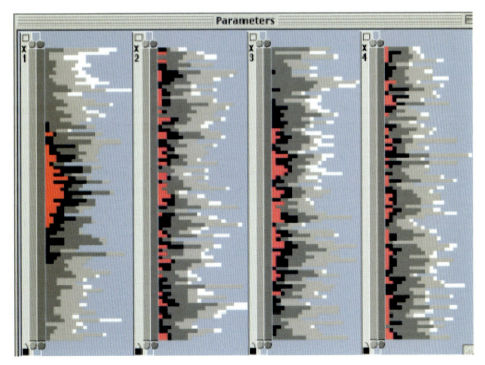

FIGURE 5.49
Limits placed on the four stresses S1 to S4 have been brushed into the parameter histograms, with red designs indicating those which satisfy all limits on S1, S2, S3 and S4

performances; some idea of permitted parameter tolerances can begin to be explored. Continuous interaction also allows the designer to explore, for example, the effect of adjusting performance limits in the same manner as limits were explored in the Attribute Explorer, perhaps with a view to negotiations with a customer regarding performance limits. Exploration of the trade-off between S4 and S3 was demonstrated in Section 5.2. The exploration facilities described above were provided by the Influence Explorer (Tweedie *et al.,* 1995, 1996).

The prosection

The same data can alternatively be displayed in the form of a prosection matrix (Figure 5.50) (Furnas and Buja, 1994; Tweedie and Spence, 1998). A prosection is associated with a pair of parameters and displays a *projection*, on to that two-dimensional parameter space, of all generated designs lying within chosen limits (i.e. a *section*) to all other parameters. Those designs that satisfy all limits on all performances – and fall within a region of acceptability – are coded red and those that fail one limit are black, etc. in the same way that colour coding was used in the Attribute Explorer.

FIGURE 5.50
A prosection matrix associated with a design involving four parameters. Red indicates the location of designs that satisfy all performance limits. Yellow defines the regions within which the designs of a mass-produced design will lie as a result of manufacturing tolerances on the parameters

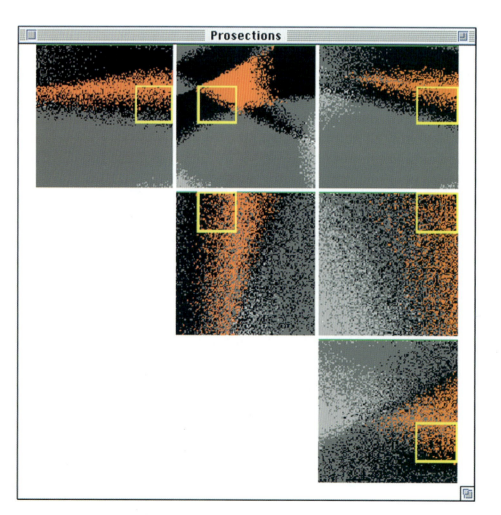

The principal advantage of the prosection matrix stems from the fact that, in conventional design, the designer has very little (or no) initial idea as to the location of the region of acceptability. With the prosection matrix the designer can now select a set of values for all parameters to place the design within the red region. More realistically the designer will recognize that parameter values can be guaranteed only within manufacturing tolerances and will therefore address the task of design for mass production by placing a high-dimensional tolerance box within the region of acceptability (Spence and Soin, 1988): the outline of such a tolerance box is coloured yellow in Figure 5.50. As the tolerance boxes are continuously moved by the designer, an indicator provides a numerical indication of the manufacturing yield of the design.

5.6 Interaction dynamics

5.6.1 *Mental models*

In Norman's Action Cycle the result of execution has been labelled either 'change in the world' or 'change in view of data' and is represented by a *single* box. This box bears more detailed examination because the change may *not* be instantaneous: indeed, as we shall show, it may be better if it is *not* instantaneous. We need to examine the transition from the old view of data to the new one (Figure 5.51).

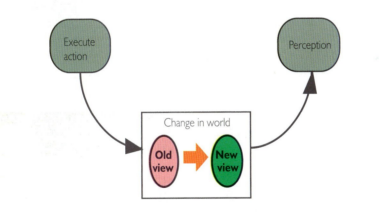

FIGURE 5.51
With information visualization, Norman's 'change in world' consists of an old view of data being replaced by a new view

The need to consider the dynamic nature of the visual change that occurs in response to stepped interaction is most cogently illustrated by the example of the cone tree (Robertson *et al.*, 1991), already discussed in Chapter 3 and illustrated again in Figure 5.52. To facilitate use of the cone tree, a command identifying a particular node will cause the rotation of as many cones as are necessary to bring the identified node, together with its superordinate nodes at each level, to the front, thereby supporting easy examination and comprehension. If another node is now identified and again, with appropriate cone rotations, is to be brought to the front, an interaction design issue immediately arises. If the second presentation occurs *immediately*, the user's previously formed internal model of the cone tree is likely to be lost or severely damaged. However, if animation – lasting

FIGURE 5.52
A cone tree

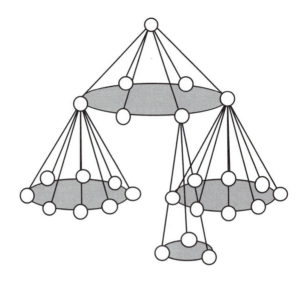

around one second – is employed to ensure a smooth transition between the two states (by rotation of the cones), then, as a result of our perception of object constancy (in other words, in the physical world, cones usually remain cones), the user's internal model derived from the first presentation suffers much less degradation and their mental model of the tree might be enhanced. A very convincing demonstration of this is provided in a video presentation of the cone tree in which Card remarks that 'without animation it takes several seconds to reassimilate the relationships between the parts of a tree' – in other words, to restore the mental model. Here is a major difference between continuous and stepped interaction: in the former an immediate response is the ideal, whereas in the latter an immediate response may well be far from ideal.

Even if there is no physical metaphor available, *artificial* animation between two discrete views achieved by stepped interaction can often help. In Figure 5.53(a), for example, a set of coloured circles might represent the gross national products (GNP) of a collection of countries, with circle diameter proportional to GNP. If, in a stepped interaction, a different year is chosen and the display is changed immediately to that of Figure 5.53(b), it may take a user a little time to assimilate what changes have taken place. However, if animation – lasting no more than one second – is introduced, by employing intermediate displays such as the sequence shown in Figure 5.53(c), then although these intermediate displays may be wholly artificial, the change between the two years represented by (a) and (b) is easier to interpret.

5.6.2 Blindness

A first requirement, of course, is that the visual change should be *noticed*; otherwise the entire reason for causing a change of view is negated. There are two phenomena which are relevant in this context. Both are remarkably counterintuitive and many people find them difficult to believe. There is every reason, therefore, to bring them to the attention of interaction designers, especially those concerned with safety-critical applications (DiVita *et al.*, 2004).

Country

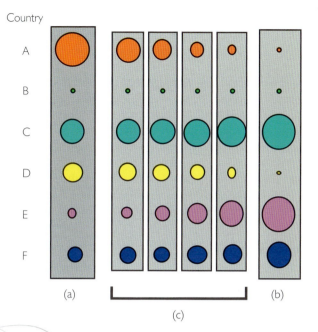

(a)

(b)

(c)

FIGURE 5.53
Replacement
of one
representation
(a) by another
(b) might best
be achieved by
animation
through the
representations
of (c)

Change blindness

We first encountered the phenomenon of *change blindness* (CB) (Rensink *et al.*, 2000; Rensink, 2002; Rensink URL) in Chapter 3: a pilot, for example, fails to notice a change in an altimeter display. One pointer towards an explanation of CB seems to lie in the fact that the human visual system does not automatically store a *detailed* memory of previously attended items. In other words, on viewing a scene a viewer does not acquire a record of all pixels constituting that scene but rather remembers a man in a blue suit standing on the pavement getting into a yellow cab. If this picture is replaced after a short interval (even as little as 40 ms) by one which is very similar except for some small detail (e.g. another pedestrian walking by), the mental model of the new scene might well be identical to that of the first and no change is noticed (Rensink's URL).

Another situation in which a change may not be noticed is when eye-gaze is undergoing a saccade. Grimes (1996) reported that changes to even realistic scenes may not be noticed when the change is made during an eye movement. In one example, 50 per cent of observers failed to notice that two people switched heads if that change was made during a saccade.

Inattentional blindness

The other 'blindness' phenomenon of which an interaction designer exploiting the potential of information visualization should be aware is *inattentional blindness* (IB). This phenomenon (Simons and Chabris, 1999) was introduced in Chapter 1 by an example in which viewers who were engaged in a task involving watching a display did not notice a person dressed as a gorilla strolling through the display. Many other examples of inattentional blindness, all astonishingly counterintuitive, are described by Varakin *et al.* (2004).

Design to counteract blindness

Durlach (2004) has provided some answers to the question 'What can I, as an interaction designer, do to minimise the problems associated with change blindness and inattentional blindness apart, of course, from careful usability testing?'. All answers have their advantages and disadvantages. For example, the provision of 'change alerts' may truly alert a user to change, but responding to these alerts may increase the user's workload. Similarly, coding information for recency may give the user some guide as to which information is newest, but can add to visual complexity and requires the interaction designer to find an unused but salient coding modality. These are just two of the potential means to facilitate change detection which Durlach (2004) lists. Although relevant research began a long time ago (e.g. Cherry, 1953) in the context of audible input, and a great deal has been written about CB and IB, many questions remain unanswered.

5.6.3 *Visual momentum*

A concept aptly named visual momentum (Woods, 1984) is relevant to visual change and was first identified in the context of scene transitions during cinematography. It is often illustrated by the simple, albeit obvious, example of the need for an actor to have the same hairstyle in one scene as in the one preceding it. That's why the proverbial 'continuity girl' is so valuable in film production. Translation of this principle to information visualization requires, for example, the style of a website to be maintained between a change from one web page to another. It would confuse the user if menus took on new locations within the page and if the colour of a header changed for no reason. More generally, high visual momentum implies that a user expends the minimum cognitive effort to place a new display in the context of previous ones. Essentially, the momentum referred to is that of a mental model. When stepping to a new and related web page, the user should not have to jettison the original model and start building a new one: rather, the user should be enabled to carry over much of the earlier mental model, throw away only part of it and direct cognitive effort to what is new and informative. The web designer, as well as the film director, needs the proverbial continuity girl!

5.7 Design for interaction

The discussion in this chapter has provided the last missing palette that the discipline of information visualization can make available to the interaction designer, that concerned with interaction. Like the previous palettes related to representation and presentation, it contains useful concepts and techniques, some of which are identified in Figure 5.54.

When designing an interaction to exploit the benefits of information visualization the effective use of all the palettes is, as a task, on a par with designing an investment portfolio, a car or a new washing machine. There are no step-by-step instructions which, when followed, will guarantee success or even an

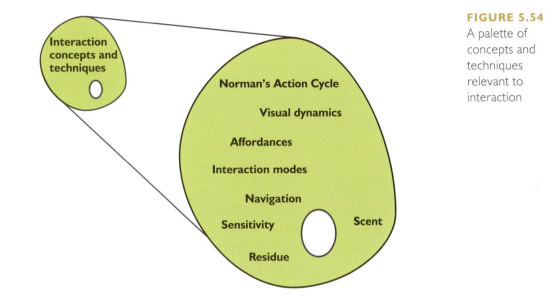

FIGURE 5.54
A palette of concepts and techniques relevant to interaction

adequate result.[8] The reason is simple: every new interface is different and usually complex; there are many requirements to satisfy (social, technological, financial, to name a few); available technology is changing with time and many different sources of expertise are drawn upon – cognitive psychology, visual design, the list is long. Design is largely a creative process and there is no 'silver bullet'. Walk into a design studio (Figure 5.55) and you will immediately be aware that design is collaborative, multidisciplinary, iterative (look at all those coloured Post-its) and demanding. And discussion with the designers will emphasize the essential ingredient of experience in a variety of disciplines.

FIGURE 5.55
Interaction design in progress. Visible features emphasize the collaborative, iterative and creative nature of design
Source: *Image courtesy of UCD network, and Alison Black*

---

[8] Doubters should try to devise a generic process that would take data from Napoleon's records and create Minard's famous map.

Some – though only a limited – idea of the complexity of interaction design undertaken to exploit the benefits of information visualization can be appreciated from the examples presented in the following chapter. The complexity arises from many sources. There is the need to fully understand the task to be supported; to review and evaluate existing techniques; to identify the nature of the user (novice? trainable? casual?); to identify the way in which a goal is formulated and the related task is carried out; and to be aware of currently available technology. What the interaction designer must do, usually collaboratively, is be aware of the many issues involved and then, in most cases, take that creative step that he or she believes will lead to a good interface design. The collaboration will often occur in an environment covered in tentative sketches and many trial designs. Even then, clients may reject or partially accept a proposed design, leading to modifications. Later, usability studies may well lead to more modifications. The route to a successful final design is certainly not straightforward.

The complexity of interaction design to exploit information visualization is to a large degree ameliorated by the many techniques and concepts available. Indeed, that is the *raison d'être* of Chapters 3, 4 and 5. Many ingredients to support representation, presentation and interaction are described in detail in these chapters: like a good chef or skilled painter, interaction designers must select appropriate ingredients from those available and use established concepts to blend them into a pleasing and effective product. And, as with cooking and painting, good interaction design can be achieved only with practice and the experience of both good and not so good results. Hopefully, the examples that follow in Chapter 6 will reinforce some of the views expressed above and provide both inspiration and guidance.

Exercises

The value of many of these exercises can be enhanced by discussing the results in open class.

◼ Exercise 5.1 (Review)

Express, in one sentence, the essential features of (1) passive interaction, (2) stepped interaction, (3) dynamic interaction.

◼ Exercise 5.2 (Review)

Describe, in one sentence, the following concepts: (1) sensitivity, (2) residue, (3) scent and (4) breadcrumbs. What is the principal function of each?

◼ Exercise 5.3

Select an interactive artefact – there's probably more than one attached to you or in your pocket or handbag (iPod, mobile, camera). The example you choose need not be overtly electronic (e.g. railway ticket machine, coffee machine, lift (elevator)).

For the artefact you choose, identify how it supports – or doesn't support very well or at all – the six stages of Norman's Action Cycle of interaction. If appropriate, indicate simple changes that could enhance the artefact. For class presentation, draw Norman's Cycle with details of its support for your chosen interactive artefact on a large sheet of paper and include your comments (and those of others) as annotations.

◼ Exercise 5.4

Select a web page (*not* a web*site*). With reference to the concepts of sensitivity, residue and scent, as well as any other relevant concepts, provide a critique of that web page and suggest how it might be enhanced.

◼ Exercise 5.5

Select the representation you designed in Exercise 3.3 for the scores in eight subjects by five students and suggest how interaction could enhance that representation. Which questions identified in Exercise 3.2 are better supported by your suggested interaction? Comment upon how the animation you suggest enhances object and/or attribute visibility and/or correlation.

■ Exercise 5.6

It is generally agreed that in a web page designed for use by the general public the Attribute Explorer technique would not be appropriate. Nevertheless, they would find sensitivity cues (as embodied, for example, in black houses) extremely valuable. Locate a website (e.g. for houses, cars or airlines) in which attribute limits are requested and which could represent similar sensitivity information in a manner easily understood by the novice user. Describe such an improved design.

■ Exercise 5.7

For a web page selected by the instructor, each student is asked to suggest modifications to it to exploit the concept of social navigation. Discussion of the various suggestions should identify both potential advantages and drawbacks of the suggested modifications.

■ Exercise 5.8

In Exercise 3.10 you were asked to suggest possible static (not interactive) representations for human relationships (including marriage, births, deaths) and identify the advantages and disadvantages of each. Now suggest how one of those representations – or a revised design – could usefully be made interactive.

Case Studies

Design

A design is a moment in time. It draws upon the past and it influences the future.

Whatever is being designed – an interface, an aircraft or a financial investment – the design activity inevitably draws upon previous designs and experiences (both successful and unsuccessful); it attempts to exploit to the best the characteristics of available components; it acknowledges current and anticipated technology and human needs; and it is cognisant of market forces. As the design proceeds, pilot evaluation and use of the designed object or scheme suggest potentially beneficial modifications.

Design is therefore a *dynamic process*. The time constants of this process – and there are many – can vary enormously: decades for aircraft, months for domestic product design and, at an extreme, days for some innovative interfaces. The one constant feature in this scenario which cannot be changed is innate human performance.

The design of an information visualization tool – on its own or as part of a more extensive application – is very much a *craft activity*. The human designer – more often a collaboration of designers – draws upon known concepts and techniques as well as fresh ideas to produce an innovative result and in this sense does what engineering designers have been doing for hundreds of years. A crucial component of this activity is the designer's vision. Design is also a collaborative activity, involving prospective users where possible[1].

---

[1] A well-known designer is reputed to wear a badge with the message (for interaction designers), 'Remember, you are not the user.' Another badge says, 'You don't even *think* like a user.'

What follows are five accounts of designs that have led to significant examples of information visualization tools and which emphasize the craft nature of design. Necessarily the designs draw upon principles and techniques from the wider context of human–computer interaction. The accounts are my own: I rejected the easy option of reprinting existing papers in favour of the freedom to emphasize what I think are the essentials of the design and the achievements of the designers, to introduce brevity and additional background where I think it appropriate, and to provide a consistency of presentation throughout the book. I have often used, verbatim, passages from the original paper which are already expressed with great clarity and which could suffer from rewriting, but in all cases I have obtained the permission to do so from the senior author. Their permission to use original figures is most gratefully acknowledged, but the reader should know that I have introduced figures of my own where I thought it might help comprehension. At the end of each case study an intentionally brief collection of relevant references is provided.

Readers who are familiar with major information visualization tools such as Spotfire and ADVIZOR may be surprised by the absence of any mention of them in this chapter. The reason is simple. Progression from the previous chapters to the present one involves a quantum leap from concepts and techniques to *the design for their use in the context of specific tasks and other constraints.* Justice could not be done to the further quantum leap to major commercial visualization tools involving a multitude of fresh contextual factors and requirements: indeed, it would be an insult to their designers to present a necessarily superficial account in the limited space that is available.

The case studies

The case studies which follow have been selected to encompass as wide a range of issues as possible. The first three, for example, address different available display areas: PDA (6.1), conventional monitor (6.2) and mobile (6.3). The tasks are equally varied, from the online purchase of objects (6.2) and calendar use (6.1) to the selection of a news channel (6.3). The data that is visualized by the user is also varied: from the communications generated by a military exercise (6.4) to the details of a huge collection of newspaper articles (6.5). Where possible I have implicitly addressed the topic of usability – worthy of a book in its own right – to show how this topic can be handled. The different sections discuss the following:

- PDA calendar (6.1) describes an application exploiting *distortion* and *suppression* to good effect within the severe constraint imposed by the display area available on a PDA.

- The online purchase of objects (6.2) provides an illustration of the representation of *hypervariate data* and the use of *interactive bargrams* to permit flexible exploration of available objects, as well as the effective use of *sensitivity cues* to facilitate a 'see-and-go' rather than a 'go-and-see' strategy.

- Mobile telephones impose a very severe constraint on available display area and provide a natural medium for exploration of the *slide-show mode* of image presentation in the context of searching for a relevant news channel (6.3).

- The exploratory analysis of vast collections of communication data arising from a military exercise (6.4) illustrates the potential of the *Attribute Explorer*, especially within the context of other tools, to support the acquisition of insight.

- In the last case study (6.5) the InfoSky system adopts a Galaxy *metaphor* to address the problem of searching and browsing a large collection of newspaper articles, illustrating the value of well-designed *semantic zoom* as well as the power of *algorithms*.

6.1 Small interactive calendars

Planning your time

Human activity, whether personal or professional, is increasingly well planned and calendars are an excellent means of facilitating such planning. When can I schedule a dental appointment? When is a good weekend to go camping this spring? I've forgotten – what's the date of the CHI conference? A calendar is virtually essential to obtain reliable answers.

The combination of plentiful memory and interactive computational power enables calendars to become more powerful, while handheld devices such as PDAs have the potential to render them mobile and permit immediacy of use. But how? Calendars are conventionally not small, especially if one needs to look ahead by up to a year, but PDAs have very limited display area. By the skilful and innovative integration of available concepts and techniques, the power of the calendar was brought to the PDA display by Bederson, Clamage, Czerwinski and Robertson in 2002. The result was first named FishCal, reflecting the principal concept on which it is based, but is now known as DateLens.

The designers made one major decision: to handle the large amount of calendar data within a small display area by exploiting the concept of the Fisheye lens: hence the name FishCal. The approach is illustrated in Figure 6.1.1 by views taken from their design. On the left is a representation of 12 weeks showing 'overview' data (e.g. the extent to which a day is already scheduled) rather than detail. On the right is the result of a single tap on the date of 2 April: all days except that one are automatically distorted (but *not* removed) to allow the selected day to be (again automatically) assigned sufficient space for the time and nature of appointments to be visible and readable.

Design philosophy

The designers acknowledged the part played by existing knowledge in influencing their design decisions:

> . . . *much of the groundwork for this design was laid by earlier work,*

a situation very common in the design of complex systems. But they rightly identified their achievement:

> . . . *while individual features of FishCal represent only variations of existing approaches, the primary contribution here is the integration of a host of*

FIGURE 6.1.1
Two views of
the FishCal
calendar,
showing the
use of
distortion

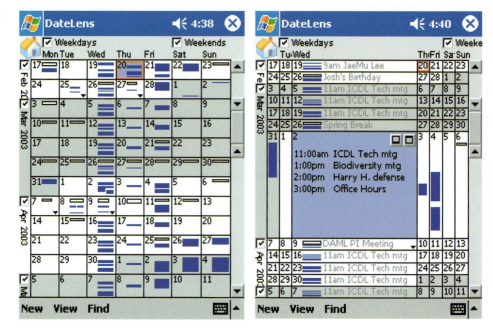

techniques to create a novel application that is both usable and useful in an important domain.

Background

It is appropriate to examine earlier work that is relevant to the development of an interactive PDA calendar.

As the designers point out, the fisheye distortion technique which underlies the design of FishCal is the bifocal display (Spence and Apperley, 1982) discussed in Chapter 4. Later, in 1986, Furnas proposed the 'degree-of-interest' concept which handles suppression to leave important data visible (also discussed in Chapter 4). A combination of distortion and suppression lies at the heart of FishCal.

The first proposal for a fisheye calendar appeared in Spence and Apperley's original 1982 paper proposing the concept of distortion and is shown in Figure 6.1.2. A rudimentary illustration presented in 1980 (Imperial College) purely for concept demonstration, it exploited both X-distortion and Y-distortion, but its implementation was severely limited by available technology. Later, Furnas (1986) described a textual program in which clicking on an individual day caused the amount of space allocated to that day to be increased (Figure 6.1.3). Impressive for its time, it did not support graphical representations or searching and it did not have widgets to control which and how many weeks to display. Furthermore it was not designed with small displays in mind. Later, Sutton and Spence (1988) described a means of suppressing detail to provide space by employing the metaphor of sliding tectonic plates: 'plates' containing the full detail of a day could be moved to provide more space for a particular day or collection of days (e.g. a week), as illustrated in Figure 6.1.4.

Since a calendar is essentially a collection of tables, the potential offered by the table lens (Rao and Card, 1994) must be considered. However, it is princi-

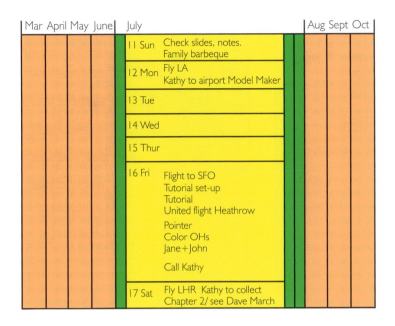

FIGURE 6.1.2
The first bifocal
calendar (1980)

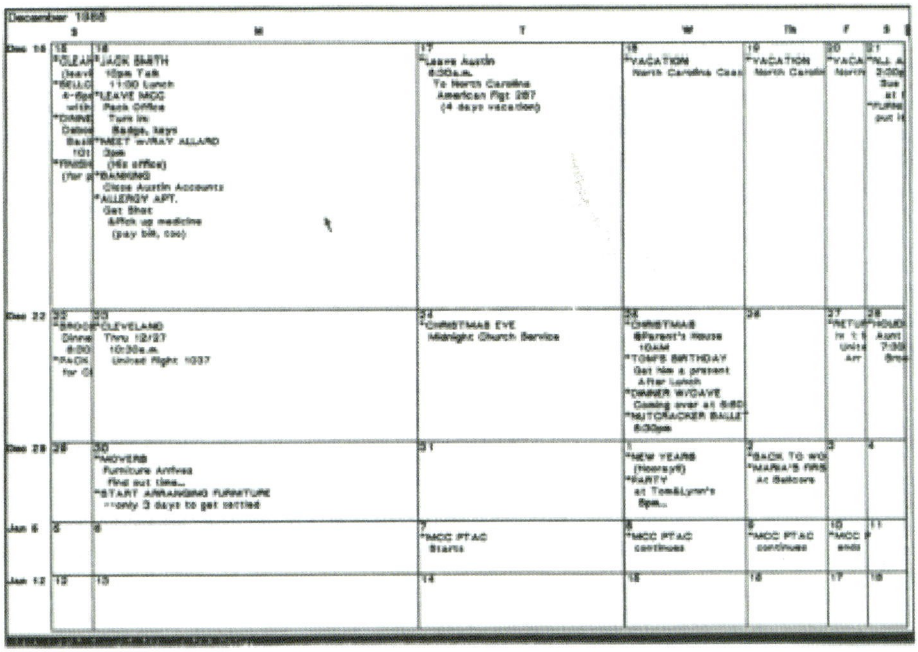

FIGURE 6.1.3
Furnas's
calendar (1986)

pally designed to support one item per cell rather than the multiple items demanded by calendars. Other early work included the first visual representation of a calendar on a small display (Plaisant and Shneiderman, 1992) and the cascade of calendar components due to Mackinlay *et al.* (1994) shown in Figure 6.1.5. The latter is not suitable for small display devices, though it does have a fisheye-like quality.

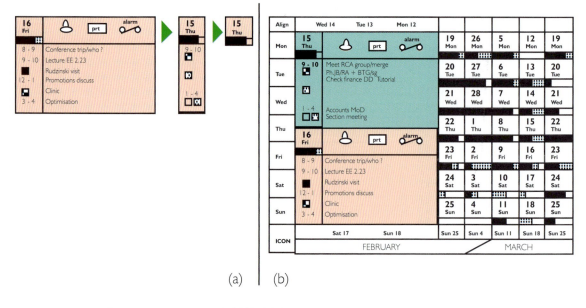

(a) | (b)

FIGURE 6.1.4 The tectonic calendar (1988). (a) Successive suppression of detail by masking; (b) the resulting tectonic calendar

FIGURE 6.1.5
The spiral
calendar (1994)

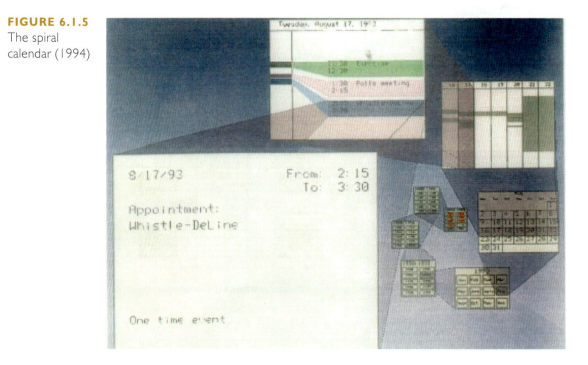

Calendar views

The designers of FishCal decided to provide four different views of the calendar called 'Tiny', 'Agenda', 'Full day' and 'Appointment detail' (Figure 6.1.6). The names are virtually self-explanatory. For example, *Appointment detail* provides detail of a particular appointment within a day; *Full day* allows a conventional full-day view, with appointments shown at relevant times. The *Agenda* view shows an ordered textual list of appointments. If space is available times are shown and a larger font is employed. The *Tiny* view offers a graphical view of the day's appointments, using colour to differentiate between different types of appointment.

Interactive control

A simple and consistent scheme is employed to achieve transition between the four views and is shown in part in Figure 6.1.6. Two buttons, always appropriately located, permit maximization and minimization, involving semantic zooming to achieve the desired view. Space limitations require a tapping action to move from *Tiny* to *Agenda* view.

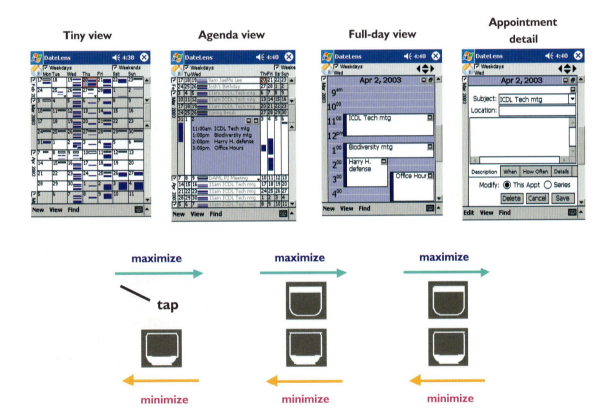

FIGURE 6.1.6 The four views offered by the FishCal calendar and some of the interactions involved in transitions between them

The time span displayed by the calendar can also be adjusted with ease, simply by moving the bottom of the scrollbar thumb, as shown in Figure 6.1.7. FishCal also exploits direct manipulation, for example by allowing a user to tap anywhere on a day to focus upon that day, simultaneously minimizing the area

FIGURE 6.1.7
Use of the
scrollbar thumb
control to
adjust the
visible time
span

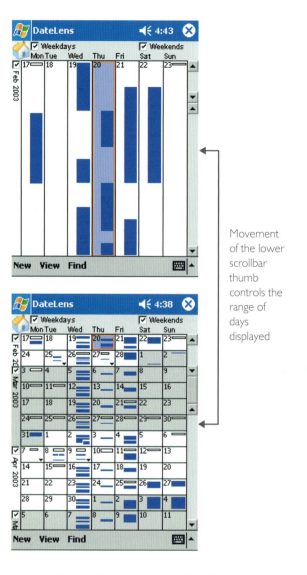

Movement
of the lower
scrollbar
thumb
controls the
range of
days
displayed

devoted to other days. Also, within a focused day (e.g. Figure 6.1.1, right) a tap on the background causes a zoom-in to a full-day view.

The designers recognized the considerable value of animated transitions between calendar views. As they point out,

> [these animated transitions] *may improve users' ability to maintain a sense of where they are.*

Search

As the designers remark, the activity of searching is important because it allows users to identify patterns and outliers within a large time span. A search in FishCal leads to the highlighting of all days that contain a matching appointment (Figure 6.1.8).

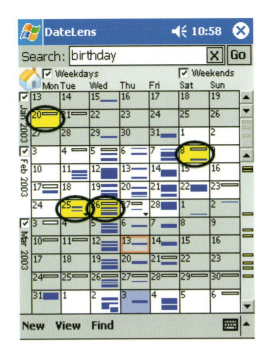

FIGURE 6.1.8
The result of
using the
FishCal search
facility

Usability study

The designers of FishCal carried out a study to compare it with the then currently available user interface of Microsoft's Pocket PC 2002™ calendar. Because relevant software was not available on the Pocket PC to run FishCal satisfactorily, both calendars were run on a PC using a mouse and keyboard. In the 1024 × 768 resolution display each calendar occupied a 240 × 320 pixel window (corresponding to standard Pocket PC resolution) centred on the display.

Six male and five female subjects, carefully chosen, were used to evaluate the new calendar. Following brief tutorials to acquaint the subjects with both calendars, each subject performed 11 tasks using each calendar. Necessarily, the order of calendar use and the task set for the calendar were counterbalanced to minimize the effects of training or the possibility of one task set being slightly more difficult than another. A limit of two minutes was set for the completion of each task, since this deadline seemed consistent with a user's expectations of being able to discover information from a calendar. Typical tasks were:

- Find the date of a specific calendar event.
- Find how many Mondays a particular month contains.
- View all birthdays for the next three months.
- Find free time to schedule an event.

Observations

What aspects of a new calendar are of principal interest and should be the concern of the calendar's designers? An obvious performance measure is the time needed to complete a task. Another is the success in completing a task. More subjective is the user's satisfaction and preference, though this was then transformed by the user to a quantitative value (1 = very difficult, 5 = very easy) for purposes of statistical analysis. Finally, in the course of observing the progress of any experiment, usability issues always arise and, indeed, point the way to potentially useful redesigns and research.

Task completion times

Statistical analysis revealed that tasks were performed faster using FishCal (49 seconds on average) than with Pocket PC (55.8 seconds on average), though the significance was borderline (Figure 6.1.9). It was also found that as the tasks became more complex the FishCal time advantage increased.

FIGURE 6.1.9
Average task completion times for the two calendars (DateLens = FishCal)

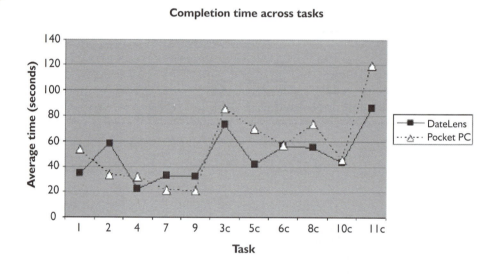

Task success

Tasks were completed successfully significantly more often using FishCal (on average, an 88.2 per cent success rate versus 76.3 per cent for the Pocket PC) (Figure 6.1.10). The more difficult and ambiguous tasks were successfully completed more often with FishCal. This was primarily because the user had the ability to get all the information across a particular time span into one view in order to answer the question; the Pocket PC user was confined to predetermined views (day, week, month and year views).

Satisfaction and preference

FishCal was rated higher across a majority of tasks, especially the most difficult one (task 11 – how many conflicts are there for the next three months?). FishCal was rated higher than the Pocket PC in terms of task-by-task satisfaction, though the significance of this result was borderline.

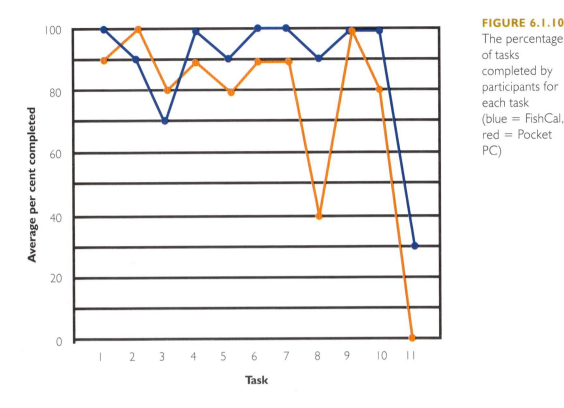

FIGURE 6.1.10
The percentage of tasks completed by participants for each task (blue = FishCal, red = Pocket PC)

Usability

The designers received good design feedback from participants suggesting how best to move towards redesign. For example, many users disliked the view of the calendar when more than six months were shown at once; they also wanted to see all 24 hours of a day in the Full view rather than just the 9am to 5pm view provided in the prototype; and users expressed strong concerns about the readability of text and the desirability of setting their own default views. Users also wanted control of the day selected for the start of a week (Sunday or Monday).

It is rare to encounter a clear-cut expression of preference, or the reverse, for a thoroughly explored innovative interface, and the outcome of an overall satisfaction questionnaire and briefing completed by participants is no exception. Responses to the questionnaire revealed no significant differences, though users preferred the Pocket PC slightly more overall. Six of the eleven participants chose the Pocket PC calendar, one abstained, saying she wanted features of both calendars in the ideal calendar, and four participants chose FishCal. It was also clear that a frequent reason cited for choosing the Pocket PC calendar was the participants' familiarity with Outlook XP calendar.

Again, as with the development of many innovative interfaces, several areas of future work were identified. Inevitably users requested a long list of desirable features and these must be examined to see how they would affect users without jeopardizing ease of use for the novice. It was also recognized that studies must be carried out on hand-held devices using pens and touch-screens rather than the mice and keyboards that necessarily had to be employed in the reported studies.

The authors' conclusions are not unusual for an innovative development of the sort described here. They have certainly revived a useful application of fish-eye technology and in so doing have produced in FishCal a viable competitor to traditional calendar interfaces. However, as they remark, since the managing of one's calendar is so important, many users will be cautious about adopting non-traditional interfaces, so that a remaining challenge is to refine FishCal so that it is appreciated by a broad spectrum of users.

Overall, FishCal – now DateLens – represents a significant design achievement, especially in view of the remark by Kent Wittenburg that must surely be echoed by many designers:

Achieving positive results for first-time users of novel visualization systems is rare.

Principal references

URL: www.cs.umd.edu/hcil/datelens

Bederson, B.B., Clamage, A., Czerwinski, M.P. and Robertson, G.G. (2003) 'A fisheye calendar interface for PDAs: providing overviews in small displays', Proceedings of Extended Abstracts of Human Factors in Computing Systems (CHI 2003), ACM Press, Demonstration, pp. 618–619.

Bederson, B.B., Clamage, A., Czerwinski, M.P. and Robertson, G.G. (2004) 'DateLens: a fisheye calendar interface for PDAs', ACM Transactions on Computer–Human Interaction, 11, 1, pp. 90–119.

Supporting references

Furnas, G.W. (1986) 'Generalized fisheye views: visualizing complex information spaces', ACM, Proceedings CHI '86, pp. 16–23.

Mackinlay, J.D., Robertson, G.G. and DeLine, R. (1994) 'Developing calendar visualizers for the information visualizer', ACM, Proceedings UIST '94, pp. 109–118.

Plaisant, C. and Shneiderman, B. (1992) 'Scheduling home control devices: design issues and usability evaluation of four touchscreen interfaces', *International Journal of Man–Machine Studies*, 36, 3, pp. 375–393.

Rao, R. and Card, S.K. (1994) 'The table lens: merging graphical and symbolic representations in an interactive focus+context visualisation for tabular information', ACM, Proceedings CHI '94, pp. 318–322.

Spence, R. and Apperley, M.D. (1982) 'Data base navigation: an office environment for the professional', *Behaviour and Information Technology*, 1, 1, pp. 43–54.

Sutton, J. and Spence, R. (1988) 'The bifocal display', Report to the UK Science and Engineering Research Council on the outcome of Grant GR/D/16499, 28 March.

6.2 Selecting one from many

The problem

The activity of selecting one object from many that are available is a common one. We go to the supermarket and select a cheese, to the department store to buy a tie, to the car showroom to select a new car and to the estate agent with a view to moving house. We have been doing these things without the help of computers, of course, for a very long time: the challenge now is to decide how best to offer an alternative by supporting these activities by computational means. In this case study we examine the development, by Wittenburg and his colleagues (2001), of a web-based application called EZChooser which facilitates the selection of one object from a collection of such objects on the basis of its attribute values. The success of EZChooser is primarily a result of the use of the *bargrams* introduced in Chapter 2, the provision of sensitivity cues, a recognition of the many and complex sub-tasks involved in the selection of an object and, consequentially, the importance of a mental model in the entire process of object selection.[2]

The task

Wittenburg and his colleagues – we shall henceforth call them 'the developers' – begin by stating in very precise terms the task they propose to facilitate (Spence, 2001, p. 73):

> *Given a collection of objects, each described by the values associated with a set of attributes, find the most acceptable such object or, perhaps, a small number of candidate objects worthy of more detailed consideration.*

As they point out, this generic task is applied very widely: to investment decisions, the choice of colleges, travel itineraries or real estate.

For many years database queries followed a rigidly prescribed procedure, but the severe limitations of these classic techniques are now well established. As the developers remark:

> *Responses to queries all too often lead to zero hits, leading to complex follow-up dialogues. A fundamental issue is that in many decision contexts users may not be sure of what they are looking for before they start. Making a good choice may depend on the total set of choices available and how individual choices compare and interact across a number of dimensions (attributes). Users will improvise as a reaction to discovered knowledge (Suchman, 1987) and, at best, classic querying provides only an indirect and tedious route towards formulating a mental model that can discover unanticipated solutions. For instance, in a car-buying context, if users discover the existence*

---

[2] Some material in this case study will constitute a repetition of material that has been presented in earlier chapters. This is intentional so that this case study can be read independently.

of a better warranty or gas mileage than they had previously supposed, they may be willing to extend their previously assumed price limit. Classic querying approaches will not easily reveal such information to a user.

Their comments are appropriately reflected by the inclusion of 'exploration' in the title of their paper. It is disappointing that many current online services appear to be unaware of what the developers state so cogently.

Existing solutions

Before the creation of EZChooser, a number of approaches designed to overcome the limitations of classic techniques were available. *Tables*, for example, constitute a data format familiar to many people and may well be useful for examining options once a sufficiently small number have been distilled by a 'whittling-down' process. Indeed, after presenting EZChooser, the developers make a comparison with the use of tables. *Guides*, which ask the user a number of questions, have the drawback that a user cannot anticipate the consequences of taking a certain path. For example, in the travel domain, a user may not feel comfortable selecting departure and arrival times before knowing the corresponding consequences for the price of the ticket. A more recent development is the provision of *agent-based recommender systems* which gather preference information from the user and respond with a 'solution'. Often, the user has the uncomfortable feeling that they could have made a better decision if only they knew more about the manner in which that solution was obtained.

The developers then pay particular attention to two visualization techniques which allow users to form better cognitive models of the decision space. They are Dynamic Queries and the Attribute Explorer.

The *Dynamic Queries* approach was named by Shneiderman and colleagues in 1992 and is illustrated in Figure 6.2.1 by a 'home-finding' example. Attribute scales on the right allow lower and upper limits on a number of attributes to be positioned by a user, whereupon dots on the map on the left represent houses that satisfy all the limits. The positions of the limits can be varied manually, with instant response on the map, hence the term *Dynamic Queries*. The *Attribute Explorer* technique (Spence and Tweedie, 1998) was

FIGURE 6.2.1

Dynamic Queries: a home-finding example. Limits placed on house attributes by a user lead to the display of houses satisfying those limits on the map

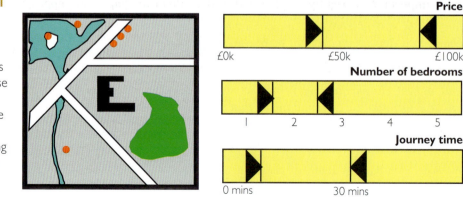

introduced in Chapter 3 and will not be discussed further here. In connection with both these techniques the developers quote Kirsch (1997) as arguing that users should be offered a sort of playground in which they can manipulate the parameters of their problem and agree that interfaces for electronic shopping should allow users 'the opportunity to "play" with electronic artifacts of their decision parameters'. Recently, other interfaces supporting the flexible exploration of multiparameter objects have been developed (see, for example, Yi, *et al.*, 2005).

Bargrams

A crucial decision taken by the developers was to adopt – and indeed to name – the concept of *bargrams*. A one-dimensional bargram (Figure 6.2.2(b)) is derived from a two-dimensional histogram (Figure 6.2.2(a)) by tipping over the columns of the histogram and laying them end-to-end, ignoring any null bins. The relative count in a bargram is shown in the relative widths of the bars, in contrast to vertical heights in a histogram. Bargrams have the following properties:

1. They carry less information about value distributions; for example, gaps are not shown, neither are outliers identified as such.
2. There is no indication of whether adjacent items are close together or far apart in value.
3. They are generic: they can be used to represent numerical values, text, ordinal data and categorical data.
4. They can be used in parallel to represent a number of attributes.
5. They are simple.
6. They occupy little space.

The advantages of 3 to 6 tend to outweigh any potential disadvantages associated with 1 and 2.

Affordances

The developers then examined the *affordances* provided by bargrams. In a realistic scenario more than one attribute is of interest, so *parallel bargrams* (whose importance is rightly emphasized in the title of the paper) are appropriate (Figure 6.2.2(c)). Since each object is represented once in each bargram, there is a *link* offering the potential for *brushing* and the display and exploration of *multi-attribute* information. Indeed, since the bin content of each bargram corresponds to the numbers of objects, it is possible – and very useful, as we shall see – to associate, with each bargram, what the developers called an *item vector* (Figure 6.2.2(d)) composed of *domain-specific glyphs*. The placement of item glyphs above the bargram now allows the bargram value bins to support informative labels (e.g. *MPG* and *Price* in the car example) as well as providing an interactive mechanism by means of which a user can form queries (Figure 6.2.2(e)). The results of those queries can then be reflected back into the item vector to indicate which objects satisfy all attribute range selections.

FIGURE 6.2.2

Development of the bargram, parallel bargrams and item vectors

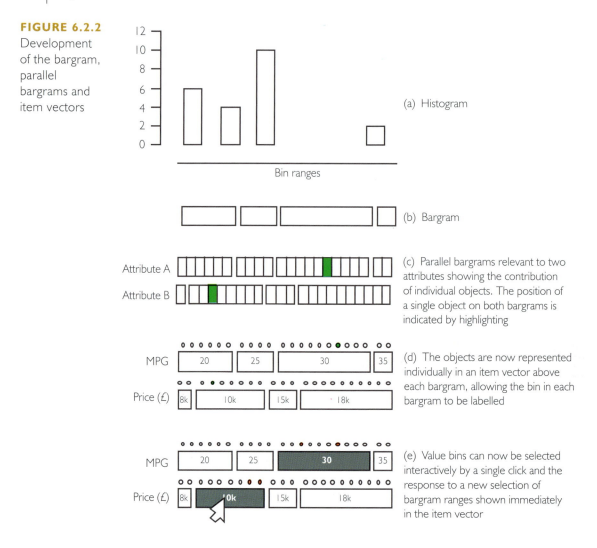

(a) Histogram

Bin ranges

(b) Bargram

Attribute A
Attribute B

(c) Parallel bargrams relevant to two attributes showing the contribution of individual objects. The position of a single object on both bargrams is indicated by highlighting

MPG
Price (£)

(d) The objects are now represented individually in an item vector above each bargram, allowing the bin in each bargram to be labelled

MPG
Price (£)

(e) Value bins can now be selected interactively by a single click and the response to a new selection of bargram ranges shown immediately in the item vector

EZChooser

By exploiting the attractive features and affordances characteristic of parallel bargrams, the developers created the EZChooser interface. It is illustrated in Figure 6.2.3 for the example of car purchase. The most noticeable addition to the parallel bargrams is the display, in the lower portion of the screen, of images of the 23 cars from which a selection is being made. The *appearance* of a car is an important attribute but is not quantifiable and would present a severe challenge to query systems that are based on conventional numeric, ordinal or categorical data. Since an attribute row (i.e. bargram plus item vector) has a minimum height, a scroll bar (Figure 6.2.3) is provided to accommodate more attributes than can be handled in the available display area.

There are many ways (some of which were described in Chapter 2) in which the data presented in EZChooser can be explored: indeed, that is one of its

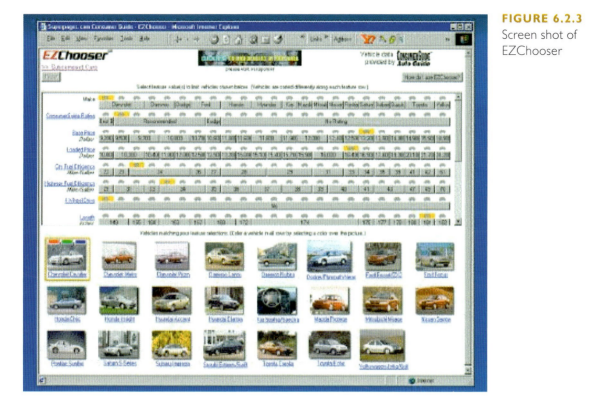

FIGURE 6.2.3
Screen shot of
EZChooser

advantages. For example, a single car can be identified by clicking it in the image set (as confirmation it is framed in yellow – see Figure 6.2.3) whereupon, in a brushing activity, the corresponding car glyphs are highlighted in the item vectors above the bargrams. It is immediately obvious that the car highlighted in Figure 6.2.3 is at the lower end of fuel efficiency and in the mid- to upper-price range compared with other available cars. Brushing can also be initiated by selecting a car glyph in an item vector. Alternatively the user might wish to identify attribute ranges reflecting his requirements in order to see how many cars satisfy those requirements, what ranges their other attribute values fall in and what they look like. In this case a user can click on any number of value bins in a bargram to impose a number of requirements; bins within a bargram are treated as a logical OR, while value restrictions between bargrams are treated as logical AND.

A valuable feature of EZChooser is the ability to make highlighting 'sticky' to serve as memory cues. We often come to a tentative conclusion about a choice and want to 'tag' it in some way so that it is both easy to return to and can serve as a basis of comparison. In fact, EZChooser can be entered directly from a web page associated with a particular car, so that a user can start with an example at a detailed level and then later acquire an overview. This feature is important, not only in that it facilitates a particular exploration style but that it emphasizes the fact that 'overview first, then details on demand' (Shneiderman, 1996) is not the only or even at times the most desirable approach to the exploration of a data set.

Sensitivity

Excellent use is made of the domain-specific glyphs (Figure 6.2.4). If a car complies with all requirements established by clicked value bins it is represented by a *full glyph* in all the item vectors and, as mentioned earlier, can be moused-over in order to establish its location in all item vectors. All full car glyphs correspond to the set displayed at the bottom of the screen. However, if a *full glyph* appears over a value bin not yet selected it is an indication that this button's additional value restriction can be invoked without yielding a null result. An *outline glyph* identifies a car which, although it does not satisfy all requirements, would do so if the value bin below it were to be selected. This is an extremely valuable feature of EZChooser and one which is regrettably absent from many websites. If there are *no glyphs* at all over a button, other restrictions have already ruled out cars with these values. Overall, this use of item vectors to encode information reinforces comments made in Chapter 5 about the value of sensitivity cues. In that context, the labelled bins together with the glyphs constitute SM encoding and the bins encode SI.

An example is shown in Figure 6.2.5. The user has selected three favourable Consumer Guide recommendation values (row 2) and also a loaded price range (row 4). Four cars whose appearance is shown at the bottom match these restrictions and their feature values are indicated in every row by filled glyphs. Outlined glyphs in rows 2 and 4 show that the user could include those cars by selecting the bin buttons underneath the outline glyphs.

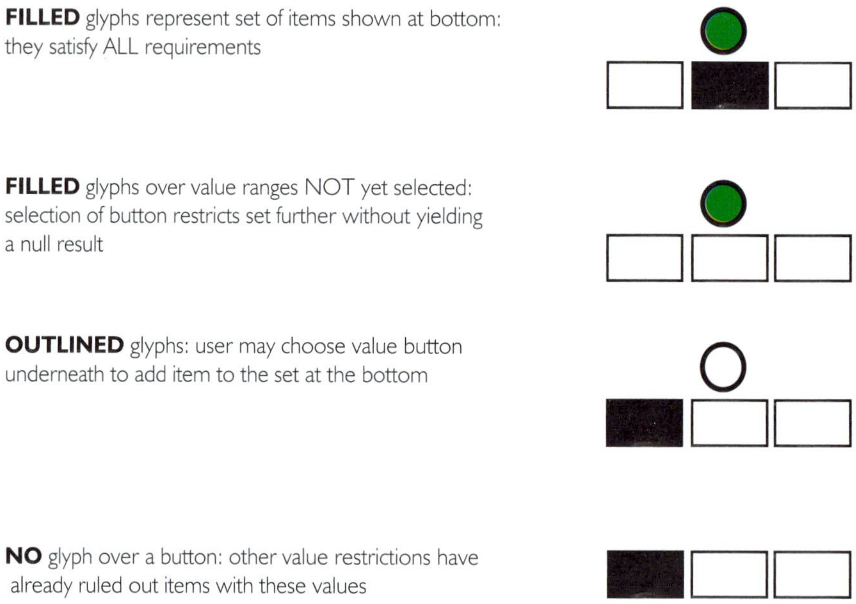

FIGURE 6.2.4
Glyph states and the information they provide

FILLED glyphs represent set of items shown at bottom: they satisfy ALL requirements

FILLED glyphs over value ranges NOT yet selected: selection of button restricts set further without yielding a null result

OUTLINED glyphs: user may choose value button underneath to add item to the set at the bottom

NO glyph over a button: other value restrictions have already ruled out items with these values

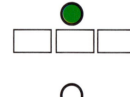

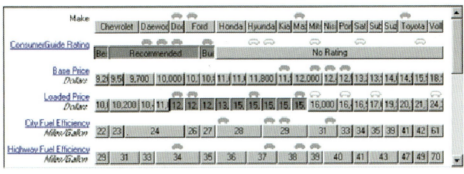

FIGURE 6.2.5
Querying with the EZChooser. A user has selected some restrictions on the set of cars. Glyphs above the rows indicate relationships among the values and guide further restrictions

Related work

After describing EZChooser it was appropriate for its developers to make a comparison with other 'query systems', though that term does not do justice to the exploration facilities and potential insight offered by an interface such as EZChooser.

Of the two other bargram-based interfaces existing at the time, one was *MultiNav* (Lanning *et al.*, 2000). Its interface can perhaps best be understood by reference to Figure 6.2.6 which illustrates the first prototype. We see a representation of three attribute values for each of 27 TV sets. Manufacturer B has been selected by clicking, thereby highlighting five objects in each of the attribute

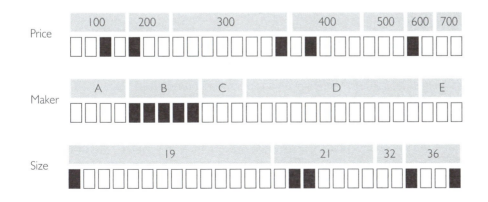

FIGURE 6.2.6
Appearance of the first MultiNav prototype. A user has clicked on Manufacturer B to highlight the corresponding products on all attribute scales

rows. While the second prototype (Figure 6.2.7) allows the same interactions, the attribute 'rods' can also be moved horizontally: in the figure a user has dragged the *Price* bar slightly to the left to bring into the central focus position a TV set costing just under $400. In response the remaining attribute 'rods' slide to bring the identified object (a 19" set from Manufacturer B) in line with that focus and the identified TV set is shown at the bottom of the screen together with more detail. Claimed advantages of MultiNav include the fact that users can observe correlations and reverse correlations by noting which rods tend to move in the same or different directions. However, a significant disadvantage is the lack of any sensitivity information that will bring a user's attention to the fact that (say) a much larger screen size becomes available if the user is prepared to spend an extra $15.

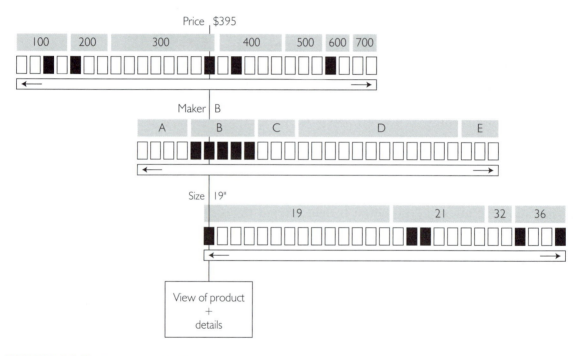

FIGURE 6.2.7 The second MultiNav prototype. A user has dragged an attribute row to position a TV costing just under $400 in the central focus position

Colleagues of the EZChooser developers carried out user tests with a view to deploying MultiNav on the Internet for consumer e-commerce applications. However, the decision to go ahead with the development of EZChooser was triggered by two usability issues associated with MultiNav. One concerned the unusual and often disconcerting sliding action which, it was felt, might be appropriate to more specialized settings but not the general user: similar dynamics are associated with the Neighbourhood Explorer (Apperley *et al.*, 2000; Spence, 2001). The other arose because, when users selected a value restriction (e.g.

Manufacturer B), they expected to see *all* valid objects at the bottom of the screen rather than just the one corresponding to the focus object. While the MultiNav technique can also be observed in the Neighbourhood Explorer, the developers of EZChooser nevertheless decided to revert to a more familiar form of interaction, namely, mouse button pressing.

The other existing system designed to support the same general task as EZChooser was *InfoZoom* (Lindner, 2000) which uses parallel bargrams for larger set sizes and focus+context tables for small ones. While it supports simple selection as well as filtering (i.e. the suppression of groups of objects), it does not include item vectors with all the advantages they offer. For example, no sensitivity information is provided, neither is the marking/tagging of objects.

The developers also provide an illuminating discussion, under the heading 'Dynamic histograms', of the advantages of coupling item vectors with bargrams: in the interests of brevity the reader is referred to the original paper (Wittenburg *et al.*, 2001, p. 57).

Evaluation

In an interesting conclusion to their discussion of EZChooser the developers conducted a preliminary evaluation by comparing it with simple tables containing the same data. Their hypothesis, confirmed by experiment, was that

> *Users prefer EZChooser over static tables for larger sets, and they are more likely to use EZChooser.*

The hypothesis that:

> *Static tables are preferable for small sets*

was not confirmed. However, the developers were quick to point out that their results were based on only two set sizes, of 3 and 50, and that many questions that spring to mind regarding the effect of set size on preference would have to wait for further research. They stress that their results are preliminary and make the interesting – and, for all developers of novel interfaces, the encouraging – comment:

> *. . . it should be noted that achieving positive results for first-time users of novel visualization systems is rare.*

Comment

In EZChooser, the developers have created an interface for the selection of one object from among many which reflects the manner in which this task is typically pursued, since it supports flexible sequencing, discovery and play. EZChooser combines the simplicity of button clicking with the potential offered by the combination of bargrams and item vectors, and crucially incorporates sensitivity information to support navigation.

Principal reference

Wittenburg, K., Lanning, T., Heinrichs, M. and Stanton, M. (2001) 'Parallel bargrams for consumer-based information exploration and choice', ACM, Proceedings of UIST '01, pp. 51–60.

Supporting references

Apperley, M.D., Spence, R. and Gutwin, C. (2000) 'The Neighbourhood Explorer', Working Paper 00/3, February, Department of Computer Science, University of Waikato, New Zealand.

Kirsch, D. (1997) 'Interactivity and multimedia interfaces', *Instructional Science*, 25, 2, pp. 79–96.

Lanning, T., Wittenburg, K., Heinrichs, M., Fyock, C. and Li, G. (2000) 'Multidimensional information visualization through sliding rods', ACM, Proceedings Conference on Advanced Visual Interfaces (AVI 2000), pp. 173–180.

Lindner, H-G. (2000) 'Knowledge reporting with InfoZoom', SAP Design Guild, Innovation Second Edition, 12/22/2000, http://www.sapdesignguild.org.

Shneiderman, B. (1996) 'The eyes have it: a task by data type taxonomy for information visualization', IEEE, Proceedings Workshop on Visual Languages '96, pp. 336–343.

Spence, R. (2001) *Information Visualization*, Harlow, Addison-Wesley,

Spence, R. and Tweedie, L. (1998) 'The Attribute Explorer: information synthesis via exploration', *Interacting with Computers*, 11, pp. 137–146.

Suchman, L.A. (1987) *Plans and Situated Actions*, Cambridge, Cambridge University Press.

Williamson, C. and Shneiderman, B. (1992) 'The Dynamic Housefinder: evaluating dynamic queries in a real estate information exploration system', ACM, Proceedings SIGIR '92, pp. 339–346

Yi, J.S., Melton, R., Stasko, J. and Jacko, J.A. (2005) 'Dust & Magnet: multivariate information visualization using a magnet metaphor', *Information Visualization*, 4, 4, pp. 239–256.

6.3 Web browsing through a keyhole

Seeking news

'Keeping up with the news' is a familiar activity and often achieved by tuning into one of many available news channels. However, it is increasingly common to view news on the display of a mobile telephone or a PDA, thereby freeing the user from any constraints on location. But the display area available on these devices is very much smaller than that on a conventional monitor, giving rise to many design challenges. An example of how they can be addressed is provided by this case study: it specifically explores the problem faced by a user who, using a PDA, wishes to assess rapidly the nature of ten or twenty news items so that one that is of interest can be selected without undue delay.

The problem

On a monitor of conventional size, a web page such as that shown in Figure 6.3.1 offers a collection of news items. Where a graphical picture and brief text constitute a link to more detail we shall refer to a 'link preview'. Without interaction (i.e. with 'passive interaction' as defined in Chapter 5) it allows the perusal of content sufficient to enable a user to choose an item of interest. If the available display area is much smaller, however, as it is with a PDA, the same approach to assessment and the formation of scent cannot take place, simply because the entire page cannot be perused without interaction of some sort.

FIGURE 6.3.1

A typical news page, with a link preview identified by the green box

One approach is to allow scrolling over the unchanged page. This is generally unacceptable in view of the time necessarily required to view content as well as navigational cues (SM and SI as introduced in Chapter 5). As well as having to engage in tedious scrolling activity the user must attempt to remember the content and cues from previously explored parts of the page.

Another approach is to avoid the need for scrolling by eliminating all or most of the graphic content of the page and providing simple textual links to news items, as shown in Figure 6.3.2. Unfortunately, pictures or icons often provide many of the principal navigational cues and their absence could severely diminish the user's ability to formulate scent sufficient to help him or her to decide which news item is relevant to his or her interest.

Not surprisingly, a number of researchers (Woodruff et al., 2001; Cockburn et al., 1999; Ayers and Stasko, 1995) have examined the benefit of using thumbnail images, in the form of reduced-size copies of target pages, to represent hyperlinks (i.e. SM and SI). Thumbnails can indeed provide powerful naviga-

FIGURE 6.3.2
The removal of graphic content to provide a complete menu in the display area, without the need for scrolling
(Courtesy Oscar de Bruijn and Chieh Hao Tong)

tional cues, but Kaasten *et al.* (2002) showed that, for them to be useful, a significant fraction of the screen area would have to be dedicated to the display of these thumbnails. With mobiles and PDAs there is simply not enough display area available.

A solution

To overcome the problems posed by small screen areas while at the same time retaining the powerful navigational cues offered by well-designed images, de Bruijn and Tong (2003) explored the potential of rapid serial visual presentation (RSVP) described in Section 4.2. Basically, instead of presenting a user with a single display containing a complete collection of link previews, those previews are instead presented *sequentially* (Figure 6.3.3). As a consequence, each link preview can now occupy the *entire* display area; indeed, roughly the same room for graphics and brief text is provided as was the case with a conventional web page (see Figure 6.3.1). This design choice is the major decision taken in this case study.

Even with the decision to explore the sequential rather than concurrent display of link previews, many problems were still faced by the investigators, most again arising from the limited display area. While the sequentially presented previews provided valuable navigational cues, other issues of navigation and interaction had to be addressed.

The application chosen as the context in which to explore the potential of RSVP is a scenario in which a user either wants to see what news is available or has a particular interest and wishes to see whether any news channel addresses that interest.

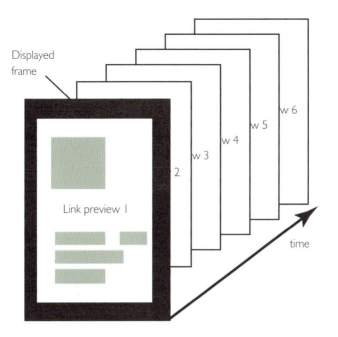

FIGURE 6.3.3
The sequential presentation of link previews, each occupying the full available display area

The RSVP Browser

The structure of the experimental system called the RSVP Browser is shown in Figure 6.3.4. In effect it provides a two-level menu system in which the available choices at each level are presented in slide-show RSVP mode rather than statically. Thus, any news item is represented by two link previews. An example of a link preview and the associated news item is shown in Figure 6.3.5. In fact, the design of each link preview need differ very little from the news item's representation on a larger screen. Indeed, as far as the user's visual processing system is concerned, the effect of a sequential presentation of the link previews of Figure 6.3.4 is very similar to that of the succession of images presented to the foveal region as the user scans a larger page such as that of Figure 6.3.1. It can in fact be argued that the sequential presentation removes the need for the user to formulate an eye-gaze strategy and provides more time for each news item to be interpreted. As de Bruijn has pointed out:

> . . . *reading content and following links are activities that can effectively be separated.*

The initial view presented to a user is a static page titled 'ITV News'. A command initiates the slide-show presentation of link previews at the first level, a presentation that continues cyclically until the user stops it at a chosen preview (B in Figure 6.3.4). After initiation, the second slide-show mode continues until stopped at the chosen news item (B2 in Figure 6.3.4), whereupon appropriate commands allow the news item to be read, and support paging if the news item extends to more than a single page.

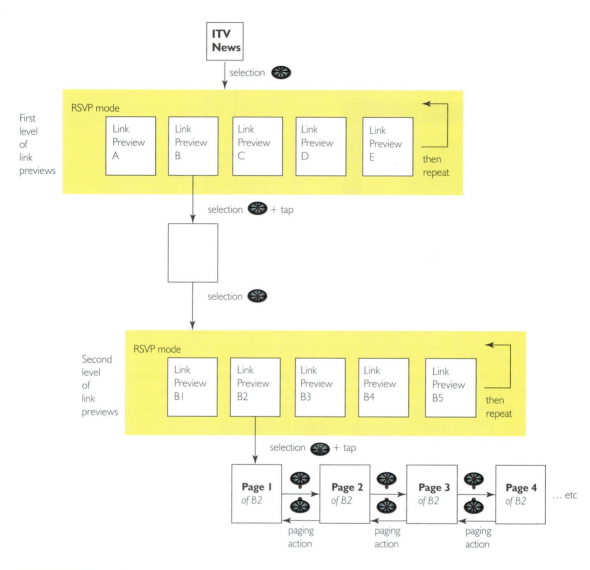

FIGURE 6.3.4 Schematic diagram of the operation of the RSVP Browser. On two levels the presentations are in slide-show mode and continue until stopped. Icons indicate the interaction required with the main control button of the PDA employed. The effect of interactions is discussed in more detail later and illustrated in Figure 6.3.7

System design

A major decision for the investigators concerned the amount of time for which each link preview should be visible. Too short a time would not enable the preview to be interpreted satisfactorily, while too long a time might be frustrating for the user. A value of half a second was chosen, a decision partly – though not wholly – justified by preferences expressed by users and discussed later in this case study.

FIGURE 6.3.5
(a) The link preview mode and (b) the page mode of a news story. The news story can contain more than one page
(Courtesy Oscar de Bruijn and Chieh Hao Tong)

Although the link previews were designed to provide powerful navigational cues, other features to enhance navigation were introduced. First, 'universe visibility' was supported by a link bar (Figure 6.3.6) containing a small rectangle for each link. To support an awareness of where in the sequence the currently displayed link preview is, the appropriate rectangle is highlighted, thereby providing some indication as to when the user might halt the sequential presen-

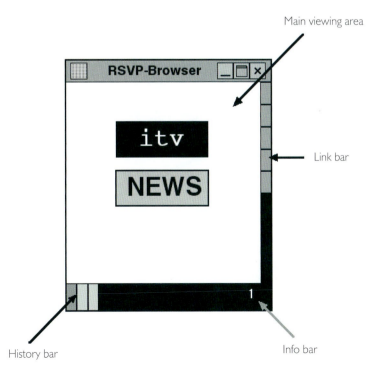

FIGURE 6.3.6
The link bar, history bar and information bar designed to assist navigation
(Courtesy Oscar de Bruijn and Chieh Hao Tong)

tation to select a desired link. Whereas link previews help to answer the question 'Where can I go from here', the developers were also well aware of the finding by Tauscher and Greenberg (1997) that a history of steps already taken provides a powerful and highly desirable navigational aid: in the RSVP Browser this information is embodied in a 'history bar' (Figure 6.3.6) in which small rectangles represent already visited pages. An information bar also provides useful navigational information: in link preview mode the bar shows the position of the currently displayed preview in the sequence, whereas in page mode it shows the position of the currently viewed page in the sequence of pages comprising a news item.

The investigators took advantage of the control buttons associated with a PDA (Figure 6.3.7) to explore the possibility of single-handed user interaction with the RSVP Browser. Most of the functionality of the final version of the Browser was accessed using the four-directional pad near the bottom of the PDA, thereby avoiding problems associated with stylus-based interaction: the latter can include the need for two-handed operation and for considerable accuracy when touching the screen.

FIGURE 6.3.7
Navigational controls of the RSVP Browser

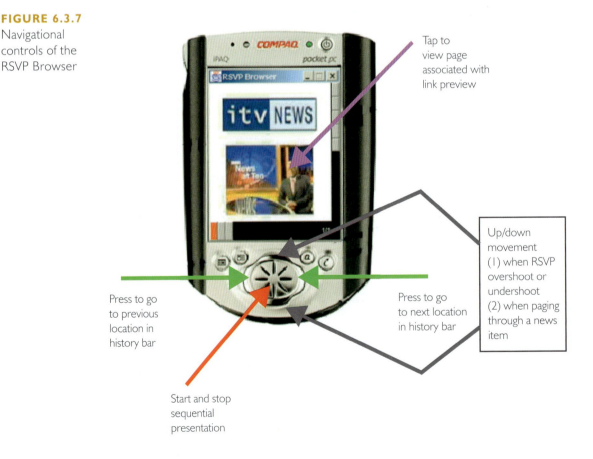

Tap to view page associated with link preview

Up/down movement (1) when RSVP overshoot or undershoot (2) when paging through a news item

Press to go to previous location in history bar

Press to go to next location in history bar

Start and stop sequential presentation

Evaluation

The RSVP Browser was evaluated by comparing it with the pocket version of the Microsoft Internet Explorer (Pocket IE), both implemented on a Compaq IPAQ PDA. Thirty subjects were involved in an experiment in which they were asked to retrieve information from a set of five news items. In this way the investigators were able to explore the RSVP interaction mode within the constraints of an existing handheld device and test it against the benchmark offered by an existing and familiar browser operating under the same constraints.

Half of the 30 subjects were randomly assigned to use the RSVP Browser and the other half to the Pocket IE. The tasks given to experimental subjects were chosen to be realistic and independent of the device to which they were assigned. Each subject answered a series of eight questions, of which a typical example is:

The cross-border train link between Belfast and Dublin has been closed after several explosions were heard near the line. Has the cause of these explosions been identified?

[Answer: No]

The procedure adopted in the evaluation is of interest (Figure 6.3.8). Initially, the subjects were given no instructions as to how to use either the RSVP Browser or the Pocket IE. This enabled the experimenters to gain some idea of the effect of a new mode of operation and to compare use at the beginning and end of a series of eight tasks. After answering the first of eight questions subjects could ask the experimenter for advice when answering questions 2 to 6. Then, for the remaining two questions, no advice was available to a subject. This scheme (Moyes and Jordan, 1993) yielded interesting insights. Video recordings were made of the actions made by subjects so that certain aspects of interaction could later be evaluated. We deal first with measurable performance and then with preferences expressed by users.

Q1	Q2 to Q6	Q7 and Q8
No instruction given	Subject could ask experimenter for advice	No advice available to subject

FIGURE 6.3.8 Advice available to subjects taking part in the experimental evaluation of the RSVP Browser

Time to solution

Not surprisingly, the time required to find the answer to the first question was an average of five times longer for the unfamiliar RSVP Browser than for the conventional Internet Explorer (Figure 6.3.9). However, following the performance of six tasks, there was no statistically significant difference between the two devices.

FIGURE 6.3.9

The average times (rounded to the nearest second) needed to answer questions 1, 7 and 8 for subjects using the RSVP Browser compared with Pocket IE

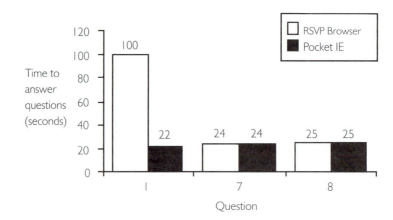

Number of steps

Figure 6.3.10 shows the number of unnecessary steps taken during the task of finding answers to questions 1, 7 and 8. An example of an unnecessary step is where an incorrect link preview is selected. What is plotted vertically is the number of unnecessary steps divided by the minimum number of steps. Again we see that familiarity acquired with earlier tasks resulted in essentially no difference between the RSVP Browser and Pocket IE in this respect.

FIGURE 6.3.10

The mean number of extra (unnecessary) steps taken by subjects in finding the answers to questions 1, 7 and 8 using either the RSVP Browser or Pocket IE

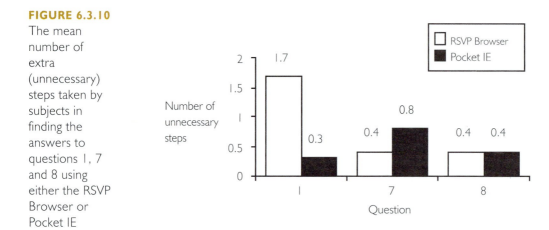

Personal preferences

As is normal in any evaluation of usability, subjects were interviewed to elicit information that cannot be measured. After finding the answers to eight questions, subjects were asked about their subjective experience of the browser they used by answering a number of questions in a questionnaire. For example, the question 'Did you find it easy to retrieve the answers to the questions?' could be answered by selecting one of the following five alternatives: 'Very easy', 'Easy', 'Indifferent', 'Difficult' and 'Very difficult'.

Participants either found the speed of the RSVP action (two per second) fast or thought it was about right (Figure 6.3.11). A presentation time of 500 ms is,

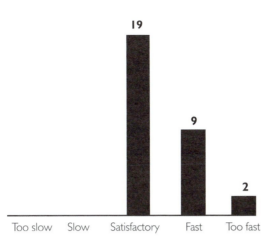

FIGURE 6.3.11
Subjects'
perception of
the speed of
the RSVP
presentation

of course, much longer than the approximate minimum of 100 ms required for the recognition of a known target (see Section 4.2) but this is to be expected since some considerable interpretation and evaluation must take place to decide which news item may be relevant to the question whose answer is sought. However, user feedback evidently suggests that 500 ms would be a minimum for the RSVP Browser. In practice, it would probably be wise to allow the user to preset their own preferred slide-show rate.

The questionnaire also revealed that more subjects who used the RSVP Browser were either confident or very confident that they knew all the functions of the browser compared with subjects who used Pocket IE.

Discussion

Both the performance measures and the subjective ratings seem to indicate that unfamiliarity with the concept underlying the RSVP Browser initially put it at a disadvantage compared with Pocket IE. That is, it appears that the Pocket IE interaction model conforms more closely to what people expect from interacting with a PDA. Nevertheless, when subjects were given time to gain experience with the RSVP Browser with or without help from the experimenter, this initial disadvantage disappeared and a number of advantages of the RSVP Browser over Pocket IE became apparent. Indeed, it seems that breaking up stories into separate pages in the RSVP Browser may significantly reduce the effort required for scrolling through text documents. Moreover, the simplicity of the interaction model underlying the RSVP Browser ensured that very little training was required to make users feel confident that they knew all the options the RSVP Browser had to offer.

Comment

As with the other case studies, a valuable aspect of the present one is that it serves to emphasize that the factors affecting design are numerous. As a consequence, at the time of writing there is still debate about the best approach to the task of viewing a web page on a PDA or mobile. At the very least the case study has shown that RSVP offers a viable alternative to the standard web browser for pocket PCs. However, the investigators acknowledge that their study leaves interesting questions to be explored.

There are other technical considerations that impinge on the feasibility of employing RSVP in the manner described, including considerations of server-client architecture and the development of web standards. The reader who wishes to dig deeper is referred to the principal reference for further details and discussion.

Principal reference

de Bruijn, O. and Tong, C.H. (2003) 'M-RSVP: mobile web browsing on a PDA', in O'Neill, E., Palanque, P. and Johnson, P. (eds) *People and Computers – Designing for Society*, London, Springer, pp. 297–311.

Supporting references

Ayers, E. and Stasko, J. (1995) 'Using graphic history in browsing the World Wide Web', in Proceedings of the 4th International WWW Conference, December.

Cockburn, A., Greenberg, S., McKenzie, B., Smith, M. and Kaasten, S. (1999) 'WebView: a graphical aid for revisiting web pages', in Proceedings OZCHI '99, November.

Kaasten, S., Greenberg, S. and Edwards, C. (2002) 'How people recognise previously seen web pages from titles, URLs and thumbnails', in *'People and Computers XVI'* (eds Faulkner, X., Finlay, F. and Detienne, F.), Proceedings HCI 2002, London, Springer, pp. 247–265.

Moyes, J. and Jordan, P.W. (1993) 'Icon design and its effect on guessability, learnability and experienced user performance', in Alty, J.L., Diaper, D. and Guest, D. (eds) *People and Computers VIII*, pp. 49–59.

Tauscher, L. and Greenberg, S. (1997) 'Revisitation: patterns in world wide web navigation', ACM, Proceedings CHI '97, pp. 399–406.

Woodruff, A., Faulring, A., Rosenholtz, R., Morrison, J. and Pirolli, P. (2001) 'Using thumbnails to search the web', ACM, Proceedings CHI 2002, pp. 198–205.

6.4 Communication analysis

Command and control

Communication is crucial to many activities and especially to the command and control of distributed safety-critical human activities such as firefighting, law enforcement and military operations. In these environments, multiple teams operate at separate locations under hazardous conditions to achieve common goals. The messages that are generated are not only essential to a successful outcome but also provide an observable trace showing how key actors performed. In this way, *communication analysis* can yield information of considerable value to the later redesign of a command and control system.

Morin and Albinsson at the Swedish Defence Research Agency created a system, called MIND, to facilitate communication analysis and have used it to support systems development, performance evaluation and training. Briefly, MIND supports two principal activities, *reconstruction* and *exploration*. The former involves several steps for constructing a multimedia model of the course of events in a distributed work session, a model that involves audio, video, photographs, statements, log files and position data from multiple sources in the operational environment. Exploration – the focus of this case study – refers to the rendering of this data in a tool that supports its explorative analysis.

System requirements

What are the requirements for such a system and what sort of questions may be asked of it? Certainly, contextual data must be preserved and be available: full understanding requires awareness, not only of the message sent but also of the *situation* in which it was sent. Contextual data must, as we saw in Chapter 4, also be available to support an analyst's navigation through a mass of data. A major problem is that of formulating – or even knowing – relevant questions to ask and suggests that queries should be dynamic. This is important when designing complex socio-technical systems where problem *setting* and problem *solving* are inherently intertwined. Often, questions cannot be anticipated, so that flexible support for analysis is required. Rapid response is also required for questions such as 'Where are the actors?', 'What are they doing?', 'What tasks have they been assigned?' and 'What is the status of the communication system?' The ability to rapidly explore the data sets and view them from different perspectives provides opportunities to both answer questions we want to ask and identify the questions we should ask.

The MIND tool

With the above and other requirements in mind, the investigators developed context-preserving methods and exploratory tools for communication analysis for the domain of emergency services and military operations, in order to identify commanders' information needs in command and control. Of particular interest in the context of this book is their choice of the Attribute Explorer discussed in Chapter 3 to support the analysis of complex and extensive communication data. The example employed below to illustrate the interface of the MIND tool is taken from a military exercise.

Exploratory analysis

Within the MIND system the Attribute Explorer facilitates the exploration of recorded communication data. This vital component of MIND is illustrated in the simple example of Figure 6.4.1, which refers to just three dimensions of some communication data. It is being used to allow examination of the communications received by a company commander *QJ* initiated by any of the other companies, as well as communication sequences that are fairly long. As shown in Figure 6.4.1, four companies have been selected in the sender dimension, *QJ* in the receiver dimension and the range from 30 seconds to 2 minutes in the

FIGURE 6.4.1
Simple illustration of the application of the Attribute Explorer technique to the study of communication system use

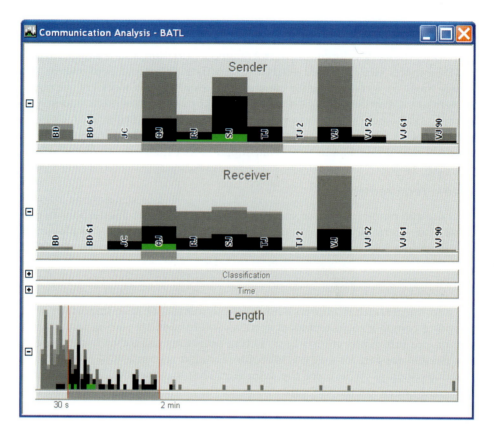

length (time duration) dimension. The green elements disclose that *RJ* and *SJ* initiated the communication and that the sequences are in the shorter half of the selected length range. Colour coding provides additional contextual hints. For example, the black elements outside the selected limits in the length dimension represent communication links that fail in this dimension only, indicating that *QJ* did receive some shorter messages as well as a few longer ones, but no considerably longer ones. Furthermore, elements in shades of light grey – for example the unit *JC* in the sender dimension – represent communication links far from a hit, which reveals that *JC* never initiated any communication to *QJ*.

Scenario

As mentioned, the Attribute Explorer is only one, albeit important, component of the MIND system, one of whose advantages is its integration of multiple representations of data. Another component representation is the node-link diagram familiar from Chapter 3. A brief description of the use of MIND in the context of a military exercise will illustrate those representations and further illustrate the advantages, for the analyst, of the Attribute Explorer.

Figure 6.4.2 shows the interface of the MIND system and illustrates how an analyst follows a company carrying out a task during a particular period of time. The period, of about half an hour, is selected in the Time dimension. By limiting the sender dimension to include only the company of current interest (*TJ*), by

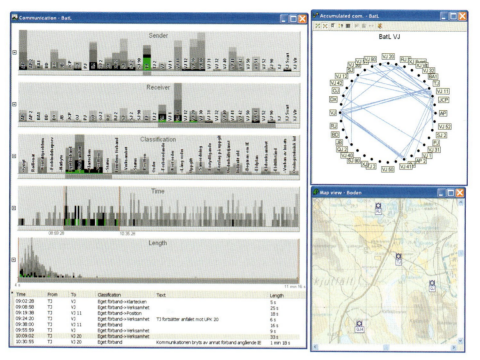

FIGURE 6.4.2
The interface of
the MIND
system
designed to
support the
analysis of
communication
behaviour

restricting the receiver dimension to include only the supervisors of *TJ* on the battalion staff, and by selecting 'reports' in the classification dimension, we see how *TJ* sent regular progress reports (represented by green elements in the time dimension). These reports are immediately accessible in the list of hits at the lower left part of the MIND interface, enabling the analyst to review and replay the original communication as well as synchronizing other MIND views to a specific communication. The interface also provides a map view of the geographical situation at the time of the selected communication. A node-link view at top right shows the accumulated report communication at the time of the selected communication. The Attribute Explorer provides other hints as well. For example, *TJ* reported only to its supervisors (three of them), which is clear from the fact that there are no black elements outside the limits of the receiver dimension. Moreover, *TJ* initiated only report communication during the selected time period, since there are no black elements outside the applied limits in the classification dimension. Examining the length dimension we also see that all reports were short except for one that was considerably longer: that link represents a concluding summary report of the company's progress.

Conclusion

The use of many such interactive displays of captured data (Albinsson *et al.*, 2003) allowed the defence authorities to identify information and support needs for commanders. The investigators valued the opportunity not only to find answers to existing questions but also to identify questions that should be asked, a feature of considerable importance when designing complex socio-technical systems where problem setting and problem solving are inherently intertwined.

They also pointed out that an annotated version of the data set can be used as a teaching tool.

The MIND framework has been welcomed as a helpful tool and is under constant development. One aspect of such future development is the potential for more powerful coordination between different views of data. With any development, of course, evaluation is always a consideration. However, the view expressed by the developers of the Attribute Explorer component of MIND makes the point that formal evaluations of the Explorer – to compare it with other techniques – could be a non-trivial task and hard to make ecologically relevant. 'Instead of trying to rationally figure out if the approach is *ideal* or *true*, we make use of the fact that it is *real* and let the ongoing use provide insight into ends as well as means', (Albinsson *et al.*, 2003).

Principal references

Albinsson, P-A., Morin, M. and Fransson, J. (2003) 'Finding information needs in military command and control systems using exploratory tools for communication analysis', Proceedings of the 47th Annual Meeting of the Human Factors and Ergonomics Society, Santa Monica, CA, The Human Factors and Ergonomics Society, pp. 1918–1922.

Morin, M. and Albinsson, P-A. (2005) 'Exploration and context in communication analysis', in Bowers, C., Salas, E. and Jentsch, F. (eds) *Creating High-Tech Teams: Practical Guidance on Work Performance and Technology*, Washington, DC, APA Press, pp. 89–112.

6.5 Archival galaxies

Large collections of documents

There are many large collections of documents which users would like to explore or search according to some precise, vague or even unarticulated criterion. They range from personal collections of articles to the archives maintained by news organizations for the benefit of journalists. It was for the latter purpose that a visualization tool known as InfoSky was designed and implemented by a team drawn from the Know-Center Graz, Hyperwave and Graz University of Technology, all in Graz, Austria.

The aim of this case study is to illustrate the value of information visualization for the exploration and searching of document collections and to draw attention to the value of specialized algorithms to organize data spatially. As with the other case studies it is our intention to show how the nature of a task influences the design of a visualization tool.

Background and requirements

The type of archive envisaged by the designers of InfoSky is exemplified by the one that was first used to demonstrate the system (Andrews *et al.*, 2002). It is a collection of 109,000 German-language news articles already manually classified into 6,900 collections and sub-collections and arranged in a hierarchical structure up to 15 levels deep.

The InfoSky system had to satisfy the following principal requirements:

- *Scalability*: it should be possible easily to visualize hierarchically structured repositories containing hundreds of thousands and even millions of documents.

- *Hierarchy plus similarity*: it is desirable to represent not only the relationships between documents implicit in their hierarchical organization but, additionally, other similarities between individual documents not accounted for in the hierarchical organization.

- *Focus+Context*: it is desirable to integrate, smoothly, both a global and a local view of the information space.

- *Stability*: a stable metaphor should be used to promote visual recall and the recognition of features. The representation should remain largely unchanged at a global level even if changes occur to the underlying document repository at a local level.

- *Exploration*: Interactions involved in both browsing and searching the repository should be intuitive.

Earlier work

About a decade before InfoSky was envisaged, a number of innovative schemes were proposed for the exploration and search of a collection of documents. Although it is unsurprising in view of their early emergence that they did not satisfy all the requirements imposed on InfoSky, it is nevertheless instructive to examine those schemes to establish their principal features.

- *BEAD* (Chalmers, 1993) – documents are automatically clustered according to their keywords and these clusters are then displayed in a 2.5D landscape with meta keywords indicating categories (Figure 6.5.1). No manual classification is involved and no advantage is taken of any hierarchical relationships: the raw data is an unstructured repository.

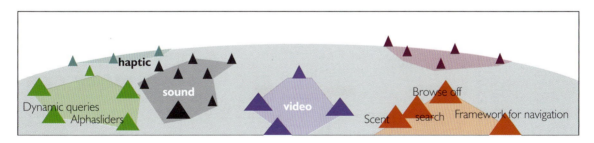

FIGURE 6.5.1 A landscape representation of data about a collection of documents

- *SPIRE* (Wise *et al.,* 1995) is illustrated in Figure 6.5.2. Documents which are 'close' in high-dimensional thematic space are automatically transformed to be close in 2D space, with theme strength indicated by elevation. Again, the operations are performed on flat, unstructured repositories; any hierarchical relations that might exist are not exploited.

FIGURE 6.5.2
A themescape
representation
of 700 articles
related to the
financial
industry

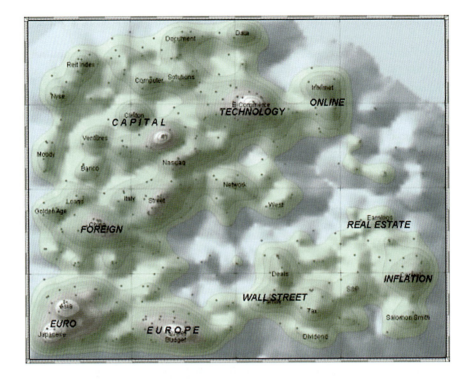

FIGURE 6.5.3
A hyperbolic
browser
representation
of a
hierarchically
ordered
collection of
documents

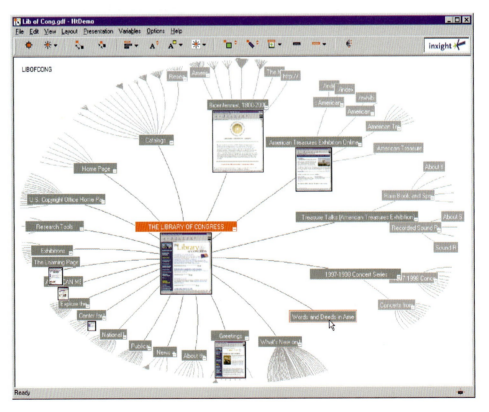

- The *hyperbolic browser* (Lamping and Rao, 1994) has been discussed in Chapter 3 (Figure 3.98, reproduced as Figure 6.5.3). It offers an interactive representation of a hierarchical system, permits smooth exploration and directed movement within the hierarchy and, as a result of the distortion involved, allows the user to focus on a selected region of the tree while keeping sight of the context. Except for any *a priori* hierarchical organization, no account is automatically taken of content or keywords or other relationships between documents. No search facility is offered, though it could be incorporated.

- The *cone tree* (Robertson *et al.*, 1991), discussed in Chapter 3 (Figure 6.5.4), compactly represents a hierarchical system. There is, however, no means of focusing on regions of interest. Apart from the hierarchy, no account is taken of content or keywords or other relationships between documents. It supports interaction and a search facility is incorporated.

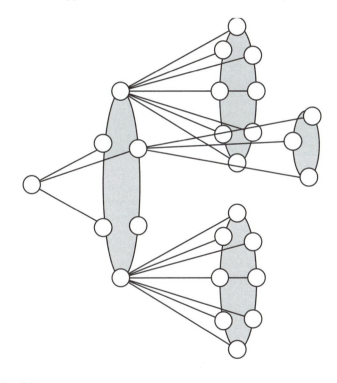

FIGURE 6.5.4
The cone tree, tilted to allow the text associated with each node to be readable. Selective distortion could be applied to allow focus on any part

Design decisions

With the above requirements in mind, the major decision made by the designers was to employ the metaphor of a *galaxy of stars* to represent the repository and its component documents; further, to employ the related metaphor of a *telescope* so that variable magnification, enhanced by *semantic zoom*, can facilitate exploration of the galaxy at any level of detail.

The top view of the galaxy is shown in Figure 6.5.5, with each star representing a document. The galaxy illustrated in this case study is derived from a collection of approximately 109,000 German-language news articles from the German daily newspaper *Süddeutsche Zeitung*. The articles have been classified thematically by the newspaper's editorial staff into around 6,900 collections and sub-collections up to 15 levels deep.

FIGURE 6.5.5
View of the entire galaxy, showing collection boundaries and titles at the top level

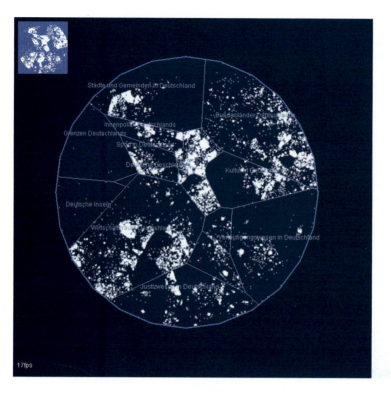

Visible in Figure 6.5.5 are the major collection titles (e.g. *Bundesländer Deutschlands*) forming the top level of the hierarchy. The corresponding sub-collections lie within the piecewise-linear boundaries. The structure is the same all the way down the hierarchy. For example, in Figure 6.5.6 the collection *Bundesländer Deutschlands* has been selected, prompting the segments within that collection to be centred in the display and the names of those segments to be displayed (e.g. *Bayern*). Selection of *Bayern* and a subsequent mouse-hover over *Wirtschaftsraum Bayern* highlights that collection (Figure 6.5.7): selection then displays the appropriately centred next level of the hierarchy as shown in Figure 6.5.8. This sequence can continue until document titles are eventually reached (Figure 6.5.9).

Interaction and search

Interaction with the galaxy is simple and consistent at all levels. A left mouse click on a collection title leads to semantic zoom to the next lower level, while a right mouse click reverses that zoom. Holding down the left mouse button causes continuous semantic zoom and allows users to reach a known position more quickly, an action that is helped by the fact that at each level of the hierarchy collections are contained within piecewise linear boundaries whose distinctive shapes make them easier to remember.

On receipt of a keyword, a search facility will highlight in yellow both relevant regions and relevant documents (Figure 6.5.10): the latter pulsate to provide differentiation. In this way search results can be viewed in context.

FIGURE 6.5.6
View of the
sub-collection
*Bundesländer
Deutschlands*

FIGURE 6.5.7
The result of
clicking on the
title *Bayern* in
Figure 6.5.6.
The mouse
now hovers
over
*Wirtschaftsraum
Bayern*

FIGURE 6.5.8
The result of
selecting
*Wirtschaftsraum
Bayern*

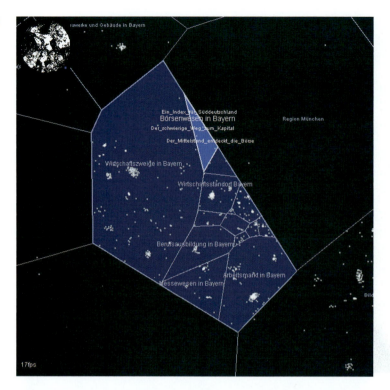

FIGURE 6.5.9
At the lowest
level titles are
visible

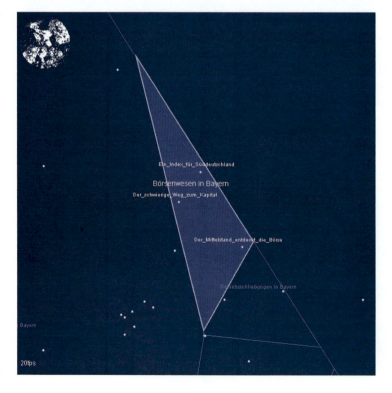

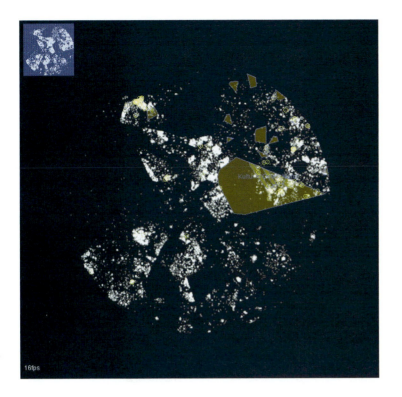

FIGURE 6.5.10
Highlighting of both relevant regions and documents follows the entry of a keyword

Layout

The piecewise-linear boundaries defining the collections at each level of the hierarchy (Figure 6.5.11) are determined by two factors. The size of each polygonal region is proportional to the number of subordinate documents in that collection. The position of the centroid of each region is influenced by the similarity between the documents within the sub-collections.

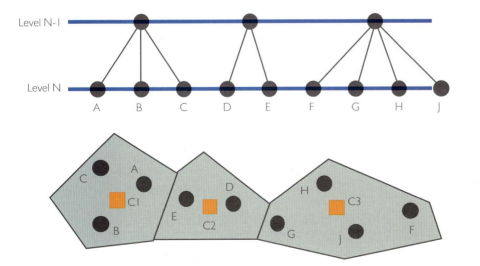

FIGURE 6.5.11
Representation of collections at two levels of the hierarchy and, for the lower level, the layout of the collections (A, B, C, etc.) and their centroids (C1, C2, C3)

There are many algorithms that can compute the similarity between documents according to a specific criterion and others that can determine the piecewise-linear boundaries. In the present case study our principal intention in this respect is to draw the reader's attention to the fact that such algorithms, as well as the skill with which they are selected and applied, can exert considerable influence on the quality of a visualization tool. For the detailed nature of the algorithms the reader is referred to the principal reference.

Evaluation

The prototype InfoSky visualization tool was first formally evaluated by comparing its use with a conventional tree viewer whose appearance at the top level is shown in Figure 6.5.12.

FIGURE 6.5.12

Appearance of the conventional tree viewer at the top level

Deutschland
 Deutschland(stars)
 Kultur in Deutschland
 Bildungswesen in Deutschland
 Bundesländer Deutschlands
 Innenpolitik Deutschlands
 Wirtschaftsraum Deutschland
 Forschungsstandort Deutschland
 Justizwesen in Deutschland
 Städte und Gemeinden in Deutschland
 Soziales Leben in Deutschland
 Kriminalität in Deutschland
 Kirche und Religion in Deutschland
 Außenpolitik Deutschlands
 Alltagsleben in Deutschland
 Gesundheitswesen in Deutschland
 Verteidigungswesen in Deutschland
 Sozialstruktur in Deutschland
 Deutsche Geschichte
 Natur und Umwelt in Deutschland
 Verkehrswesen in Deutschland
 Katastrophen und Unglücke in Deutschland
 Öffentliche Verwaltung in Deutschland
 Sport in Deutschland
 Statistik in Deutschland
 Grenzen Deutschlands
 Landschaften in Deutschland
 Deutsche Inseln
 Seen und Flüsse in Deutschland

Eight subjects were divided randomly into two groups and were each invited to perform two equivalent sets of five tasks using both the InfoSky tool (called the Telescope browser TS) and the Tree Viewer (TV). They were not allowed to use the browsers concurrently, neither could they make use of the search facility. Two sets, each of two subjects, employed TS first and TV second; the other two sets used the browsers in the reverse order. The two sets of tasks were designed to be equivalent in the sense that their solutions lay at the same level of the hierarchy and involved approximately the same number of choices at each level. Again, the order in which the two sets of tasks were undertaken was evenly distributed over the sets of subjects and browsers. Two minutes of introduction to the Telescope Browser were provided before the experiment. The actions of the subjects were videotaped and interviews took place after the tasks were performed. The time taken to locate a solution to each task was recorded.

Of the 80 task solutions (8 subjects, 2 sets of 5 tasks), allowing 40 comparisons of the task completion time, only in 8 cases was the solution found more rapidly with the Telescope browser. On average, the Tree browser performed better than the prototype Telescope browser for each of the tasks tested and this difference was statistically significant ($p<0.05$). The average time taken for task solution with the Telescope browser ranged from 36 per cent to 186 per cent greater than for the Tree browser.

The developers point to two principal reasons for the apparently disappointing performance of the Telescope browser. First, subjects had had many hours of experience in the past with traditional tree browsers and had become familiar with their metaphors and controls. The developers pointed out that, in comparison, 'two minutes' training could not make up the deficit'. Second, the Telescope browser was at a fairly early stage of development, with numerous bugs and issues affecting usability. Examples included small polygon sizes and 'jumping titles'.

The results of the evaluation should *not* call into question the inherent value of the galaxy and telescope metaphor, for many reasons. First, it was a prototype that was evaluated. Second, its use involved unfamiliar controls and metaphors. Third, the tasks did not test the value of the Telescope browser for finding related or similar documents or sub-collections. Fourth, the search facility was not provided to subjects. And fifth, concurrent use of the two browsers was not permitted in the evaluation. In view of all these constraints, the evaluation results are far from discouraging and the galaxy+telescope metaphor could eventually become a preferred method for browsing and searching large hierarchical collections of documents. The encouraging results of more recent evaluations can be found in the supporting references of Granitzer *et al.* and Kappe *et al.*

Principal reference

Andrews, K., Kienreich, W., Sabol, V., Becker, J., Droschl, G., Kappe, F., Granitzer, M., Auer, P. and Tochtermann, K. (2002) 'The InfoSky visual explorer: exploiting hierarchical structure and document similarity', *Information Visualization*, 1, 3/4, pp. 166–181.

Supporting references

Chalmers, M. (1993) 'Using a landscape metaphor to represent a corpus of documents', in 'Spatial information theory – a theoretical basis for GIS',

Proceedings of the European Conference COSIT '93, Springer-Verlag, Lecture Notes in Computer Science, pp. 377–388.

Granitzer, M., Kienreich, W., Sabol, V., Andrews, K. and Klieber, W. (2004) 'Evaluating a system for interactive exploration of large, hierarchically structured document repositories', IEEE, Proceedings InfoVis 2004, pp. 127–133.

Kappe, F., Droschl, G., Kienreich, W., Sabol, V., Becker, J., Andrews, K., Granitzer, M., Tochtermann, K. and Auer, P. (2003) 'InfoSky: visual exploration of large hierarchical document repositories', Lawrence Erlbaum Associates, Proceedings HCI International 2003, pp. 1268–1272.

Lamping, J. and Rao, R. (1994) 'Laying out and visualising large trees using a hyperbolic space', ACM, Proceedings UIST '94, pp. 13–14.

Robertson, G.G., Mackinlay, J.D. and Card, S.K. (1991) 'Cone trees: animated 3D visualizations of hierarchical information', ACM, Proceedings CHI '91, pp. 189–194.

Wise, J.A., Thoma, J.J., Pennock, K., Lantrip, D., Pottier, M., Schur, A. and Crow, V. (1995) 'Visualising the non-visual: spatial analysis and interaction with information from text documents', IEEE, Proceedings InfoVis '95, pp. 51–58.

Exercises

The value of these projects can be enhanced by having the outcomes presented in open class

Each of the following design exercises will involve about five days of full-time work by a group of three or four students. The objective is *not* to test programming skills but rather to consider a (possibly somewhat ill-defined) commission, decide the nature of the user(s) and the tasks, identify the design issues, make major decisions about a possible design and then describe that design. Continuous creative design and evaluation will be involved. Brain-storming and the production of many intermediate (hand) sketches (preferably maintained in constant view as in a real design house) are encouraged. An intermediate requirement is the *oral presentation* (with questions) by the group of progress to date (after about two or three days of design). The final requirement is an account of the group's work in *four pages* (no more) in ACM conference format: no additional appendices or figures or print-outs are allowed. The projects emphasize the use of information visualization, but not to the exclusion of other issues: they place information visualization in context.

◼ Design 1 Flower power

A company which owns a number of garden centres is considering whether to make it possible for customers to explore the products on offer via a large touch screen-operated display. Most of its customers have very little knowledge of plants and bushes or of the conditions necessary for their optimum growth. The company would like to see one or more possible designs for such an interface.

◼ Design 2 What's interesting?

Design a means of providing, on a PDA display, information about local services within a specifiable distance from the location of the PDA. Assume the PDA is fitted with a GPS or European satellite navigation system.

◼ Design 3 Rail travel

Select a major rail station. Design a printed display of train times to facilitate fast acquisition of travel information.

■ Design 4 Find that photo

Most people possess a huge number of photographs and it is rare for them to be classified in any way except possibly by date. Finding one to show to a friend is difficult. Design an interface to support such a search. It can be for a mobile, a PDA or a standard monitor and an assumption can be made that pictures taken will be automatically classed according to date and location (via GPS). Recollections such as 'it was in Italy last summer . . .' should be considered.

■ Design 5 Journal search

Given a research question in (say) biology, there are many scientific papers that could be relevant to one or more keywords and those keywords could be entered and removed according to their perceived relevance and the number of papers identified. Devise an interface to support the researcher.

■ Design 6 Postgraduate study

Anyone contemplating postgraduate study must visit a large number of websites in order to come to some conclusion regarding universities to which a first approach might be made. Suggest a design for a website directed at such a person.

■ Design 7 Travel by bus

In a major city such as London a bus ride can be a very pleasant way of travelling between one location and another. The major question is 'Which bus?' and the answer – especially where a change from one bus route to another is involved – is often difficult to find. Devise a bus map (for the centre of London, New York, Paris – the choice is yours) that will help the visitor to find a suitable bus route. It may be best to test your initial ideas with a small and fictitious city and to see how your ideas scale up.

■ Design 8 Online shopping

A store that sells home furnishings (tables, chairs, beds, bookcases, carpets, lighting, etc.) requires a website to be designed so that customers can decide what purchases they wish to make. Suggest a possible design for that website.

■ Design 9 The Web on a mobile

Web pages are large compared with the display area of a mobile. Also, there is usually no direct interaction device (such as a stylus) available with a mobile. Design a scheme that will allow web pages to be satisfactorily viewed and acted upon using a mobile or a PDA.

■ Design 10 Email records and their exploration

Most users of email possess records of received and sent emails stretching back over a long time. First, make a list of tasks that the owner of such a record might want to undertake (aim for about ten) and the questions they might ask. Then, design an interactive representation of such records to support those tasks and questions as well as others that occur during the design.

■ Design 11 Mobiles for very young children

Consider the possible advantages and disadvantages of making some type of mobile phone available for children between three and five years old and suggest some possible designs.

Glossary

Key:
Dict = dictionary definition
IV = definition in context of information visualization

attribute (page 17)

Dict: a quality or characteristic belonging to a person or thing.

attribute visibility (dimension visibility) (page 59)

IV: representation of data such that the distribution of objects' attribute values in each attribute dimension is clear.

breadcrumb trail (page 163)

IV: representation of a path already traversed in discrete information space. (*Often loosely applied to paths that could be traversed.*)

browse (page 142)

Dict: [www.etymonline.com] 'peruse'.
IV: an activity involving the (usually visual) perception, interpretation and evaluation of content, including navigational cues.

Typically involves eye-gaze movement both during the perusal of a static display and during the perusal of a sequence of displays.

Browsing can be qualified according to the underlying intent or absence of such. It may be *opportunistic* (where content is unknown), *exploratory* (with a view to forming a mental model of some space) or, in a special case where it is undirected, *involuntary*.

brushing (page 30)

IV: a change in the encoding of one or more items essentially immediately following, and in response to, an interaction with another item.

conceptual short-term memory (page 130)

IV: a model of the human sensory system accounting for performance during a period of up to one second from an initial stimulus.

derived value (page 30)

IV: one or more values derived from an existing set of values.
Example: average, variance.

detail (n) (page 18)

IV: information about a number of attributes of a single member of a set.

dynamic query (page 154)

IV: an interface in which a continuous manual adjustment of one or more data values results responsively (e.g. well within one second) in a visual representation of some function(s) of those data values.

exploration (page 151)

IV: navigation and browsing undertaken solely with the aim of forming a mental model of part or all of an information space.

fixation (page 125)

Dict: the dwelling of eye-gaze on an essentially fixed point.

glyph (page 69)

IV: a graphical object designed to convey multiple data values (Ware, 2004, p. 145).

insight (page 5)

IV: an enhancement of an internal model of some data (could involve additions to or removals from an internal model). Understanding.

navigation (page 25)

IV: directed movement in discrete or continuous information space.

object visibility (page 59)

> IV: the representation of an object as a single coherent visual entity so that its attributes are clear.

overview (n): (page 19)

> IV: the assessment of one or more attributes of a set of objects. Concerns the acquisition of knowledge about metadata or scope. There is often an implication that the assessment is rapid and preferably pre-attentive. The assessment could be conscious or unconscious (pre-attentive).

pre-attentive processing (page 47)

> IV: perceptual and cognitive processing that occurs prior to conscious attention (Ware, 2004, p. 149).

presentation (page 98)

> Dict: to offer to view: display.
> IV: the selection of encoded data and its layout on a display.

pursuit (page 151)

> IV: a navigational step undertaken with the sole aim of enhancing some aspect of movement towards a target.

relation (page 71)

> Dict: a logical or natural association between two or more things; relevance of one to another; connection.

represent (page 29)

> Dict: to depict, portray.
> Dict: to present clearly to the mind.
> IV: to encode data in visual, aural or any other sensory medium.

residue (page 156)

> IV: an indication of distant content in the SM encoding.

saccade (page 125)

> Dict: ballistic movements of the eye.

scent (page 160)

> IV: the perceived benefit associated with a movement in information space, evaluated following interpretation of one or more cues.

search (page 137)

Dict: to make an examination in order to find something.

Search is directed and associated with a specific target. Within informatics the word often implies an *automatic* search carried out by a machine. If carried out by a human being it could involve one or more forms of browsing and navigation.

sensitivity (page 151)

IV: a movement in discrete information space and the interaction required to achieve it.

suppression (page 22)

IV: removal from view of a representation of data, according to some automatic or manually chosen criterion.

tree (page 84)

IV: a network of nodes and links containing no loops.

visualization tool (page 8)

IV: a software system, usually involving a visual display, which allows a user to interact with and change the view of some data with a view to forming a mental model of that data.

visualize (page 5)

Dict: to form a mental model of something.

wayfinding (page 151)

IV: a combination of exploration and pursuit.

Appendix – Videos

Short videos (e.g. <5mins) and video clips (from 10 to 30 seconds) can lend very effective support to the teaching of information visualization.

The titles of 37 freely available videos and clips, all provided on the DVD accompanying this book, are listed below. Then, separately for each clip, the chapter within *Information Visualization* (Spence, 2007) to which the clip is relevant is stated and a relevant journal reference is given. There follows its format, file size and duration, as well as a discussion of the background to each video, the action that is to be seen and, briefly, the concepts that are illustrated.

V1   Qualitative Representation
V2   Dynamic Exploration of Relationships
V3   Encoding by Sound: a Brain Tumour
V4   Visualization 2020AD
V5   Attribute Explorer
V6   Attribute Explorer: a Short Demo
V7   Infocanvas
V8   Interactive Venn Diagram
V9   The Cone Tree
V10   FundExplorer
V11   Bifocal Display I
V12   Bifocal Display II

VI Qualitative Representation

Chapter 3(1)

Spence, R. and Drew, A. (1971) 'Graphical exploration in electrical circuit design and modelling', NRC, Ottawa, Proceedings 2nd Man-Computer Communications Seminar, pp. 61–70.

QuickTime Movie, 14.9 MB, 60 seconds (silent at first, then with sound)

Background

MINNIE is an interactive-graphic computer-aided design system facilitating the design of electronic circuits. It was created in 1968 and became a commercial product in 1985. The video dates to circa 1973.

Action

The size of each circle is a measure of the effect, on some property of an electronic circuit (here, its amplification), of small changes in the component on which the circle is superimposed. At any moment the display refers to one frequency in the range from bass to treble. Animation appropriately changes the circle sizes as an indicator (on right) moves through the frequency range from bass to treble.

Illustrates

Representation by size, especially where qualitative insight is important; the use of animation to handle an additional dimension (here, frequency).

Notes

A designer finds such sensitivity information extremely useful when deciding what component value to change if the circuit's performance is unacceptable. Also, since the designer probably has an *a priori* idea about the effect of each component, any departure from this (e.g. a large circle where a small one is expected) has a useful educational effect.

V2 Dynamic Exploration of Relationships

Chapter 1

Spence, R. and Apperley, M.D. (1974) 'On the use of interactive graphics in circuit design', IEEE, Proceedings of the International Symposium on Circuits and Systems, pp. 558–563.

QuickTime Movie 3.5 MB, 38 seconds (silent)

Background

There are many occasions when an engineering designer can benefit immensely by being able to explore the relationship between some property of the artefact that is being designed and a single parameter whose value must be chosen. The designer's mental model of the relationship can be enhanced if the designer can manually vary the parameter value and immediately see the effect on the artefact's property.

Action

The clip, converted from a film (ca 1974) of the MINNIE CAD system for electronic circuit design, shows an electronic circuit designer exploring, interactively, the relation between the performance of an electronic circuit and the value of a component, by adjusting the value of that component continuously.

Illustrates

Responsive interaction; dynamic querying.

V3 Encoding by Sound: A Brain Tumour

Courtesy Institute for Visualization and Perception Research, University of Massachusetts, Lowell, USA.

Chapter 3(1).

QuickTime Movie, 15.8 MB, 1 minute 14 seconds

Background

The term 'visualization' is usually interpreted, though incorrectly, to imply the sole use of visual images to represent data. Such use is indeed very common, but it is also possible to encode data by sound.

Action

The video demonstrates the encoding of data in sound in the context of the exploration of a brain scan. As a cursor is moved between different parts of the brain, the skull and a tumour, distinctive sonorities convey appropriate information.

Illustrates

The encoding of data by sound.

V4 Visualization 2020AD

Chapter 3(1).

Spence, R. (1995) 'Visions of design', *Journal of Engineering Design*, 6, 2, pp. 125–137.

QuickTime Movie, 9.88 MB, 45 seconds

Background

In 1995, 12 eminent engineering designers were asked for their visions regarding the way engineering design would be carried out 25 years later, in the year 2020. The visions were presented via a video showing a dinner party taking place in the year 2020, during which leading engineering designers of that year describe how they undertake design. One common vision had to do with the visualization of data, using large displays, collaborative working and the use of sound to encode data.

Action

Three designers involved in engineering design interact with visually and aurally presented data.

Illustrates

Collaborative working; visual and aural encoding of data.

 # V5 Attribute Explorer

Chapter 3(1)

Spence, R. and Tweedie, L. (1998) 'The Attribute Explorer: information synthesis via exploration', *Interacting with Computers*, 11, pp. 137–146.

QuickTime Movie, 36.8 MB, 3 minutes 32 seconds

Background

There are many situations in which a user must select one object from among many on the basis of the values of a number of attributes. Typical examples include house and car purchase and the selection of a mobile phone to buy.

Action

For all objects, each attribute is displayed in the form of a histogram and limits can be placed on an attribute to select a range and, consequently, the objects for which the attribute lies within the chosen range. When more than one attribute is explored, the histograms are linked so that a selection based on one attribute is 'brushed' into the other histograms. Through interaction with the attribute limits the user can form a mental model of the data and gradually whittle down the large number of objects to one or a few worth further and more detailed examination.

Illustrates

Dynamic querying by direct manipulation; colour-encoded sensitivity to guide the user, especially in a 'zero hits' situation; the fact that a user will typically not be familiar with the data and will therefore initially (qualitatively) explore to form a mental model before making a quantitative decision concerning objects worthy of further examination.

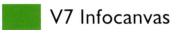

V6 Attribute Explorer: a Short Demo

Chapter 3(1)

Spence, R. and Tweedie, L. (1998) 'The Attribute Explorer: information synthesis via exploration', *Interacting with Computers*, 11, pp.137–146.

QuickTime Movie, 72.2 MB, 1 minute 35 seconds (silent)

Background

There are many situations in which a user must select one object from among many on the basis of the values of a number of attributes. Typical examples include house and car purchase and the selection of a mobile phone to buy.

Action

This short clip (without sound) shows some of the major features of the Attribute Explorer.

Illustrates

Some major features of the Attribute Explorer; colour-coded sensitivity information.

V7 Infocanvas

Courtesy John Stasko.

Chapter 3(1)

Miller, T. and Stasko, J. (2001) 'Information conveyance through personalised, expressive art', ACM, Proceedings CHI '01, pp. 305–306.

MPEG movie, 70.8 MB, 6 minutes 37 seconds

Background

There is often some information that a user might wish to refer to quite frequently without the need to do more than simply glance at a display: traffic conditions, the weather, stock prices, breaking news.

Action

The solution offered is to create, from a conventional monitor, a wall-hanging display in which information of interest is portrayed artistically within an attractive scene.

Illustrates

Artistic encoding of frequently but casually accessed data.

V8 Interactive Venn Diagram

Courtesy Ron Bird and Ken Chahhawata.

Chapter 3(2)

Quicktime Movie, 15.1 MB, 58 seconds (silent)

Background

A Venn diagram need not be static: it can benefit considerably if it is interactive, allowing a user to flexibly explore the data.

When an interaction designer must convey an interface design to a client, much time can be saved if an animated presentation – *not* a fully implemented application – can be shown, especially since considerable modification to the design might well be suggested.

Action

The video illustrates, in a financial context, a design in which interaction allows Venn diagram representations of a body of data to be flexibly examined.

Illustrates

Venn diagrams; the use of an animated sketch when presenting a first proposed design to a client.

V9 The Cone Tree

Courtesy of Stu Card.

Chapter 3(2) and 5(6)

Robertson, G.G., Mackinlay, J.D. and Card, S.K. (1991) 'Cone trees: animated 3D visualizations of hierarchical information', ACM, Proceedings CHI '95, pp. 189–194.

Quicktime Movie, 10.5 MB, 1 minute 5 seconds

Background

The representation of hierarchically structured data by means of a tree has the drawback that, as soon as the tree becomes realistically large, it is difficult to display it in its entirety on a conventional display. The cone tree offers a solution to this problem. All nodes subordinate to a given node are arranged in a circle underneath it, the corresponding links thereby identifying a cone. Such a conceptual 3D arrangement, viewed on a 2D display, is called a cone tree.

Action

When a query is entered to identify one node of a tree, all cones revolve in such a way as to bring the relevant node to the fore. Most importantly, when another node is identified, the new view of the cone tree does not appear immediately: animation lasting about one second ensures a smooth transition between the two views, thereby helping to maintain the user's mental model of the tree.

Illustrates

A means of presenting hierarchically structured data; the use of animation to help preserve a mental model during a transition between two views.

V10 FundExplorer

Courtesy John Stasko.

Chapter 3(2)

Csallner, C., Handte, M., Lehmann, O. and Stasko, J. (2003) 'FundExplorer: supporting the diversification of mutual fund portfolios using context treemaps', IEEE, Proceedings of Information Visualization 2003, pp. 203–208.

MPEG movie, 87.8 MB, 3 minutes 57 seconds

Background

An equity mutual fund is a financial instrument that invests in a set of stocks. Any two different funds may partially invest in some of the same stocks, so that overlap is common.

Action

The video describes a system called FundExplorer that implements a distorted treemap to allow a user to explore both the amount of money invested and the context of remaining market stock. The system allows people to interactively explore diversification possibilities with their portfolios.

Illustrates

Treemaps; interactive exploration; context.

 V11 Bifocal Display I

Chapter 4(1)

Spence, R. and Apperley, M.D. (1982) 'Data base navigation: an office environment for the professional', *Behaviour and Information Technology*, 1, 1, pp. 43–54.

QuickTime Movie, 2.78 MB, 13 seconds

Background

The Bifocal Display, invented in 1980, was arguably the first demonstration of the use of distortion to provide a focus+context view of an electronic information space. A user can focus on (e.g. read) one or two documents and, at the same time, have an overall view of the whole of the information space.

Action

The video (quality dates from 1980) shows a simulation of the scrolling action which brings a desired item from the distorted region into the focus region.

Illustrates

Focus+context; distortion; smooth transition from distortion to focus region.

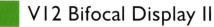 V12 Bifocal Display II

Chapter 4(1)

Spence, R. and Apperley, M.D. (1982) (as for V11 Bifocal Display I)

QuickTime Movie, 12.2 MB, 60 seconds

Background

As for V11 (Bifocal Display I).

Action

A demonstration, using a paper representation of information space, of the concept of the Bifocal Display.

Illustrates

As for V11 (Bifocal Display I).

 V13 Flip Zoom on a Mobile

Courtesy Ron Bird.

Chapter 4(1)

Holmquist, L.E. (1997) 'Focus+Context visualization with flip-zooming and zoom browser', Exhibit, CHI '97.

Quicktime Movie, 11.7 MB, 1 minute 57 seconds (silent)

Background

Many solutions have been proposed for the focus+context problem, a significant number involving distortion. The interesting feature of the flip-zoom technique is that equal X- and Y-distortion is used, so that what results in the 'distorted' region is a recognizable miniature, especially valuable if the result is an undistorted, albeit smaller, image.

Action

The clip shows an animated sketch prepared as a proposal by an interaction designer to a manufacturer of mobile phones. It presents a suggested (and accepted) means whereby the mobile user can scan through a collection of stored photographs.

Illustrates

The flip-zoom technique; presentation of an image collection; the use of animated sketches in the 'proposal' stage of interaction design.

 V14 Distorted Map on a PDA

Courtesy David Baar, IDELIX Software, Inc.

Chapter 4(1)

Same reference as for V11 (Bifocal Display I).

AVI, 2.1 MB, 52 seconds (silent)

Background

The focus+context concept first embodied in the Bifocal Display, together with the technique of suppression, has been applied by IDELIX and is illustrated in the demanding requirement to present a useful map of Boston on a PDA.

Action

A user is seen moving rectangular areas around a (principally transportation) map of Boston, showing how parts can be selectively magnified and, concurrently, filled with appropriate data. It also shows to good effect the continuity between regular and distorted regions which is an essential feature of the distortion technique.

Illustrates

Distortion, continuity; suppression.

V15 Pliable Display Technology on a Table

Courtesy Chia Shen.

Chapter 4(1)

Same reference as for V11 (Bifocal Display I). Videos V14 and V16 are also relevant.

Quicktime Movie, 15.9 MB, 3 minutes 1 second

Background

As for V11 (Bifocal Display I).

Action

The video shows an effective combination of distortion technology and an interactive table. A video projector positioned above a table projects a map on to the table surface. The map can, however, be distorted in a rubber sheet manner through the action of a user's fingers placed on the surface of the table.

Illustrates

Distortion; focus+context; interaction; collaboration.

V16 Rubber Sheet Map Distortion

Courtesy David Baar, IDELIX Software, Inc.

Chapter 4(1)

Same reference as for V11 (Bifocal Display I).

Quicktime Movie, 5 MB, 33 seconds (silent)

Background

The focus+context concept first embodied in the Bifocal Display, and the technique of suppression, have been applied by IDELIX and are illustrated in the context of exploring a conventional map. A magnification region is moved over a map, using distortion to maintain context, to a location of interest, whereupon a magnified portion of that map is presented.

Action

A highly magnified region is moved over a conventional map while maintaining full context and continuity. When a feature of interest is found, it and its immediately surrounding area are displayed conventionally.

Illustrates

Distortion; continuity; suppression.

V17 The Perspective Wall

Chapter 4(1)

Mackinlay, J.D., Robertson, G.G. and Card, S.K. (1991) 'Perspective Wall: detail and context smoothly integrated', ACM, Proceedings CHI '91, pp. 173–179.

QuickTime, 11.3 MB, 54 seconds

Background

See background for V11 (Bifocal Display I).

Action

Demonstrates, with a real implementation, the 3D effect characteristic of the Perspective Wall, the variable distortion, the encoding and the movement to bring a desired item into the central region.

Illustrates

Distortion of information space.

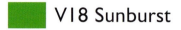 # V18 Sunburst

Courtesy John Stasko.

Chapter 4(1)

Stasko, J. and Zhang, E. (2000) 'Focus+context display and navigation techniques for enhancing radial, space-filling hierarchy visualizations', IEEE, Proceedings of Information Visualization 2000, pp. 57–65.

MPEG movie, 37.9 MB, 3 minutes 53 seconds

Background

Radial representations of hierarchical data suffer from the problem that, as the hierarchy grows in size, many items become small peripheral slices that are difficult to distinguish.

Action

Three techniques are demonstrated that provide flexible browsing of a radial representation, allowing the examination of small items in detail while providing context within the entire hierarchy.

Illustrates

Hierarchical data representation; focus+context techniques.

V19 Combined Zoom and Pan

Courtesy Andy Cockburn.

Chapter 4(1)

Cockburn, A. and Savage, J. (2003) 'Comparing speed-dependent automatic zooming with traditional scroll, pan and zoom methods', in *People & Computers XVII*, pp. 87–102.

MPEG Movie, 30.8 MB, 3 minutes 5 seconds (silent)

Background

Zooming and panning are well-known techniques made familiar through cinema and television. A combination of the two, and especially where zoom takes place automatically according to the nature of a panning action, can offer advantages.

Action

The short video presents the technique of automatic zooming during panning. It demonstrates two different forms of automatic zooming: speed-dependent zooming and displacement-dependent zooming.

Illustrates

Automatic zooming during panning.

V20 Floating RSVP

Courtesy Kent Wittenburg.

Chapter 4(2)

Wittenburg, K., Chiyoda, C., Heinrichs, M. and Lanning, T. (2000) 'Browsing through rapid-fire imaging: requirements and industry initiatives', SPIE, Proceedings of Electronic Imaging, pp. 48–56.

MPEG movie, 6.1 MB, 30 seconds (silent)

Background

Rapid serial visual presentation (RSVP) is a means of presenting a collection of images in rapid sequence and exploits the fact that the human being needs sight of an image for only around 100 milliseconds to be able to identify it as an image being sought.

Action

Shows a user browsing through a department store's contents using the Floating RSVP technique. Manual control allows the user to control the forward and backward movement of all the items and to stop the display when they see an item of interest.

Illustrates

The Floating RSVP mode of image presentation; a situation wherein a user's goal may not have been precisely identified and which benefits from the ability to explore rapidly.

▮ V21 Image Browsing – Video on Demand

Chapter 4(2)

Lam, K. and Spence, R. (1997) 'Image browsing – a space–time trade-off', Proceedings INTERACT '97, pp. 611–612.

Quicktime Movie, 21.4 MB, 1 minute 55 seconds

Background

Riffling the pages of a book is quite an efficient – and very common – way of rapidly obtaining an overall understanding of the nature of that book. Electronic riffling can be an equally valuable means of browsing an information space. This method of presentation is called Rapid Serial Visual Presentation, or RSVP.

Action

The video shows how RSVP supports the act of browsing and how it additionally provides a trade-off between space and time, a trade-off of especial value when – as with a mobile or a PDA – available space is very limited.

Illustrates

RSVP; the activity of browsing; the space–time trade-off inherent in RSVP; a video-on-demand interface based on RSVP.

▮ V22 Navigation via a Small Display

Chapter 4(2)

de Bruijn, O. and Spence, R. (2001) 'Movement in the web', extended abstracts, CHI 2001 Companion Proceedings, pp. 209–210.

QuickTime Movie, 34.1 MB, 2 minutes 22 seconds

Background

There is an increasing need to be able to navigate through vast quantities of information (e.g. the Web) via a small display such as that associated with a mobile or a PDA.

Action

A solution is to use the space–time trade-off provided by Rapid Serial Visual Presentation (RSVP). RSVP can be used both to look ahead at outlinks (i.e. images representing possible destinations one click away) and to look at 'footprints', images representing previously visited locations in information space.

Illustrates

RSVP; space–time trade-off; navigation.

V23 to V28 Image Presentation Modes

Chapter 4(2)

Cooper, K., de Bruijn, O., Witkowski, M. and Spence, R. (2006) 'A comparison of static and moving image presentation modes for image collections', ACM, Proceedings AVI 2006, pp. 381–388.

AVI movies, about 5 MB each. Duration between 3 and 4 seconds each (silent)

Background

Rapid serial visual presentation (RSVP), involving the presentation of images in a rapid sequence, can take on many different forms. These video clips offer a selection but include, for comparison, the Tile image presentation mode in which all images are presented concurrently.

Action

A set of six very short clips showing image-collection presentation modes (three 'static' modes followed by three 'moving' modes):

V23 Slide-show
V24 Tile
V25 Mixed
V26 Diagonal
V27 Ring
V28 Stream

Illustrates

The image presentation technique generally known as Rapid Serial Visual Presentation (RSVP).

◼ V29 Opportunistic Browsing with a Coffee Table

Chapter 5(0)

Stathis, K., de Bruijn, O. and Macedo, S. (2002) 'Living memory: agent-based information management for connected local communities', *Interacting with Computers*, 14, 6, pp. 663–688.

QuickTime Movie 13.6 MB, 1 minute 3 seconds

Background

An important mode of interaction is that called opportunistic browsing (OB). In OB, the user is unaware that an image on which his or her eye is temporarily fixated is being categorized and consolidated to see whether it is relevant to one of the user's interests.

Action

The video shows people engaging in conversation around a table on to which images describing news items are projected. The images move slowly around the table and are eventually replaced by other images. If a person notices an information item that is of interest they can 'push' it, with their finger, into the centre of the table where it increases in size and provides more detail.

Illustrates

Opportunistic and involuntary browsing.

◼ V30 Discovery via Dynamic Representation

Chapter 5(2)

Spence, R. and Drew, A. (1971) 'Graphical exploration in electrical circuit design and modelling', NRC, Ottawa, Proceedings 2nd Man-Computer Communications Seminar, pp. 61–70. (as for V1 Qualitative Representation)

QuickTime Movie, 4.77 MB, 18 seconds

Background

See V1 Qualitative Representation.

Action

See V1 Qualitative Representation.

Illustrates

How the unexpected can usefully occur in a visualization tool. Two circles suddenly expanding and contracting indicates a (usually) undesirable effect (resonance) in a circuit (similar to the destructive resonance of the Tacoma Narrows bridge). Subsequent manual variation of the frequency indicator can then identify the frequency at which resonance occurred.

 # V31 Influence Explorer

Chapter 5(2), 5(5)

Tweedie, L., Spence, R., Dawkes, H. and Su, H. (1996) 'Externalising abstract mathematical models', ACM, Proceedings CHI '96, pp. 406–412.

QuickTime Movie, 47.8 MB, 4 minutes 53 seconds

Background

An engineering designer has to choose the values of a number of parameters to ensure that the corresponding values of some performances lie within prescribed limits. For the Influence Explorer a large number of designs are selected (i.e. parameter value sets are chosen to 'cover' a large exploratory region of parameter space) and the corresponding performances calculated. The Influence Explorer visualization tool then allows the pre-calculated data to be fluently explored in the same way as with the Attribute Explorer.

Action

The video relates to the design of a structure, about 4 inches long, which supports the filament of an electric lamp. The parameters, four in number, are various dimensions of the structure whereas the performances, also four in number, are the stresses at various points of the structure (Su *et al*., 1996).

Illustrates

Exploration to discover trade-offs between performances, and correlations between parameters and performances; the transformation of performance limits to the location of satisfactory designs in parameter space; the process of selecting tolerance ranges for the parameters with a view to achieving a high manufacturing yield.

V32 Model Maker

Chapter 5(3)

Smith, A.J., Malik, Z., Nelder, J. and Spence, R. (2001) 'A visual interface for model fitting,' *Quality and Reliability Engineering International,* 17, pp. 85–91.

QuickTime Movie, 47.5 MB, 4 minutes 51 seconds

Background

A frequent requirement in scientific investigation, engineering design and data mining is for a mathematical relation to be fitted to measured or simulated data. This task is difficult for a user unfamiliar with statistics. The Model Maker 'hides' the underlying theory and algorithms and makes good use of the user's domain expertise.

Action

Each term in the mathematical model (e.g. a polynomial) is represented by a square. The circle inside each square indicates, by its size, how important the term is in achieving a good fit to the data. Black circles indicate terms already in the model, whereas white ones refer to terms which are not yet included in the model.

Illustrates

Encoding by size (value of term to the model); encoding by colour (term is already within model or not); direct manipulation (click on square) to include or remove term from model.

Notes

The interface displays the effect of all possible single changes to an existing model and significantly reduces the statistical knowledge required to find a model.

V33 Human Guidance of Automated Design

Chapter 5(4)

Colgan, L., Spence, R. and Rankin, P.R. (1995) 'The cockpit metaphor', *Behaviour and Information Technology*, 14, 4, pp. 251–263.

QuickTime Movie, 79 MB, 5 minutes 40 seconds

Background

So-called 'optimization algorithms' exist which, given an electronic circuit design, will automatically and iteratively change the values of its components so that the circuit is 'better' in some sense. However, such 'automated design' has many drawbacks: the human designer has no idea how the new circuit was obtained (Were any significant trade-offs encountered, for example? Could a vast improvement have been obtained if a parameter limit were minimally relaxed?) and it is far from easy to define 'better'.

An optimization algorithm can be employed more effectively if its progress can be monitored and, if necessary, modified, by bringing to bear the domain expertise of a human designer. The interface linking the optimization algorithm and the human designer is called the cockpit.

Action

Following an introduction showing the relevance of the topic to many areas of design, the video addresses, in some detail, the (real) task of improving the design of a circuit on a silicon chip.

Illustrates

The human guidance of automated design; encoding by size and colour; the complexity of a real visualization tool.

V34 Prosection Matrix

Chapter 5(5)

Tweedie, L. and Spence, R. (1998) 'The prosection matrix: a tool to support the interactive exploration of statistical models and data', *Computational Statistics*, 13, pp. 65–76.

QuickTime Movie, 28.6 MB, 2 minutes 52 seconds

Background

As for the Influence Explorer, but the same pre-calculated data is now examined by means of a visualization tool called a prosection matrix. A prosection refers to a pair of parameters and shows, by colour coding, the location of satisfactory designs in that two-dimensional space, but only those designs selected by limits placed on the remaining parameters. In the same two-dimensional space is shown a yellow rectangle defined by the tolerance on the two parameters and within which all mass-produced versions of the design will lie. Thus, to achieve a high manufacturing yield, the yellow rectangles should be positioned to lie, as far as possible, totally within the red (acceptable) regions.

Action

The video provides a summary and demonstration of the prosection matrix.

Illustrates

The simplification of a difficult cognitive problem by replacing it with a simpler perceptual task.

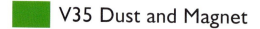 V35 Dust and Magnet

Courtesy John Stasko.

Chapter 6(2)

Yi, J.S., Melton, R., Stasko, J. and Jacko, J.A. (2005) 'Dust and magnet: multivariate information visualization using a magnet metaphor', *Information Visualization*, 4, 4, pp. 239–256.

QuickTime Movie, 46.6 MB, 4 minutes 46 seconds

Background

Data which is multidimensional in nature is difficult to represent in a manner that is easy for the general population to understand. Dust and magnet is a visualization technique which uses a 'magnet' metaphor and appropriate interaction techniques and allows a user to flexibly explore alternative objects on the basis of their attributes.

Action

The video presents many examples of the use of the dust and magnet interface, including unanticipated strategies employed by users.

Illustrates

A multidimensional and interactive representation technique; the exploration that often occurs when a user formulates questions as he or she explores the data.

V36 RSVP Browser

Chapter 4(2), 6(3)

DeBruijn, O. and Tong, C-H. (2003) 'M-RSVP: mobile web browsing on a PDA', in O'Neill, E., Palanque, P. and Johnson, P. (eds) *People and Computers – Designing for Society*, Springer, pp. 297–311.

V22 (Navigation via a small display) is also relevant.

QuickTime movie, 2 MB, 6 seconds (silent)

Background

There is an increasing need to be able to navigate through vast quantities of information (e.g. the Web) via a small display such as that associated with a mobile or a PDA.

Action

The video illustrates the application of Rapid Serial Visual Presentation (RSVP) to the presentation of news items on the display of a PDA. The user sees a series of 'previews', each comprising an informative image and few but relevant words, so that the choice of a news item can be made without undue delay.

Illustrates

RSVP; space–time trade-off

V37 Infosky Visual Explorer

Courtesy Keith Andrews.

Chapter 6(5)

Andrews, K., Kienreich, W., Sabol, V., Becker, J., Droschl, G., Kappe, F., Granitzer, M., Auer, P. and Tochtermann, K. (2002) 'The InfoSky visual explorer: exploiting hierarchical structure and document similarity', *Information Visualization*, 1, 3/4, pp. 166–181.

AVI movie, 25.2 MB, 2 minutes 34 seconds

Background

There is an ongoing challenge posed by the need for users to visualize the structure and content of very large hierarchical databases. An example is a large collection of newspaper articles.

Action

The video demonstrates the use of the InfoSky visual explorer in the exploration and search of a hierarchically structured collection of over 100,000 newspaper articles. The Explorer employs a 'galaxy and telescope' metaphor. Exploration and search are additionally enhanced by the fact that articles are also positioned in space according to their similarity.

Illustrates

The galaxy and telescope metaphor; semantic zoom; algorithmic placement according to similarity of data items.

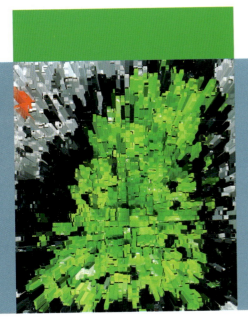

References

Ahlberg, C. (1996) 'Dynamic Queries', PhD dissertation, Chalmers University of Technology, Sweden.

Ahlberg, C. and Shneiderman, B. (1994) 'Visual information seeking: tight coupling of dynamic query filters with starfield displays', ACM, Proceedings CHI '94, pp. 313–317.

Ahlberg, C., Williamson, C. and Shneiderman, B. (1992) 'Dynamic queries for information exploration: an implementation and evaluation', ACM, Proceedings CHI '92, pp. 619–626.

Albinsson, P-A., Morin, M. and Fransson, J. (2003) 'Finding Information Needs in Military Command and Control Systems using Exploratory Tools for Communication Analysis', Proceedings of the 47th Annual Meeting of the Human Factors and Ergonomics Society, Santa Monica, CA: The Human Factors and Ergonomics Society, pp. 1918–1922.

Andrienko, G. and Andrienko, N. (2003) 'Informed spatial decisions through coordinated views', *Information Visualization*, 2, 4, pp. 270–285.

Apperley, M.D., Tzavaras, I. and Spence, R. (1982) 'A bifocal display technique for data presentation', Proceedings Eurographics, pp. 27–43.

Arnold, C.J. (1997) *An Archaeology of the Early Anglo-Saxon Kingdoms*, London, Routledge, p. 216.

Baudisch, P. and Rosenholtz, R. (2003) 'Halo: a technique for visualizing off-screen locations', ACM, Proceedings CHI '03, pp. 481–488.

Becker, R.A. and Cleveland, W.S. (1987) 'Brushing scatterplots', *Technometrics*, 29, 2, pp. 127–142.

Bederson, B.B., Clamage, A., Czerwinski, M.P. and Robertson, G.G. (2003) 'A fisheye calendar interface for PDAs: providing overviews in small displays', Proceedings of Extended Abstracts of Human Factors in Computing Systems (CHI 2003), ACM Press, Demonstration, pp. 618–619.

Bederson, B.B., Clamage, A., Czerwinski, M.P. and Robertson, G.G. (2004) 'DateLens: a fisheye calendar interface for PDAs', ACM Transactions on Computer-Human Interaction, 11, 1, pp. 90–119.

Bendix, F., Kosara, R. and Hauser, H. (2005) 'Parallel sets: visual analysis of categorical data', IEEE, Proceedings Information Visualization '05, pp. 133–140.

Bertin, J. (1967) Semiologie graphique, Paris, Editions Gauthier-Villars.

Bertin, J. (1981) Graphics and Graphic Information-Processing, Berlin, Walter de Gruyter: a translation of La Graphique et le Traitement Graphique de l'Information, Paris, Flammarion (1977).

Bertin, J. (1983) Semiology of Graphics (translation by W.J. Berg), University of Wisconsin Press.

Bier, E.A., Stone, M.C., Fishkin, K., Buxton, W. and Baudel, T. (1994) 'A taxonomy of see-through tools', ACM, Proceedings CHI '94, pp. 358–364.

Bjork, S., Holmquist, L.E., Redstrom, J., Bretan, I., Danielson, R., Karlgren, J. and Franzen, K. (1999) 'WEST: A web browser for small terminals', ACM, Proceedings UIST '99, pp. 187–196.

Bolt, R.A. (1984) The Human Interface, Belmont, CA, Lifetime Learning Publications, p. 2.

Brayton, R.K. and Spence, R. (1980) Sensitivity and Optimization, Amsterdam, Elsevier.

Bryson, B. (1998) Notes From a Small Island, London, Black Swan.

Cairns, P. and Craft, B. (2005) 'Beyond guidelines: what can we learn from the visual information seeking mantra?', IEEE, Proceedings Information Visualization IV05, pp. 110–118.

Chernoff, H. (1973) 'The use of faces to represent points in k-dimensional space graphically', Journal of the American Statistical Association, 68, pp. 361–368.

Cherry, E.C. (1953) 'Some experiments on the recognition of speech with one and with two ears', Journal of the Acoustical Society of America, 25, pp. 975–979.

Chi, E.H., Pirolli, P., Chen, K. and Pitkow, J. (2001) 'Using information scent to model user information needs and actions on the web', ACM, Proceedings CHI '01, pp. 490–497.

Cleveland, W.S. (1993) Visualizing Data, Summit, NJ, Hobart Press.

Cleveland, W.S. (1994) The Elements of Graphing Data (Revised Edition), Summit, NJ, Hobart Press.

Cleveland, W.S. and McGill, R. (1984) 'Graphical perception: Theory, experimentation and application to the development of graphical methods', Journal of the American Statistical Association, 79, 387, pp. 531–554.

Cockburn, A. and Jones, S. (1996) 'Which way now? Analysing and easing inadequacies in WWW navigation', International Journal of Human–Computer Studies, 45, 1, pp. 105–129.

Cockburn, A., McKenzie, B. and JasonSmith, M. (2002) 'Pushing back: evaluating a new behaviour for the back and forward buttons in web browsers', International Journal of Human–Computer Studies, 57, pp. 397–414.

Cockburn, A., Greenberg, S., Jones, S., McKenzie, B. and Moyle, M. (2003) 'Improving web page revisitation: analysis, design and evaluation', *IT & Society*, 1, 3, pp. 159–183.

Cockburn, A. and Savage, J. (2003) 'Comparing speed-dependent automatic zooming with traditional scroll, pan and zoom methods', *People & Computers* XVII, pp. 87–102.

Cockburn, A., Gutwin, C. and Alexander, J. (2006) 'Faster document navigation with space-filling thumbnails', ACM, Proceedings CHI 2006, pp. 1–10.

Coekin, J.A. (1969) 'A versatile presentation of parameters for rapid recognition of total state', IEE, Proceedings of International Symposium on Man–Machine Interaction, Cambridge, England.

Colgan, L., Spence, R. and Rankin, P.R. (1995) 'The cockpit metaphor', *Behaviour and Information Technology*, 14, 4, pp. 251–263.

Coltheart, V. (1999a) 'Introduction: perceiving and remembering brief visual stimuli', in Coltheart, V. (ed.) *Fleeting Memories: Cognition of Brief Visual Stimuli*, Cambridge, MA, MIT Press, pp. 1–12.

Coltheart, V. (1999b) *Fleeting Memories: Cognition of Brief Visual Stimuli*, Cambridge, MA, MIT Press.

Cooper, K., de Bruijn, O., Spence, R. and Witkowski, M. (2006) 'Static and moving images', ACM, Proceedings of the Conference on Advanced Visual Interfaces (AVI 2006), pp. 381–388.

Csallner, C., Handte, M., Lehmann, O. and Stasko, J. (2003) 'FundExplorer: supporting the diversification of mutual fund portfolios using context treemaps', IEEE, Proceedings of Information Visualization 2003, pp. 203–208.

Czerwinski, M.P., van Dantzich, M., Robertson, G. and Hoffman, H. (1999) 'The contribution of thumbnail images, mouse-over text and spatial location memory to web page retrieval in 3D', in Sasse, A. and Johnson, C. (eds) 'Human–Computer Interaction', Proceedings of INTERACT '99, Scotland, IOS Press, pp. 163–170.

Dahlback, N. (1988) 'On spaces and navigation in and out of the computer', in Dahlback, N. (ed.) 'Exploring navigation: towards a framework for design and evaluation of navigation in electronic spaces', SICS technical report T98:01, ISSN: 1100–3154.

Davidson, C. (1993) 'What your database hides away', *New Scientist*, 9 January, pp. 28–31.

Dawson, R.J.McG. (1995) 'The "Unusual Episode" data revisited', *Journal of Statistics Education*, 3, 3 (online).

de Bruijn, O. and Spence, R. (2001) 'Serendipity within a ubiquitous computing environment: a case for opportunistic browsing', in Abowd, G.D., Brumitt, B. and Shafter, S. (eds) UBICOMP 2001: Ubiquitous Computing, Springer, LNCS 2201, pp. 362–369.

de Bruijn, O. and Tong, C.H. (2003) 'M-RSVP: mobile web browsing on a PDA', in O'Neill, E., Palanque, P and Johnson, P. (eds) *People and Computers – Designing for Society*, London, Springer, pp. 297–311.

De Soete, G. (1986) 'A perceptual study of the Flury-Riedwyl faces of graphically displaying multivariate data', *International Journal of Man–Machine Studies*, 25, pp. 549–555.

DiVita, J., Obermayer, R., Nugent, W. and Linville, J.M. (2004) 'Verification of the change blindness phenomenon while managing critical events on a combat information display', *Human Factors*, 46, pp. 205–218.

Dix, A., Finlay, J., Abowd, G. and Beale, R. (1998) *Human–Computer Interaction*, London, Prentice-Hall.

Dourish, P. and Chalmers, M. (1994) 'Running out of space: models of information navigation', Proceedings HCI '94.

Durlach, P.A. (2004) 'Change blindness and its implications for complex monitoring and control systems design and operator training', *Human-Computer Interaction*, 19, pp. 423–451.

Eick, S.G. (1994) 'Data visualization sliders', ACM, Proceedings UIST '94, pp. 119–120.

Farrand, W.A. (1973) 'Information display in interactive design', Doctoral Thesis, University of California at Los Angeles.

Fawcett, C., Craft, B., de Bruijn, O., Witkowski, M. and Spence, R. (2004) 'Image presentation in space and time: errors, preferences and eye-gaze activity', ACM, Proceedings of the Conference on Advanced Visual Interfaces, AVI 2004, pp. 141–149.

Feiner, S.K. and Beshers, C. (1990) 'Worlds within worlds: metaphors for exploring n-dimensional virtual worlds', ACM, Proceedings of the Symposium on User Interface Software and Technology, pp. 76–83.

Field, G.E. and Apperley, M.D. (1990) 'Context and selective retreat in hierarchical menu structures', *Behaviour and Information Technology*, 9, 2, pp. 133–146.

Fluit, C., Sabou, M. and von Harmelen, F. (2003) 'Ontology-based information Visualization', in Geroimenko V. and Chen C. (eds) *Visualizing the Semantic Web*, London, Springer, pp. 36–48.

Fowlkes, E.B. (1969) 'User's manual for a system for interactive probability plotting on Graphic–2', Technical Memorandum, Murray Hill, NJ, Bell Telephone Laboratories.

Freeman, L.C. (2000) 'Visualizing social networks', *Journal of Social Structure*, 1 (online).

Freeman, L.C. (2005) 'Graphical techniques for exploring social network data', in Carrington, P.J., Scott, J. and Wasserman, S. (eds) *Models and Methods in Social Network Analysis,* Cambridge, Cambridge University Press, pp. 248–269.

Friendly, M. (1992) 'Mosaic displays for loglinear models', in ASA, Proceedings of the Statistical Graphics Section, pp. 61–68.

Friendly, M. (1994) 'Mosaic displays for multi-way contingency tables', *Journal of the American Statistical Association (Theory and Methods)*, 89, 425, pp. 190–200.

Friendly, M. (2000) *Visualizing Categorical Data*, Cary, NC: SAS Institute Inc.

Friendly http://www.math.yorku.ca/SCS/friendly.html [accessed 19 July 2006]

Furnas, G.W. (1981) 'The FISHEYE view: a new look at structured files', Bell Laboratories Technical Memorandum No. 81-11221-9, 12 October.

Furnas, G.W. (1986) 'Generalized fisheye views: visualizing complex information spaces', ACM, Proceedings CHI '86, pp. 16–23.

Furnas, G.E. and Buja, A. (1994) 'Prosection views: dimensional inference through sections and prosections', *Journal of Computational and Graphical Statistics*, 3, 4, pp. 323–353.

Furnas, G.W. and Bederson, B.B. (1995) 'Space-scale diagrams: understanding multi-scale interfaces', ACM, Proceedings CHI '95, pp. 234–241.

Furnas, G.W. (1997) 'Effective view navigation', ACM, Proceedings CHI '97, pp. 367–374.

Garland, K. (1994) *Mr Beck's Underground Map: a history*, Harrow Weald, Capital Transport Publishing.

Gibson, J.J. (1977) 'The theory of affordances', in Shaw, R.E. and Bransford, J. (eds) *Perceiving, Acting and Knowing*, Hillsdale, NJ, Lawrence Erlbaum Associates.

Goodman, T.G. and Spence, R. (1978) 'The effect of computer system response time on interactive computer-aided problem solving', ACM, Proceedings SIGGRAPH '78.

Grimes, J. (1996) 'On the failure to detect changes in scenes across saccades', in Atkins, K. (ed.), *Vancouver Studies in Cognitive Science: Vol. 2. Perception*, New York, Oxford University Press, pp. 89–110.

Hearst, M.A. (1995) 'TileBars: visualization of term distribution in full text information access', ACM, Proceedings CHI '95, pp. 59–66.

Herot, C.F. (1980) 'Spatial management of data', ACM, Transactions on Database Systems, 5, 4, pp. 493–514.

Herot, C.F., Carling, R., Friedell, M., Kramlich, D. and Rosenberg, R.L. (1981) 'Overview of the spatial data management system', Technical Report CCA-81-08, November, Computer Corporation of America.

Hochheiser, H. and Shneiderman, B. (2004) 'Dynamic query tools for time series data: Timebox widgets for interactive exploration', *Information Visualization*, 3, 1, pp. 1–18.

Holmquist, L.E. (1997) 'Focus+Context visualization with flip-zooming and zoom browser', Exhibit, CHI '97.

Hook, K., Benyon, D. and Munro, A. (2003) *Designing Information Spaces: the social navigation approach*, London, Springer.

i2: www.i2.com [accessed 6 January 2006]

Imperial College Television Studio (1980) 'Focus on information: the office of the professional' (video), Production number 1003.

Inselberg, A. (1985) 'The plane with parallel coordinates', *The Visual Computer*, 1, pp. 69–91.

Inselberg, A. (1997) 'Multidimensional detective', IEEE, Proceedings of Information Visualization '97, pp. 100–107.

Intraub, H. (1980) 'Presentation rate and the representation of briefly glimpsed pictures in memory, *Journal of Experimental Psychology: Human Learning and Memory*, 6, pp. 1–12.

Irani, P.P. and Eskicioglu, R. (2003) 'A space-filling visualization technique for cellular network data', International Conference on Knowledge Management (IKNOW-03), Springer Verlag, Graz, Austria, pp. 115–120.

Johnson, B. and Shneiderman, B. (1991) 'Tree-maps: a space-filling approach to the visualisation of hierarchical information structures', IEEE, Proceedings Information Visualization '91, pp. 284–291.

Jul, S. and Furnas, G.W. (1997) 'Navigation in electronic worlds: a CHI workshop', New York, ACM SIGCHI Bulletin, 29, pp. 44–49.

Kaasten, S., Greenberg, S. and Edwards, C. (2002) 'How people recognise previously seen web pages from titles, URLs and thumbnails', in 'People and Computers XVI' (eds Faulkner, X., Finlay, J. and Detienne, F.), Proceedings HCI 2002, London, Springer, pp. 247–265.

Kadmon, N. and Shlomi, E. (1978) 'A polyfocal projection for statistical surfaces', *The Cartographic Journal*, 15, 1, pp. 36–41.

Keim, D.A., Kreigel, H.-P. and Seidl, T. (1993) 'Visual feedback in querying large databases', IEEE, Proceedings Visualization '93, pp. 158–165 and colour plate CP-15.

Komlodi, A. and Marchionini, G. (1998) 'Key frame preview techniques for video browsing', ACM, Proceedings of Digital Libraries '98, pp. 118–125.

Lam, K. and Spence, R. (1997) 'Image browsing – a space-time trade-off', Proceedings INTERACT '97, pp. 611–612.

Lamping, J. and Rao, R. (1994) 'Laying out and visualising large trees using a hyperbolic space', ACM, Proceedings UIST '94, pp. 13–14.

Lamping, J., Rao, R. and Pirolli, P. (1995) 'A Focus+Context technique based on hyperbolic geometry for visualizing large hierarchies', ACM, Proceedings CHI '95, pp. 401–408.

Lamping, J. and Rao, R. (1996) 'The hyperbolic browser: a Focus+Context technique based on hyperbolic geometry for visualising large hierarchies', *Journal of Visual Languages and Computing*, 7, 1, pp. 33–55.

Leung, Y.K. and Apperley, M.D. (1994) 'A review and taxonomy of distortion-oriented presentation techniques', ACM Transactions on Computer Human Interaction, 1, 2, pp. 126–160.

Leung, Y.K., Spence, R. and Apperley, M.D. (1995) 'Applying bifocal displays to topological maps', *International Journal of Human-Computer Interaction*, 7, 1, pp. 79–98.

Lewis, D. (1994) *We, the Navigators*, Honolulu, University of Hawaii Press.

Li, Q. and North, C. (2003) 'Empirical comparison of dynamic query sliders and brushing histograms', IEEE, 2003 Symposium on Information Visualization, pp. 147–154.

Living Memory (2000) http://www.design.philips.com/lime

MacEachren, A.M. (2004) *How Maps Work: Representation, Visualization and Design*, New York, Guilford Press.

Mackinlay, J. (1986) 'Automating the design of graphical presentations of relational information', ACM, Transactions on Graphics, 5, 2, pp. 110–141.

Mackinlay, J.D., Robertson, G.G. and Card, S.K. (1991) 'Perspective wall: detail and context smoothly integrated', ACM, Proceedings CHI '91, pp. 173–179.

Malone, T.W. (1983) 'How do people organise their desks? Implications for the design of office information systems', ACM, Transactions on Office Information Systems, 1, pp. 99–112.

McGuffin, M. and Balakrishnan, R. (2002) 'Acquisition of expanding targets', ACM, Proceedings CHI 2002, pp. 57–64.

Miller, T. and Stasko, J. (2001) 'Information conveyance through personalised, expressive art', ACM, Proceedings CHI '01, pp. 305–306.

Mitta, D.A. (1990) 'A fisheye presentation strategy: aircraft maintenance data', in Diaper, D., Gilmore, D., Cockton, G. and Shackel, B. (eds) *Human–Computer Interaction – INTERACT '90*, Amsterdam, Elsevier, pp. 875–878.

Moreno, J.L. (1934) *Who Shall Survive?*, Washington, DC: Nervous and Mental Disease Publishing Company.

Morin, M. and Albinsson, P-A. (2005) 'Exploration and context in communication analysis', in Bowers, C., Salas, E. and Jentsch, F. (eds) *Creating High-Tech Teams: Practical Guidance on Work Performance and Technology*, Washington, DC, APA Press, pp. 89–112.

Morris, C.J., Ebert, D.S. and Rheingans, P. (1999) 'An experimental analysis of the pre-attentiveness of the features in Chernoff faces', IEEE, Proceedings of Applied Imagery Pattern Recognition '99: 3D Visualization for Data Exploration and Decision Making, October 1999.

Munro, A.J., Hook, K. and Benyon, D. (eds) (1999) *Social Navigation of Information Space*, London, Springer.

Newton, C.M. (1978) 'Graphics: from alpha to omega in data analysis', in Wang, P.C.C. (ed.) *Graphical Representation of Multivariate Data*, Orlando, Academic Press, pp. 59–92.

Nielsen, J. (2000) 'Is navigation useful?', Jakob Nielsen's Alertbox, 9 January. http://www.Useit.com/alert-box/20000109.html [accessed 6 August 2004]

Nielsen, J. and Tahir, M. (2002) *Homepage Usability*, Indianapolis, New Riders.

Nightingale, F. (1858) *Notes on Matters Affecting the Health, Efficiency and Hospital Administration of the British Army*, London, Harrison and Sons.

Norman, D.A. (1988) *The Design of Everyday Things*, New York, Doubleday (also published as *The Psychology of Everyday Things*, New York, Basic Books).

Norman, D.A. (2004) http://www.jnd.org/dn.mss/affordances_and.html [accessed 26 December 2005]

Norman, K.L. (1991) *The Psychology of Menu Selection*, Bristol, Intellect.

Norman, K.L. and Chin, J.P. (1988) 'The effect of tree structure on search in a hierarchical menu selection system', *Behaviour and Information Technology*, 7, 1, pp. 51–65.

Ovenden, M. (2003) *Metro Maps of the World*, Harrow Weald, Capital Transport Publishing.

Pirolli, P. and Card, S.K. (1999) 'Information foraging', *Psychological Review*, 106, 4, pp. 643–675.

Potter, M. (1993) 'Very short-term conceptual memory', *Memory and Cognition*, 21, pp. 156–161.

Potter, M. (1999) 'Understanding sentences and scenes: the role of conceptual short-term memory', in Coltheart, V. (ed.) *Fleeting Memories: Cognition of Brief Visual Stimuli*, Cambridge, MA, MIT Press, pp. 13–46.

Potter, M.C. (1976) 'Short-term conceptual memory for pictures', *Journal of Experimental Psychology – Human Learning and Memory*, 2, pp. 509–522.

Potter, M.C. and Levy, E.I. (1969) 'Recognition memory for a rapid sequence of pictures', *Journal of Experimental Psychology*, 81, pp. 10–15.

Potter, M.C., Staub, A., Rado, J. and O'Connor, D.H. (2002) 'Recognition memory for briefly presented pictures: the time course of rapid forgetting', *Journal of Experimental Psychology – Human Perception and Performance*, 28, pp. 1163–1175.

Pu, P. and Lalanne, D. (2000) 'Interactive problem solving via algorithm visualization', IEEE, Proceedings InfoVis 2000, pp. 145–153.

Rao, R. (1999) 'See & go manifesto', ACM, Interactions, September and October, p. 64 onwards.

Rao, R. and Card, S.K. (1994) 'The table lens: merging graphical and symbolic representations in an interactive focus+context visualization for tabular information', ACM, Proceedings CHI '94, pp. 318–322.

Raymond, J.E., Shapiro, K.L. and Arnell, K.M. (1992) 'Temporary suppression of visual processing in an RSVP task – an attentional blink', *Journal of Experimental Psychology – Human Perception and Performance*, 18, pp. 849–860.

Rensink, R.A. (2002) 'Change detection', *Annual Review of Psychology*, pp. 245–277.

Rensink, R.A. http://www.usd.edu/psyc301/ChangeBlindness.htm [accessed 24 December 2005]

Rensink, R., O'Regan, J.K. and Clark, J.J. (2000) 'On the failure to detect changes in scenes across brief interruptions', *Visual Cognition 7* (1/2/3), pp. 127–145.

Robertson, G.G., Mackinlay, J.D. and Card, S.K. (1991) 'Cone trees: animated 3D visualizations of hierarchical information', ACM, Proceedings CHI '91, pp. 189–194.

Ryall, K., Morris, M.R., Everitt, K., Forlines, C. and Shen, C. (2005) 'Experience with and observation of direct touch tabletops', Mitsubishi Electric Research Laboratories, Report TR2005-108, December.

Schon, D.A. (1983) *The Reflective Practitioner: How Professionals Think in Action*, New York, Basic Books.

Shneiderman, B. (1996) 'The eyes have it: a task by data type taxonomy of information visualizations', IEEE, Proceedings Visual Languages '96, pp. 336–343.

Siirtola, H. (2000) 'Direct manipulations of parallel coordinates', IEEE, Proceedings Information Visualization 2000 (IV00), pp. 373–378.

Siirtola, H. (2005) 'The effect of data-relatedness in interactive glyphs', IEEE, Proceedings IV05, pp. 869–876.

Siirtola, H. (2006) 'Interacting with parallel coordinate', *Interacting with Computers* (forthcoming).

Simon, H. (1996) *The Sciences of the Artificial* (3rd Edition), Cambridge, MA, MIT Press.

Simons, D.J. and Chabris, C.F. (1999) 'Gorillas in our midst: sustained inattentional blindness for dynamic events', *Perception*, 28, 9, pp. 1059–1074.

Smith, A.J., Malik, Z., Nelder, J. and Spence, R. (2001) 'A visual interface for model fitting', *Quality and Reliability Engineering International*, 17, pp. 85–91.

Smith, D. (1999) *The State of the World Atlas* (6th Edition), London, Penguin.

Snowberry, K., Parkinson, S.R. and Sisson, N. (1983) 'Computer display menus', *Ergonomics*, 26, 7, pp. 699–712.

Snowberry, K., Parkinson, S.R. and Sisson, N. (1985) 'Effects of help fields on navigating through hierarchical menu structure', *International Journal of Man-Machine Studies*, 22, pp. 479–491.

Spence, R. (1999) 'The facilitation of insight for analog design', IEEE, Transactions on Circuits and Systems II, 46, 5, pp. 540–548.

Spence, R. (2002) 'Rapid, serial and visual: a presentation technique with potential', *Information Visualization*, 1, 1, pp. 13–19.

Spence, R. (2004) 'Sensitivity, residue and scent', *Information Design Journal*, 12, 3, pp. 163–180.

Spence, R. and Apperley, M.D. (1974) 'On the use of interactive graphics in circuit design', IEEE, Proceedings of the International Symposium on Circuits and Systems, pp. 558–563.

Spence, R. and Apperley, M.D. (1977) 'The interactive man–computer dialogue in computer-aided electrical circuit design', IEEE, Transactions on Circuits and Systems, CAS-24, 2, pp. 49–61.

Spence, R. and Apperley, M.D. (1982) 'Data base navigation: an office environment for the professional', *Behaviour and Information Technology*, 1, 1, pp. 43–54.

Spence, R. and Drew, A.J. (1971) 'Graphical exploration in electrical circuit design and modelling', NRC, Ottawa, Proceedings 2nd Man–Computer Communications Seminar, pp. 61–70.

Spence, R. and Parr, M. (1991) 'Cognitive assessment of alternatives', *Interacting with Computers*, 3, 3, pp. 270–282.

Spence, R. and Soin, R.S. (1988) *Tolerance Design of Electronic Circuits*, London, Addison-Wesley.

Spence, R. and Tweedie, L. (1998) 'The Attribute Explorer: information synthesis via exploration', *Interacting with Computers*, 11, pp. 137–146.

Spoerri, A. (1993) 'InfoCrystal: a visual tool for information retrieval', IEEE, Proceedings Visualisation '93, pp. 150–157.

Spotfire: www.spotfire.com [last accessed 24 April 2006]

Stasko, J. and Zhang, E. (2000) 'Focus+Context display and navigation techniques for enhancing radial, space-filling hierarchy visualizations', IEEE, Proceedings of Information Visualization 2000, pp. 57–65.

Stathis, K., de Bruijn, O. and Macedo, S. (2002) 'Living memory: agent-based information management for connected local communities', *Interacting with Computers*, 14, 6, pp. 663–688.

Stephens, D.W. and Krebs, J.R. (1986) *Foraging Theory*, Princeton, NJ, Princeton University Press.

Stock, D. and Watson, C.J. (1984) 'Human judgement accuracy, multidimensional graphics and humans versus models', *Journal of Accounting Research*, 22, 1, pp. 192–206.

Stone, M., Fishkin, K. and Bier, E. (1994) 'The movable filter as a user interface tool', ACM, Proceedings CHI '94, pp. 306–312.

Su, H., Nelder, J., Wolbert, P. and Spence, R. (1996) 'Application of generalized linear models to the design improvement of an engineering artefact', *Quality and Reliability Engineering International*, 12, pp. 101–112.

Sun, L. and Guimbretiere, F. (2005) 'Flipper: a new method of digital document navigation', ACM, Proceedings CHI '05, Late Breaking Results: short papers, pp. 2001–2004.

Sutherland, I.E. (1963) *SKETCHPAD: A Man-Machine Graphical Communication System*, Spring Joint Computer Conference, Baltimore, Spartan Books.

Tauscher, L. and Greenberg, S. (1997) 'Revisitation: patterns in world wide web navigation', ACM, Proceedings CHI '97, pp. 399–406.

Teoh, S.T. and Ma, K-L. (2005) 'Hifocon: object and dimensional coherence and correlation in multidimensional visualization', Proceedings International Symposium on Visual Computing (ISVC '05), December, pp. 235–242.

Tory, M. and Moller, T. (2004) 'Rethinking visualization: a high-level taxonomy', IEEE, Proceedings of the Symposium on Information Visualization, pp. 151–158.

Tse, T., Marchionini, G., Ding, W., Slaughter, L. and Komlodi, A. (1998) 'Dynamic key frame presentation techniques for augmented video browsing', ACM, Proceedings of the Conference on Advanced Visual Interfaces, pp. 185–194.

Tufte, E.R. (1983) *The Visual Display of Quantitative Information*, Cheshire, CT, Graphics Press.

Tufte, E.R. (1997) *Visual Explanations*, Cheshire, CT, Graphics Press.

Tversky, B. (1993) 'Cognitive maps, cognitive collages and spatial mental models', in 'Spatial information theory – a theoretical basis for GIS', Proceedings of the European Conference COSIT '93, Springer-Verlag, Lecture Notes in Computer Science, pp. 14–24.

Tweedie, L.A. (1997) 'Characterizing interactive externalizations', ACM, Proceedings CHI '97, pp. 375–382.

Tweedie, L. and Spence, R. (1998) 'The prosection matrix: a tool to support the interactive exploration of statistical models and data', *Journal of Computational Statistics*, 13, 1, pp. 65–76.

Tweedie. L., Spence, R., Dawkes, H. and Su, H. (1995) 'The influence explorer', ACM, Companion Proceedings CHI '95, pp. 129–130.

Tweedie, L., Spence, R., Dawkes, H. and Su. H (1996) 'Externalizing abstract mathematical models', ACM, Proceedings CHI '96, pp. 406–412.

Tweedie, L., Spence, R., Williams, D.M.L. and Bhogal, R. (1994) 'The Attribute Explorer', ACM, Conference Companion Proceedings CHI '94, pp. 435–436. Also Video Proceedings.

Varakin, D.A., Levin, D.T. and Fidler, R. (2004) 'Unseen and unaware: implications of recent research on failures of visual awareness for human–computer interface design', *Human–Computer Interaction*, 19, pp. 389–422.

Ware, C. (2004) *Information Visualization: Perception for Design* (2nd Edition), Amsterdam, Morgan Kaufman.

Ware, C. and Lewis, M. (1995) 'The DragMag image magnifier', ACM, Video Program and Companion Proceedings CHI '95, pp. 407–408.

Watson, M., Russell, W.J. and Sanderson, P. (1999) 'Ecological interface design for anaesthesia monitoring', IEEE, Proceedings of the 11th Australia–New Zealand Conference on Computer–Human Interaction (OzCHI '99), Wagga Wagga, New South Wales, pp. 78–84

Watson, M. and Sanderson, P. (2004) 'Sonification helps eyes-free respiratory monitoring and task timesharing', *Human Factors*, 46, 3, pp. 497–517.

Wegman, E.J. (1990) 'Hyperdimensional data analysis using parallel coordinates', *Journal of the American Statistical Association*, Theory and Methods, 85, 411, pp. 664–675.

Westphal, C. and Blaxton, T. (1998) *Data Mining Solutions: Methods and Tools for Solving Real-World Problems*, New York, Wiley.

Wildbur, P. and Burke, M. (1998) *Information Graphics: Innovative Solutions in Contemporary Design*, London, Thames & Hudson.

Williamson, C. and Shneiderman, B. (1992) 'The dynamic housefinder: evaluating dynamic queries in a real estate information exploration system', ACM, Proceedings SIGIR '92, pp. 339–346.

Wittenburg, K. (1997) 'Navigation and search: what's the difference?', Position paper for the CHI '97 Workshop on Navigation in Electronic Worlds (March 23–24, 1997, Atlanta, GA). [See Jul and Furnas, 1997.]

Wittenburg, K., Ali-Ahmad, W., LaLiberte, D. and Lanning, T. (1998) 'Rapid-fire image previews for information navigation', ACM, Proceedings of the Conference on Advanced Visual Interfaces (AVI-1998), pp. 76–82.

Wittenburg, K., Chiyoda, C., Heinrichs, M. and Lanning, T. (2000) 'Browsing through rapid-fire imaging: requirements and industry initiatives', SPIE, Proceedings of Electronic Imaging, pp. 48–56.

Wittenburg, K., Forlines, C., Lanning, T., Esenther, A., Harada, S. and Miyachi, T. (2003) 'Rapid serial visual presentation techniques for consumer digital video devices', ACM, Proceedings Symposium on User Interface Software and Technology (UIST), pp. 115–124.

Wittenburg, K., Lanning, T., Heinrichs, M. and Stanton, M. (2001) 'Parallel bargrams for consumer-based information exploration and choice', ACM, Proceedings of UIST '01, pp. 51–60.

Woods, D. (1984) 'Visual momentum: a concept to improve the cognitive coupling of person and computer', *International Journal of Man–Machine Systems*, 21, 3, pp. 229–244.

Woods, D.D. and Watts, J.C. (1997) 'How not to have to navigate through too many displays', in Helander, M.G., Landauer, T.K. and Prabhu, P. (eds), *Handbook of Human–Computer Interaction* (2nd Edition), Amsterdam, Elsevier Science.

Wright, H., Brodlie, K. and David, T. (2000) 'Navigating high-dimensional spaces to support design steering', IEEE, Proceedings Symposium on Information Visualization, pp. 291–296.

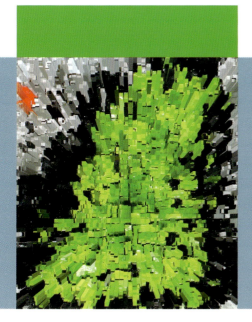

Index

Note: Figures are indicated by *italic page numbers*, glossary terms by **emboldened numbers**, footnotes by suffix 'n'

Licensing Agreement

This book comes with a DVD package. By opening this package, you are agreeing to be bound by the following: